EXCELLENCE
THROUGH
EQUITY

Dedication

When my grandmother Sarah returned to her small apartment in Oaxaca, Mexico, to find a woman taking food from her refrigerator, she opted to find out why. When she was told that it was for the woman's own hungry children, my grandma decided to prepare a meal for her to take to them each day. Compassion and understanding—especially for "the underdog"—took Grandma places others would not go and enriched her own life as much as those she helped.

Grandma Sarah's unconditional love for me as a child, likewise, enabled me to make it through.

When Dr. Myland Brown, an African American from Alabama, offered me a way out of the group home in which I lived, via a scholarship to go to college, I saw both an open door and another open heart.

In working on this book, it is my hope that many more such doors and hearts will open to millions of children, including my own: Sarah and Ava. This book is in memory of Grandma Sarah;

In honor of Dr. Myland Brown;

and in awe of Sarah and Ava—all of whom are about TRUE excellence, which is always rooted in equity.

—Alan M. Blankstein

This book is dedicated to my five children, Joaquin, Amaya, Antonio, Naima, and Ava, who are the living embodiment of excellence through equity. Much of what I have learned about equity I have learned from raising them. Watching them grow and develop and guiding them on the complicated path to adulthood has been my greatest challenge and pleasure.

—Pedro Noguera

EXCELLENCE THROUGH EQUITY

Five Principles of Courageous Leadership
to Guide Achievement for Every Student

ALAN M. BLANKSTEIN

PEDRO NOGUERA

with Lorena Kelly

Foreword by Archbishop Desmond Tutu

Alexandria, Virginia USA

FIRST ASCD EDITION: FEBRUARY 2016

ASCD®

1703 N. Beauregard St. • Alexandria, VA 223111714 USA
Phone: 800-933-2723 or 703-578-9600 • Fax: 703-575-5400
Website: www.ascd.org • E-mail: member@ascd.org • Author guidelines:
www.ascd.org/write

Deborah S. Delisle, *Executive Director,* Robert D. Clouse, *Managing Director, Digital Content & Publications;* Stefani Roth, *Publisher;* Genny Ostertag, *Director, Content Acquisitions;* Julie Houtz, *Director, Book Editing & Production;* Mike Kalyan, *Manager, Production Services;* Keith Demmons, *Production Designer*

PAPERBACK ISBN: 978-1-4166-2250-5   ASCD product #116070   n2/16

PDF E-BOOK ISBN: 978-1-4166-2256-7; see Books in Print for other formats.

Quantity discounts available: e-mail programteam@ascd.org. For desk copies, go to www.ascd.org/deskcopy.

Library of Congress Control Number for the Corwin edition: 2015936174

25 24 23 22 21 20 19 18   4 5 6 7 8 9 10 11 12

Contents

Foreword

Archbishop Desmond Tutu

Having helped to act as a catalyst and to shepherd one of the world's few peaceful transitions from a colonial occupation to a democratically elected president, I can say that a movement is born out of the convergence of dire conditions, a powerful idea, and people committed to carrying out that idea. This landmark book, edited by Alan M. Blankstein and Pedro Noguera, may be a similar catalyst to such a movement. Complete with a bold and compelling vision, cases of success throughout the world, and a guide to action for the reader, *Excellence Through Equity: Five Principles of Courageous Leadership to Guide Achievement for Every Student*, offers a powerful way forward and new hope for millions of children.

The timing for this book is on target, as America may be reaching a breaking point. Some of the signs—growing economic disparities, segregated housing, police brutality, and inequitable education for children—are well known to me and all South Africans who suffered 4 decades of apartheid. Unlike America, the inequities and brutality endured by our people were systematic and officially state-sanctioned. Yet America's challenges may still feel similar to the children, families, and communities that endure them. Looking from afar at cities throughout America like Ferguson, Missouri, it would seem so.

When a growing number of a country's citizenry feel overwhelmed, disenfranchised, angry, or hopeless, the possible roads forward are finite and known. Overall economic decline due to neglect of infrastructure and support for the common good is one; violent struggle for power is another. We in South Africa, however, chose a road less traveled. Probably unique in the history of colonialism, White settlers voluntarily gave up their monopoly of political power. The final transfer of power was remarkably peaceful; it is often described as a "miracle" because many thought that South Africa would erupt into violent civil war.

The challenges in choosing the road to higher moral ground and prosperity for all are many. They include confronting old zero-sum game thinking in which someone must lose. Blankstein and Noguera tackle this head-on and provide a more compelling reality in evidence in schools throughout the world. It more closely aligns with our own most highly held tradition of Ubuntu: "I am because you are." This view of a united community was a saving grace in South Africa.

Ubuntu was drawn on by our first popularly elected president, Nelson Mandela, and served as an underpinning of our work in the Truth and Reconciliation Commission, in which we ourselves were wounded healers of our people. We attempted to repair the gap between the races by getting the ugly truth of the apartheid regime and of the liberation movements out into the open, granting amnesty even to the worst offenders, and then seeking to find ways of reconciling the conflicting parties. We realized that everyone in the room—from the most powerful leader, to the most victimized young person—had much to learn, and we modeled an environment of equity and equality. We made sure when we had these public hearings that even the furniture layout demonstrated this. We didn't sit on a platform higher than, but we deliberately sat on a level *with* the victims.

Fortifying this reality of being stronger united than separated similarly, the authors of this book demonstrate in case after case how every student advances when learning in an equitable system. In such an environment, everyone learns and each person counts.

Allowing for this brighter reality in which all of God's rainbow children succeed within an equitable environment alarms those who fear for the loss of resources for their *own* child. Blankstein and Noguera rise to the challenge and, along with their coauthors, offer up schools, districts, and even nations that have discovered a more powerful secret: when done well, school communities focused on equity actually better educate wealthy majority students as well as those who are less privileged!

Following one's moral compass to an enlightened but less traveled road to success takes courage. Even if the mind is captured by a glorious vision that the heart is morally compelled to pursue, the body will need specific direction and courage to make the journey successfully in the face of many obstacles. *Equity Through Excellence* takes this into consideration, spotlighting how pioneers in this venture have successfully moved forward, and framing all of this in five principles of Courageous Leadership.

In their section on "The Arguments for Equity," Blankstein and Noguera share an insight that was also critical to our successful transition of power: We didn't struggle in order just to change the complexion of those who sit in the Union buildings; it was to change the quality of our community and society. We wanted to see a society that was a compassionate society, a caring society, a society where you might not necessarily be madly rich, but you knew that you counted. *Excellence Through Equity* provides direction for those bent on creating such a society for generations to come. Letting go of a system of winners and losers in favor of what is proposed in this book is a courageous leap forward that we all must take together. Let this bold, practical book be a guide; and may you travel into this new exciting vista, in which every child can succeed, with Godspeed.

God bless you.

Acknowledgments

This work was catalyzed by many who have taught me about the power of equity, inequity, systems, organizational culture, and leadership. The Jewish Child Care Agency advanced much of this by taking me in as a teenager. The late W. Edwards Deming, my personal mentor, decried the prevailing system of winners and losers and had the courage to do so—and often prevail—in corporate Japan, corporate America, and throughout the world. Archbishop Desmond Tutu, Nelson Mandela, and the amazing cadre of South African leaders that overthrew apartheid did so to replace that system—not perpetuate it with leaders of a different color. Desmond Tutu's work, in particular, has moved me and influenced this work since our first meeting in 1994.

It has been a joy to work with and learn from the work of all the authors in this book, particularly my coauthor, colleague, and longtime friend, Pedro Noguera, whose brilliance and passion for this work is superseded only by his love of family and compassion for those in need. I've been uplifted for decades by Andy Hargreaves's work *and* his support of my own; intellectually stretched by Michael Fullan's work and honored by his support throughout those same decades; and deeply touched by the humility and humanity of Marcus Newsome. Behind the scenes, this book has been informed and supported by longtime friends and colleagues Jay McTighe and Andy Cole.

At Corwin/Sage the mission for social equity began at the top and long ago. Sara McCune, herself a first-generation American, was imbued with this value and has pursued it relentlessly in her life and work. She is an inspiration and conduit for others committed to justice and advancing the human condition. In keeping with these values, Blaise Simqu and David McCune have unflinchingly followed the moral high ground and demonstrated courageous leadership and integrity in tackling critical challenges while running the Sage Corporation. This particular book is also owed to the affirmative decision and actions of Mike Soules and Lisa Shaw early on—thank you! Dan Alpert, assisted by Cesar Reyes, has been an invaluable advocate of this work, along with Lorena Kelly, who stepped in and stepped up at every turn, helped to bring this book to light in record speed.

I would like also to thank Deb Delisle, Executive Director of ASCD, for her interest in and support of the work. ASCD's commitment to educational and social equity is a hallmark that has always been evident through their work and dedication to the Whole Child approach. Our partnership with this preeminent organization and with Deb directly is a thrilling prospect for advancing "the movement" Archbishop Tutu refers to in our foreword.

On a personal note, Sue-Je Gage helped me to realize that an inequitable system—no matter who is on top at any given moment—is still inequitable. Special acknowledgments go to Nancy Shin, also "Nana" to both of my children, who has been an unflinching and essential supporter of equity, and my work in general, since I was a pup—in 1988!

—*Alan M. Blankstein*

I would like to thank the educators who have collaborated with us over the years; who have allowed us to enter their classrooms and schools; who have confided in us, sharing their fears, challenges, hopes, and dreams. Your hard work and commitment to excellence through equity is a constant reminder of the power and potential of education. Those who dedicate their professional lives to working in the trenches of education and who do so with an unswerving commitment to serving *all* children well are true heroes and beacons of hope. You are the ones who give us reason to believe that the future for this country may be more just and equitable than the present.

There are a few individuals I worked with at the beginning of my career who I want to single out for additional recognition: George Perry, the former principal of East Campus Continuation School, who used his demotion by the district to become an incredible leader for the most underserved children; Timiza Wagner, who treated each child she encountered with love, dignity, and respect and showed me through her example what it means to truly serve as a role model for young people; Afriye Quamina, who showed me how teaching could be a healing profession; Verde Delp, an English teacher who maintained high standards for all students and provided high levels of support; and Joan Cone, the social studies teacher who single-handedly led the effort to detrack her high school and won over her colleagues and parents in the process.

—*Pedro Noguera*

About the Editors

Award-winning author and educational leader **Alan M. Blankstein** served for 25 years as president of the HOPE Foundation, which he founded and whose honorary chair is Nobel Prize winner Archbishop Desmond Tutu. A former high-risk youth, Alan began his career in education as a music teacher. He worked for Phi Delta Kappa, March of Dimes, and Solution Tree, which he founded in 1987 and directed for 12 years while launching Professional Learning Communities beginning in the late 1980s. He is the author of the best-selling book *Failure Is Not an Option®: Six Principles That Guide Student Achievement in High-Performing Schools*, which received the Book of the Year award from Learning Forward. Alan is senior editor, lead contributor, and/or author of 18 books. He has also authored some 20 articles in publications including *Education Week, Educational Leadership, The Principal*, and *Executive Educator*. Alan has provided keynote presentations and workshops for virtually every major U.S. education organization and throughout the United Kingdom, Africa, and the Middle East. Alan has served on the Harvard International Principals Center's advisory board and the Jewish Child Care Agency, where he once was a youth in residence.

Pedro Noguera is a Distinguished Professor of Education in the Graduate School of Education and Information Sciences at UCLA. His research focuses on the ways in which schools are influenced by social and economic conditions, as well as by demographic trends in local, regional and global contexts. He is the author of eleven books and over 200 articles and monographs. He serves on the boards of numerous national and local organizations and appears as a regular commentator on educational issues on CNN, MSNBC, National Public Radio, and other national news outlets. Prior to joining the faculty

xiv • Excellence Through Equity

at UCLA he served as a tenured professor and holder of endowed chairs at New York University (2003–2015) Harvard University (2000–2003) and the University of California, Berkeley (1990–2000). From 2009–2012 he served as a Trustee for the State University of New York (SUNY) as an appointee of the Governor. In 2014 he was elected to the National Academy of Education. Noguera recently received awards from the Center for the Advanced Study of the Behavioral Sciences, from the National Association of Secondary Principals, and from the McSilver Institute at NYU for his research and advocacy efforts aimed at fighting poverty.

 **Lorena Kelly** is an assistant principal in Virginia Beach, Virginia. She began her career in education as an elementary teacher. After 9 years of teaching, she became an instructional specialist. Her interest in curriculum, specifically literacy, led to a position as a language arts curriculum coordinator. She used this opportunity to work with colleagues and partners to enhance learning for all students. She continues to follow her dreams by returning to a school as a school-level administrator.

Dr. Kelly holds a PhD in education with a concentration in educational leadership. Her interests include literacy, finance, and policy. Currently, she is focusing on literacy and job-embedded professional development to support teachers as they strive to help all students reach their maximum potential.

About the Contributors

Dr. Ann H. Bacon is the director of curriculum in Abington School District. Prior to assuming her current position, Dr. Bacon was the coordinator of mathematics, K–12, and a secondary school mathematics teacher in the district. Dr. Bacon graduated from Chestnut Hill College with a bachelor of science degree in mathematics and earned a master's degree in education and a doctorate in education from the University of Pennsylvania. She is a recipient of the Pennsylvania Council of Supervisors of Mathematics Hall of Fame Award, the Outstanding Contributions to Mathematics Education Award given by the Association of Teachers of Mathematics of Philadelphia and Vicinity, the Pennsylvania Council of Teachers of Mathematics Hall of Fame Award, and the Educational Service Award presented by the Willow Grove Branch of the NAACP. Dr. Bacon has served as the president of the Association of Teachers of Mathematics of Philadelphia and Vicinity and of the Pennsylvania Council of Teachers of Mathematics. In addition, she has been a member of the Mathematics Advisory Council for the Pennsylvania Department of Education and has given presentations at national, state, and local conferences. Dr. Bacon is an adjunct instructor in the School of Graduate and Professional Studies at Delaware Valley College.

Avram Barlowe has taught history and other social studies subjects in New York City public high schools for 33 years. He is a founding member of the Urban Academy Laboratory High School and an active participant in the New York Performance Standards Consortium. Both the Urban Academy and the Consortium have been featured in the media and several publications. Mr. Barlowe is the author of three publications in the *Teacher to Teacher* series, distributed by Teachers College Press. His American history class was one of those featured on Public Television's Teaching Channel.

Darlene Berg has had a teaching career in elementary schools that has spanned two continents. She has worked in public and private schools in the United States, in the state of New Jersey, and in schools outside of Lisbon, Portugal. Her experiences with teaching children from divergent social and cultural backgrounds, as well as opportunities to work with the New Jersey Department of Education's Collaborative Assessment and Planning for Achievement (CAPA) teams, prepared her for the work she went on to do with the students and teachers of West Orange, New Jersey. She began her career in West Orange 10 years ago, as their elementary math coach. Ms. Berg received a graduate degree in Educational Leadership from Montclair State University and is currently the Math Supervisor (K–5) for the West Orange Public Schools. Darlene and her husband have two children and reside in New Jersey.

Carol Corbett Burris has served as principal of South Side High School in the Rockville Centre School District in New York since 2000. She received her doctorate from Teachers College, Columbia University, and her dissertation, which studied her district's detracking reform in math, received the 2003 National Association of Secondary Schools' Principals Middle Level Dissertation of the Year Award. In 2010, she was named Educator of the Year by the School Administrators Association of New York State, and in 2013, she was named SAANYS New York State High School Principal of the Year. Dr. Burris is the coauthor of *Detracking for Excellence and Equity* (2008, ASCD) and *Opening the Common Core: How to Bring ALL Students to College and Career Readiness* (2012, Corwin). Her new book, *On the Same Track: How Schools Can Join the 21st Century Struggle Against Re-segregation*, is available from Beacon Press.

Ann Blakeney Clark brings a quarter-century of experience in Charlotte-Mecklenburg Schools (CMS) to her role as deputy superintendent. Clark has held a variety of teaching and administrative positions in CMS since joining the district in 1983 as a teacher of behaviorally and emotionally handicapped children.

Clark's extensive education background includes serving as principal at elementary, middle, and high schools. She most recently served as the chief academic officer, overseeing the district's curriculum, professional development, classroom instruction, and school zones.

She graduated from Davidson College with a BA in English and earned a master's degree in special education from the University of Virginia. She also holds administrator and curriculum and supervision certification from the University of North Carolina at Greensboro.

In addition to her work with CMS, Clark serves on multiple community boards, including Communities in Schools, Children's Theatre, the Davidson College Board of Visitors, and Levine Museum of the New South.

Her achievements in education and the community have been widely recognized. She has been named a Broad Superintendent Fellow, Charlotte Woman of the Year, the Thomas Jefferson Distinguished Alumnae Award from University of Virginia, National Principal of the Year (1994), and William Friday Fellow and Council for Great City Schools Outstanding Urban Educator Award winner.

Ann Cook is the director of the New York Performance Standards Consortium, a nationally recognized coalition of New York State public secondary schools that uses a system of performance-based assessment in lieu of high-stakes tests. She is the cofounder of the Urban Academy Laboratory High School. Ms. Cook is the editor of the *Teacher to Teacher* series distributed by Teachers College Press, which includes seven booklets and four DVDs. She is author of several books for children including the *Monster* series, as well as numerous articles and education publications.

Lucy N. Friedman is the founding president of The After-School Corporation (TASC), which is dedicated to expanding the school day to give disadvantaged kids more opportunities to discover and develop their talents, more support to overcome the challenges of poverty, and more time to achieve at the high levels essential for success in the global workplace. Before joining TASC, Ms. Friedman was the founding executive director of Safe Horizon (formerly known as Victim Services), a crime victim assistance and advocacy organization. She serves on several boards including the Afterschool Alliance, Leadership Enterprise for a Diverse America (LEDA), and the Human Services Council. She is cochair of the New York State Afterschool Network (NYSAN). Ms. Friedman received a BA from Bryn Mawr College and a PhD in social psychology from Columbia University.

Michael Fullan, OC, is Professor Emeritus of the Ontario Institute for Studies in Education of the University of Toronto. Recognized as a worldwide authority on educational reform, Michael is engaged in training, consulting, and evaluating change initiatives around the world, and his books have been published in many languages. He holds five honorary doctorates.

Michael Fullan is currently adviser to the Premier, and to the Minister of Education in Ontario. His book, *Leading in a Culture of Change,* was awarded the 2002 Book of the Year Award by the National Staff Development Council (NSDC), and *Breakthrough* (with Peter Hill and Carmel Crévola) won the 2006 Book of the Year Award from the American Association of Colleges for Teacher Education. *Change Wars* with Andy

Hargreaves won the 2009 NSDC book of the year award, and *Turnaround Leadership in Higher Education* with Geoff Scott won the 2009 Bellwether book of the year. His latest publications are *Change Leader, Stratosphere, Professional Capital* (with Hargreaves), and *The Principal Leadership*.

More information can be found at www.michaelfullan.ca.

Andy Hargreaves is the Thomas More Brennan Chair in the Lynch School of Education at Boston College and adviser in education to the Premier of Ontario. Before that, he was the cofounder and codirector of the International Centre for Educational Change at the Ontario Institute for Studies in Education.

Andy was the founding editor-in-chief of the *Journal of Educational Change*. His books have achieved outstanding writing awards from the American Educational Research Association, the American Libraries Association, the National Staff Development Council, the International Leadership Association, and the American Association of Colleges for Teacher Education, and are translated into many languages. His most recent books are *Uplifting Leadership* (with Alan Boyle and Alma Harris, Wiley Business), *Professional Capital: Transforming Teaching in Every School* (with Michael Fullan, Teachers College Press 2012), and *The Global Fourth Way* (with Dennis Shirley, Corwin, 2012).

Andy consults widely with educational systems and organizations across the world and is one of the best known and most respected figures in the fields of educational change, leadership, and development.

You can follow Andy on Twitter @HargreavesBC.

Dr. Linda Harper is an award-winning secondary school administrator with a career spanning more than 20 years. She has served in many key educational leadership roles. In 2009, while serving as principal of Oak Hill School, the special needs and alternative school programs (STARS Academy) were recognized by the Council of Leaders for Alabama Schools (CLAS) as a CLAS Banner Award recipient. Under her leadership, students in the special needs program successfully met all reading and math goals as well as received local, state, and national recognitions in the area of Special Olympics. Both programs were featured in the National Association of Elementary School Principals Journal. She worked with her leadership team to develop and expand Success Prep Academy. The Academy was featured as an effective program at the 2013 School Superintendents of Alabama Conference. It was also one of the few programs in the state and the only program in the city to receive the Preparing Alabama Students for Success Grant. Success Prep Academy was featured in the 2013 Edition of Voices for Alabama Children, Success Stories as well as featured at the National Alternative Education Conference. It was also honored as a 2013 CLAS Banner Award recipient. Dr. Harper presented the system's Success Prep Academy model at the 2014 International Institute for Restorative Practices Conference, in Bethlehem, Pennsylvania. With proven results, it continues to be a model program for supporting students at risk of leaving high school. She is currently the principal of Paul W. Bryant High School and lives in Tuscaloosa, Alabama, with her two amazing children, Stephen and Hayleigh.

Dennis Littky is the cofounder and codirector of The Met School, Big Picture Learning and College Unbound. He is nationally known for his extensive work in secondary education in urban, suburban, and rural settings, spanning more than 40 years. As an educator, Dennis has a reputation for working up against the edge of convention and out of the box, turning tradition on its head and delivering concrete results. From 2000 to 2010, The Bill and Melinda Gates Foundation gave Big Picture Learning 25 million dollars to replicate The Met School nationally and internationally. Currently there is a network of 113 schools, 52 across the country, 40 in Australia, and 21 in the Netherlands.

Presently, Dennis's focus has been to expand the Big Picture Learning design to include a program, College Unbound, for adults, that allows them to earn a bachelor's degree while working full time. He also leads the Rhode Island Partnership Project, which is charged with identifying the barriers to access and completion of college degrees for adult learners in Rhode Island, and has recently started a Gateway Course for those interested in returning to school.

Dr. Littky holds a double PhD in psychology and education from the University of Michigan. His work as a principal at Thayer Junior/Senior High School in Winchester, New Hampshire, was featured in an NBC movie, *A Town Torn Apart*, based on the book *Doc: The Story of Dennis Littky and His Fight for a Better School*. In 2004, he wrote (along with Samantha Grabelle) *The Big Picture: Education Is Everyone's Business*, which went on to win the Association of Educational Publishers' top award for nonfiction in 2005. In 2003, Dennis was recognized as a leader in education and awarded the Harold W. McGraw Jr. Prize in Education. *Fast Company* ranked Littky #4 among the top 50 Innovators of 2004, and the George Lucas Educational Foundation recently selected Dennis as part of their Daring Dozen. Locally, Dennis was awarded the Local Hero Award by Bank of America in 2008 and College Unbound was awarded The Innovative and Creative Program Award by UPCEA, New England. Most recently, Dennis was awarded the New England Higher Education Excellence Award in 2011.

Marcus J. Newsome serves as superintendent of Chesterfield County Public Schools in Central Virginia, one of the 100 largest systems in the United States—and a national model for high performing school districts. He is a creative, innovative. and forward-thinking educator who has served as a consultant and adviser to governors, members of the United States Congress, and business leaders around the globe on solutions to close achievement gaps, narrow the digital divide, assessment design, professional development, and 21st century teaching and learning. Dr. Newsome began his career as a teacher in the District of Columbia Public Schools and later served as a curriculum writer, principal, and district administrator in a variety of positions that include superintendent of Newport News Public Schools.

Estrella Olivares-Orellana is a doctoral candidate in Curriculum and Teaching at Teachers College, Columbia University. Her scholarly interests are in the areas of bilingual and bicultural education, science education in bilingual settings, and the academic experiences of immigrant students. Presently, she is conducting qualitative research with students who have been classified as presenting interrupted formal education. Estrella is a part-time instructor in the department of Arts & Humanities at Teachers College, Columbia University, a full-time bilingual science teacher at a high school in the suburbs of New York, and a contributing editor for *Esteem Conversations Between Educators Journal*. Estrella holds an EdM in International Educational Development from Teachers College and a BS in Biochemistry from SUNY, Stony Brook.

Paul Reville is the Francis Keppel Professor of Practice of Educational Policy and Administration at Harvard University's Graduate School of Education (HGSE). He is the director of HGSE's Education Redesign Lab. He recently completed nearly 5 years of service as the Secretary of Education for the Commonwealth of Massachusetts. As Governor Patrick's top education adviser, Reville established a new Executive Office of Education and had oversight of higher education, K–12, and early education in the nation's leading student achievement state. Prior to joining the Patrick administration, Reville chaired the Massachusetts State Board of Education, founded the Rennie Center for Education Research and Policy, cofounded the Massachusetts Business Alliance for Education (MBAE), chaired the Massachusetts Reform Review Commission, chaired the Massachusetts Commission on Time and Learning, and served as executive director of the Pew Forum on Standards-Based Reform, a national think tank which convened the United States' leading researchers, practitioners, and policy makers to set the national standards agenda. Reville's career, which combines research, policy, and practice, began with service as a VISTA volunteer/youth worker. He served as a teacher and principal of two urban alternative high schools. Some years later, he founded a local education foundation which was part of the Public Education Network. He holds a BA from Colorado College, an MA from Stanford University, and five honorary doctoral degrees.

Dr. Amy F. Sichel was elected as the 2013–2014 president of the national organization, AASA, The School Superintendents Association, which represents 13,000 school superintendents from across the country. She has been a member of the Abington School District for 37 years and Superintendent of Schools for 14 years. During her tenure in the district, she has served as assistant superintendent, director of pupil services, a school psychologist, and an elementary school counselor. Dr. Sichel is an adjunct associate professor for the Graduate School of Education at the University of Pennsylvania and an adjunct instructor in the School of Graduate and Professional Studies at Delaware Valley College. She graduated from Lafayette College with a major in psychology, and majoring in School Psychology at the University of Pennsylvania, she earned her MS and PhD degrees. Dr. Sichel was selected from among the leaders of the 500 school districts in Pennsylvania as the 2010 Pennsylvania Superintendent of the Year and was also named a 2010 eSchool News Tech-Savvy Superintendent Award winner in recognition of her vision, leadership, and accomplishments in educational technology. In addition, Dr. Sichel received from AASA and Farmers Insurance the Women in School Leadership Award in 2012 as a finalist in recognition of outstanding talent, creativity, and vision. Other awards include recognition by the Pennsylvania State Education Association for outstanding service, an educational leadership award from the Graduate School of Education at the University of Pennsylvania, and recognition by the local chapter of the NAACP. Dr. Sichel was the president of the Pennsylvania Association of School Administrators (PASA) in 2010 to 2011. Dr. Sichel and the Abington School District are recognized nationally for the district's work in narrowing the achievement gaps for historically underrepresented students.

Dr. Susan Szachowicz retired after serving as the principal of Brockton High School, a large (4,200 students) comprehensive urban high school, and is currently a senior fellow with the International Center for Leadership in Education. At Brockton High for 39 years, Sue describes herself as Brockton High's greatest cheerleader. Originally a history teacher, she was the social science department head for many years, and then became a housemaster. In 1999, she was appointed the associate principal for curriculum and instruction and directed the school's literacy initiatives to improve student achievement. She was appointed principal on January 1, 2004, and in that capacity led the academic turnaround of Brockton High. She has served on numerous state commissions on education reform. Her leadership at Brockton High was committed to "high expectations, high standards—no excuses." Under her leadership, Brockton High received many state and national honors including recognition as a Massachusetts Compass School, a National Model School by the International Center for Leadership in Education for 12 years in a row, recipient of the National School Change Award, five times the Bronze Medal from U.S. News and World Report as one of America's Best High Schools, and the Gould Education Award from the Associated Industries of Massachusetts.

Sue received both her BA in History and Sociology and MA in History from Bridgewater State College and earned her doctorate in Educational Leadership and Administration from the University of Massachusetts Amherst.

Saskia Traill is the vice president, policy and research, at The After-School Corporation (TASC), dedicated to giving all kids opportunities to grow through expanded learning opportunities that support, educate, and inspire them. She is currently leading research and policy efforts for TASC's ExpandED Schools, a reinvention of urban public schools by bringing together all members of the school and community to expand the day and increase learning options for students. Saskia also leads research and policy efforts in summer learning, high school expanded learning models, and opportunities for children to engage in quality science, technology, engineering, and math (STEM). Prior to working at TASC, Saskia was a program manager for the Insight Center for Community Economic Development, working to build state systems for early care and education. She has authored and coauthored articles for peer-reviewed journals, policy briefs, and reports on a range of issues, including family economics, how to fund innovative education strategies, and engaging kids in STEM. She received her BA from Columbia University and a PhD in research psychology from Stanford University.

Allison Zmuda is an author and independent consultant based in Virginia who works with schools and districts to create dynamic learning environments for like-minded educators, parents, and kids. Allison received her undergraduate degree at Yale University and graduated with her teaching certification. She then became a public high school social studies teacher for 8 years and earned National Board Teaching

Certification during that time. Allison went directly from the classroom to being a consultant and author. Allison collaborates with school staff on curriculum assessment and instructional practices to make learning more purposeful, relevant, and engaging for students. She has written seven books to date, most notably *The Competent Classroom* (2001), *Transforming Schools* (2004), *Breaking Free From Myths About Teaching and Learning* (2010), and *Learning Personalized: The Evolution of the Contemporary Classroom* (early spring 2015). Her latest project is the founding and curating of a website, learningpersonalized.com—a community where students, parents, and educators can view blog posts, share stories, contribute resources, and pose questions for further discussion. Allison can be reached at zmuda@competentclassroom.com. Her Twitter handle is compclass.

PART I

For Every Student

A journey of a thousand miles begins with one step.

—Lao-tzu

Powerful leaders are those who have the courage to take the step and embark on the journey. Courage is derived from the French word *coeur*, meaning heart. In many early Native American societies, having "heart" was considered one of the greatest virtues. The primary attributes of this virtue were to strengthen oneself by serving others and to face fears. Educators often make sacrifices and face their fears in service to the success of children. Courageous leadership is necessary to foster change in our educational system.

In the opening section of this book, the authors announce their call to action. A new paradigm is described: one addressing among the most charged issues of our time, enhancing success for all students through equity. Each author highlighted in this book demonstrates one or more of the core principles of Courageous Leadership (Blankstein, 2004, 2010, 2013). Alan M. Blankstein and Pedro Noguera challenge the notion of zero-sum thinking (the "haves" versus the "have nots") and explain the new paradigm grounded in child development, neuroscience, and environmental influences.

In the opening chapter, we outline the makings of a new paradigm and a vision of reaching *Excellence Through Equity* for every student. We also provide a framework of Courageous Leadership as the engine to get us to this vision. Each of the five principles of courage (Blankstein, 2004, 2010, 2013) are exemplified in subsequent chapters by an array of extraordinary contributors to this book. As you will see, these principles are interactive, and more than one of them is present in each of these chapters. These principles serve as a frame of reference rather than as a discrete set of activities. Thus, when we describe "getting to your core" as a leader, we recognize that there will be overlap with what it takes for "making organizational meaning" for the entire learning community.

We begin this section from two contributing authors whose chapters demonstrate at the school and system levels, respectively, the interaction of the five principles of courage. Susan Szachowicz, principal of Brockton High School, shows how these core principles have guided the largest high school in Massachusetts from being named one of the lowest performing schools in the state, to being cited as among the top high schools in the country by U.S. News and World Report. The fact that progress continues to be made at the school even after Szachowicz's retirement is further illustration of her effective leadership.

In Brockton High School, the leadership displayed the "Cycle of Courage" described in this chapter in which the leadership was faced with a crisis brought on by compelling facts, chose to **face their fears and the facts** of the situation, **got to their core,** and **created organizational meaning** and **sustained relationships** around the **purpose and plan** to which they held tightly. The plan, developed to serve all students at Brockton High School, also illustrates how the three principles of the new paradigm, a focus on the malleability of the brain, the developmental needs of students (adolescents in this case), and the contextual obstacles they face, were integral to their action plan.

Michael Fullan's chapter focuses on the big picture by providing the whole-system approach to achieving greater equity. He provides principles that not only increase the chances of achieving greater equity, but he elaborates on how to foster conditions that sustain continuing improvements.

This section lays the foundation upon which the remainder of the book is built. Each section will highlight principles of Courageous Leadership and examples from various perspectives that will help other leaders take the first step for their journey.

REFERENCE

Blankstein, A. (2004, 2010, 2013). *Failure is not an option.* Thousand Oaks, CA: Corwin.

Introduction

Achieving Excellence Through
Equity for Every Student

Alan M. Blankstein and Pedro Noguera

In education circles, the word *equity* is often controversial and confusing. When it is brought up to an economically diverse audience, those with affluence and privilege often become squeamish and start looking for the exits, while those in financial need often become more engaged, hoping that a focus on equity will bring relief and attention to what they lack. Such responses tend to occur because when the term *equity* is raised, it often evokes a zero-sum scenario; a perception that if we do more for those who are disadvantaged it will mean there will be less for the advantaged. When this occurs and the pursuit of equity—which we define as a commitment to ensure that every student receives what he or she needs to succeed—is subverted by the assumption that there must be winners and losers, rarely is any progress achieved. Invariably, conversations about equity either degenerate into acrimonious debate over how to serve the needs of both privileged and disadvantaged children, objectives that are typically perceived as irreconcilable, or we lapse hopelessly into a state of paralysis.

This book offers a way to move beyond zero-sum thinking and compelling reasons to do so. In the following chapters we provide *practical*, detailed accounts of what schools, districts, classrooms, and community-based organizations are doing to promote excellence through equity. We also show through these cases that overcoming the impasse between the pursuit of excellence and equity is essential if we are to avoid remaining trapped on a path that is not only generating greater inequality in academic outcomes but also contributing to deeper inequality within our society generally.

U.S. EDUCATORS ARE SWIMMING
AGAINST A WAVE OF POOR POLICY

The persistence of disparities in learning opportunities and academic out-comes has contributed to America's decline in educational performance in comparison with other nations. Results from the Program in International Student Assessment (PISA) reveal that American students have made little progress, and in some cases declined, relative to children in several other wealthy nations (Organisation for Economic Co-operation and Development [OECD], 2012). Closer examination of the results shows that growing inequality is a central factor contributing to America's edu-cational decline. Recent results from scores on the ACT show that only 39% of those students who recently took the exam were deemed college ready. Of these, only 11% of African Americans and 18% of Latinos passed with scores that met the college-ready threshold, while 49% of Whites and 57% of Asians met the mark (Resmovitz, 2014). Given that the majority of children in our nation's schools are presently students of color (National Center for Education Statistics, 2013), and people of color are projected to make up the majority of the U.S. population by the year 2041 (Frey, 2013), these trends are especially troubling.

Furthermore, our nation has higher levels of child poverty than most other wealthy nations, with 23%, or almost one in four children, coming from households in poverty. In the nation's largest urban school districts the number of children from impoverished families is considerably higher. Unlike many nations that outperform us, we tolerate gross inequities in school funding, in access to quality preschool, and in health care (Sahlberg, 2011). Despite compelling evidence that growing poverty and inequality are at least partially responsible for our decline in educational performance (Barton & Coley, 2010), policy makers have largely ignored the issue. Instead, they have fixated on the idea that slippage in academic performance can be reversed simply by raising academic standards and increasing accountability on educators despite consistent evidence that the strategy has not worked (Fullan & Boyle, 2014).

There is compelling evidence based on comparisons with nations that have outperformed ours that the policy direction we have pursued has contributed to our decline relative to other nations (Darling-Hammond, 2011). Despite this evidence, policy makers from both major parties have been unwilling to consider a new set of strategies or to change course. A recent report commissioned by the U.S. Department of Education called for greater focus on equity in funding and educational opportunities (Equity and Excellence Commission, 2013). Despite the report, the federal government has not called for a change in policy, and we continue to focus narrowly on accountability and standards. Instead of building the capacity of schools and providing them with additional support to meet the complex needs of students, we continue to rely on pressure and humiliation as a means of prodding schools to improve. The strategy hasn't worked, and it is increasingly clear that it never will. Ignoring equity, not merely in education but in wages, housing, health, and quality of life, has contributed to widening levels of inequality and is undermining our well-being and our future as a nation.

AN EQUITY TIDE LIFTS ALL BOATS

There is an alternative to growing inequality (in education at least) or remaining trapped indefinitely in a zero-sum quagmire. The alternative is to recognize that equity and excellence are not at odds, and that the highest level of excellence will actually be obtained *through* the pursuit of equity. To many, excellence through equity may seem like an implausible or even a radical concept. In some ways it is, given the policy direction we have pursued in recent years, but closer examination reveals that it has been a central part of the human experience for centuries. It was inherent in the message and the ethos that Franklin Delano Roosevelt used to push through the New Deal, that made it possible for a president from Texas (LBJ) to overcome powerful opposition in Congress to obtain approval of the Civil Rights Act, and that compelled the U.S. government to cooperate with Martin Luther King Jr. as he and others marched and organized for a peaceful end to American apartheid. In all three examples it is clear that by advancing equity the greater good of society would be furthered, or as Eleanor Roosevelt put it: "We do well when we all do well."

Similarly, a commitment to excellence and equity has been central to many of our nation's advances in education. The idea that we could achieve excellence through equity made it possible for President Lyndon Johnson to overcome opposition from southern legislators and enact Title I, the Elementary and Secondary Education Act, as a key provision of the effort to expand civil rights and launch the war on poverty. Later, the principle of excellence through equity served as an essential premise for advancing the educational rights of women (Title IX), linguistic minorities (Lau v. Nichols, 1974), and the disabled (National Center for Learning Disabilities, 2014). It served as an effective rationale once again when the Clinton administration moved to significantly expand access to the internet for poor children in American schools during the 1990s (Tyack & Cuban, 1995) and when President Obama launched the Promise Neighborhoods initiative.

What each of these examples has in common is recognition that societal progress is contingent upon expanding opportunities for all. These examples also remind us that in certain crucial aspects of life, the advancement of a small group cannot be achieved or *sustained* unless the larger population, including the most vulnerable, is allowed to share in the benefits. FDR didn't demand a New Deal for Democrats or northerners. Martin Luther King Jr. did not organize to demand a better life for Blacks alone while poor Whites and others languished in poverty. These visionary leaders understood that *everyone* would benefit when justice and opportunity was available to all. In a similar way, advancements in educational opportunities that have helped to eliminate structural barriers related to race, gender, poverty, and learning differences have benefited our entire society. In the United States, measures to expand civil rights for some have incrementally enlarged rights for all people and increased our ability to provide quality education to all children. Equity-based reforms have strengthened our democracy by reducing some, though by no means all, of the blatant injustices. They have also increased the ability of those who were once discriminated against and excluded to contribute to the advancement of the very society that had previously held them back.

When seen in this context, the notion that excellence can be pursued through equity is an idea that is neither novel nor far-fetched; it has been central and essential to human progress throughout time. When the idea has been applied to education it has allowed our society to move closer to living up to its democratic ideals, and it has increased the number of people who are able to participate fully in our society as genuine enfranchised members (Katznelson & Weir, 1985).

Throughout this book, we advance the idea that expansion of equity in education does not pose a threat to those with power and wealth. Instead, we argue that when equity is advanced it actually benefits those who are able to provide their children with the very best opportunities. It does so by helping them to develop a sense of empathy and compassion toward those who are less fortunate and to acquire emotional and intellectual skills that are essential to success in the 21st century (Wagner, 2008). As we will show, when the privileged are denied the opportunity to work with people from diverse backgrounds, they lose the ability to effectively interact with the vast majority of the population with whom they will ultimately have to share the planet.

We have ample evidence that by focusing narrowly on what we perceive as our self-interests, we are not only harming the *common* good but undermining the best interests of our *own* children. The efforts of affluent parents to secure a place for their children in elite preschools while poor and middle-class parents struggle to secure adequate care for their babies undermines our ability to provide each child with the opportunity to succeed in life. Similarly, when economically disadvantaged parents surreptitiously enroll their children in affluent school districts only to be removed and charged with crime upon discovery, it should serve as a reminder that we cannot afford to secure educational advantages for the few while others put up with woefully inadequate conditions. Certainly, most parents will do whatever it takes to secure excellent educational opportunities for *their* children. The mythology that must be challenged is that we can afford to take care of our children while ignoring the needs of others, and we must do so by showing that by helping others it is actually beneficial to our *own* children.

This book challenges the mythology that "haves" and "have nots" are divided by insurmountable barriers and difference. In its place we put forward the premise that it is in our *common interest* to ensure that all young people receive an education that allows them to cultivate their talent and potential. Finding ways to do this should be the mission of education, and it is indeed becoming the focus of the most successful schools and districts in America and beyond. History has shown us that separation and segregation will never provide a road that leads to excellence. Nor will maintaining the either/or dichotomy that keeps us looking out for ourselves and prevents us from pursuing strategies that benefit all. This book demonstrates how adopting the win-win paradigm based on the pursuit of excellence through equity can lead to better outcomes for *every* student.

In the 21st century, demography need not determine destiny, and a child's race and class *can* be decoupled from how well they will do in school or college. A vast body of research has shown us that talent and ability are present among all types of children (Boykin & Noguera, 2011; Darling-Hammond, 2011). As we show in the pages ahead, we now have strategies and interventions that make it possible to meet the educational needs of a wide variety of learners. The real issue is how to make these resources available to educators rather than rehashing the debate over whether or not we can or should educate all children. In the following section, we review and challenge some of the common beliefs that are barriers to the attainment of excellence through equity.

THE ARGUMENTS FOR INEQUITY

In the prevailing paradigm, it is widely believed that there are limited resources available and that it is necessary, though perhaps unfortunate, for scarce resources to be distributed in a manner that assures success of some and likely failure of others. The operating assumption is that if we redistribute resources in a more equitable manner, those who gained in the past will begin to lose, and those previously short-changed will advance at their expense. This mental model forms the basis of the following arguments:

If we spend money in one place, we don't have it to spend elsewhere— it's that simple. This presumption leads many to advocate for resources and policies that will benefit their child—even when it clearly comes at the expense of other children. Under this scenario, only the most high-minded and altruistic people would conceive of yielding resources for their children in order to advance the interests of others. Yet, this is only part of the picture. While financial resources are indeed essential to obtain resources such as technology or to support excellent instruction, there is considerable evidence that staff morale, school culture, and collaborative relationships premised on trust and respect among teachers and parents are as important if not more so than financial resources alone, as demonstrated by several of the examples used in this book. Moreover, there is evidence that suggests that when highly qualified educators are deliberately placed in low-performing schools, *all schools* benefit, as was the case in the award-winning Charlotte-Mecklenburg schools—the subject matter of Chapter 6.

If my child is forced to collaborate with poor students, he or she will be pulled down academically. In the past decade, the number of school districts that have considered socioeconomic status (SES) in student placement has grown from a few to more than 80 (Kahlenberg, 2012). This has made it possible to carry out more research on the impact of diversity (based on race, SES, and perceptions of ability) in the classroom. Some research shows that a mix of students by SES, race, and ethnicity can improve performance in higher math courses among students who were previously low achievers (Mickelson & Bottia, 2010). Several of the chapters featured in the pages ahead show that when students from diverse backgrounds learn together and are taught by teachers who know how to provide differentiated support, all children can benefit. Furthermore, research shows that in schools that are diverse with respect to race and SES, the achievement of advantaged students has not been harmed by desegregation policies (Harris, 2008, p. 563).

Subsequent chapters demonstrate how classrooms have been structured to improve math and literacy skills and performance of students at all levels simultaneously; how tapping students' native language and culture advances their achievement while enriching classes for students overall; and how systems of engagement, assessment, and project-based learning can effectively be deployed for all kinds of students, creating equity within several schools in the largest system in the United States—the New York City Public Schools.

Changing paradigms is difficult, especially when it involves changing attitudes about race and resources! Indeed this is the case, and for that reason we have framed this book around the theme of "courage." As we will show, pushing for excellence through equity requires great courage and conviction. We provide the five principles of Courageous Leadership at the end of the chapter as a guide for others who seek to follow this path. Interestingly, we were surprised to find that many of the leaders in this book who embraced these principles—intentionally or not—found far less resistance to their shift to equity than they had expected. This is true in the case studies of several of the districts, one state, and at least two countries described in coming chapters.

THE ARGUMENTS FOR EQUITY

It's the right thing to do. That members of a society share a moral imperative to assure that every child gets what he or she needs to succeed is in many ways the most important, and—until recently—the major argument that has been advanced by human rights movements throughout much of the world. While some comply with equity mandates as a result of external pressure or desegregation orders, we would argue that the courageous action and leadership that is required to enact excellence through equity can only be *sustained* if they are grounded in clear and unflinching moral reasoning. Several of the leaders profiled in subsequent chapters were successful in overcoming opposition by framing the need for change as a moral imperative. This book is rooted in the moral high ground but also based on evidence that shows that advancing equity is both *morally* and *practically* the "right thing to do."

The most advantaged and successful students do even better in an equitable school setting. Schools committed to equity don't do so by limiting opportunities for the most advanced students. On the contrary, by providing differentiated support to all students, academically advanced students can have a richer educational experience. When efforts are made to integrate students from a variety of backgrounds, the learning environment becomes more compelling and enriched. When Langston Hughes's poetry is analyzed by Black, brown, and White students together, all students gain more than when they learn in homogeneous settings. Chapter contributors Dennis Littky and Darlene Berg share examples in which the social/emotional skill development critical to a 21st century education becomes integral to learning when students communicate with others across cultures and economic status. Similarly, teaching strategies become much more complex and sophisticated as teachers are challenged to reach every student and incorporate every learning style.

Financial support for schools may actually increase. It is often the case that those who do well get more attention and opportunities to do even better. Many of the educators, schools, and districts highlighted in this book have won prestigious awards, recognition, and additional funding to expand the meaningful work they were already doing on behalf of children in greatest need. For example, Brockton High School, the largest high school in the state of Massachusetts, has received numerous awards for its success in serving a racially and socioeconomically diverse student population. Charlotte-Mecklenburg just received the Broad Prize based on the outcomes of their equity agenda. And in suburban Abington, Pennsylvania, students attending private and charter schools were drawn back to the public schools by parents who were impressed with the philosophy and student gains experienced by this equity-embracing district!

Parental, staff, and community support grows. In other chapters that follow, leaders describe their initial fears and the ensuing conflict and anger that erupted in the community over educational changes, like making AP classes accessible to all students in the district. In such cases, even some of the most ardent detractors to equity eventually became champions of change.

The alternative to equity is catastrophic. In *The Art of War*, Sun Tzu describes the "nine fighting grounds" and the pros and cons of each. The ninth, in which the trapped enemy has no means of escape, was described as the most treacherous to the apparent victor, and should be avoided at all costs, because the prevailing army would face an enemy with "nothing to lose."

As we have seen inequities widen and despair grow in communities where poverty has become deeply entrenched, more and more people have come to the conclusion that they have no possibility of improving their lives. When hope disappears, some become despondent and turn to substance abuse while others come to the conclusion that they want change now and that they have nothing to lose. In some countries, this has led to revolutions (most recently, the "Arab Spring"), and more recently it has produced social upheaval in the United States in communities like Ferguson, MO. However, we also have rare examples like that of South

Africa, where we have seen hope expand through advances in equity (albeit very slowly). This was made possible by the enlightened leadership of the African National Congress, which assumed power without punishing the White minority. Rather than trading places with their former oppressors and inflicting pain on the White minority, Mandela and his allies opted to dismantle the system of apartheid instead.

It is increasingly clear that if we do not address the profound inequities in education, the disparities in learning opportunities that are behind the so-called achievement gap, our entire society will be imperiled. Pursuing excellence through equity is a genuine alternative. In the pages ahead we demonstrate how this can be done by nothing less than a paradigm shift from our current one-size-fits-all factory model, the inevitable outcome of which is failure and hopelessness for increasing numbers of children, to a system that celebrates individual differences and serves the needs of every student.

A NEW PARADIGM

The transition from a paradigm in crisis to a new one from which a new tradition of normal science can emerge is far from a cumulative process . . . Rather it is a reconstruction of the field from new fundamentals, a reconstruction that changes some of the field's most elementary theoretical generalizations . . . When the transition is complete, the profession will have changed its view of the field, its methods, and its goals.

— Thomas S. Kuhn, *The Structure of Scientific Revolutions* (1962), 84–85

What we want to achieve in our work with young people is to find and strengthen the positive and healthy elements no matter how deeply they are hidden.

— Karl Wilker, 1921

This book is about how to create schools and learning communities where all students are able to thrive. Instead of being defined by their behavior (e.g., hyperactive, disruptive, etc.), labeled because of their needs (e.g., slow, insolent, etc.), and discarded, all children must be served by schools that are organized to meet their needs. This means that educators must take time to get to know all students so that they can spend time cultivating talents and build on their potential. By building on strengths and addressing the factors that underlie learning difficulties and behavior problems, educators are in a better position to instill confidence and, ultimately, promote independence.

Instead of schools that practice a form of triage—giving the best resources to those regarded as having the most potential, and the least to those perceived as too troubled or inferior to be worthy of a quality education, we need schools that are committed to the success of every child; where the learning needs of *all children* can be served. Equity is premised upon a recognition that because all children are different there must be a deep commitment to meet the needs of every child in order to ensure that each student receives what he or she needs to grow and develop and ultimately to succeed.

As we have stated, creating a school community in which excellence through equity is the ultimate objective would be transformational, not only for the disadvantaged but for all students. The good news is that this is an attainable goal. We know this because this goal is steadfastly being pursued in a small number of classrooms, schools, and districts right now. It is also a central feature of educational policy in some nations. This book includes many illustrations of how the commitment to excellence through equity is being achieved with different types of children. The contributors provide insights into the strategies that have been used and the challenges they have faced. We are convinced that by exercising persistence and courageous leadership (the subject of the final section of this chapter), these successes can be replicated in other settings across the United States.

However, we realize that for the pursuit of excellence and equity to occur on a larger scale we need much more than a new set of reform strategies. We need a new paradigm to guide us; one that can help us to escape the assumption that there must be winners and losers and that can free us from zero-sum thinking that presently limits us. A new paradigm is much more than a new policy, strategy, or set of practices and techniques. A new paradigm is premised on a different epistemological outlook that makes it possible for us to see our work through a different lens. According to Thomas Kuhn, author of *The Structure of Scientific Revolutions* (1962), shifts in paradigms occur when scientists encounter anomalies that can no longer be explained by the paradigm that previously provided the framework for scientific inquiry. A paradigm, in Kuhn's view, is an entire worldview that defines the basic features of the landscape of knowledge that scientists can identify around them.

Although Kuhn thought of paradigms exclusively in reference to science, we can apply the concept, with some degree of modification, to education. In American education, the paradigm that has guided our thinking about teaching and learning has been rooted in the belief that intelligence is an innate property that can be measured and assessed (Lehman, 1996). It is also intimately tied to the concept of meritocracy, the notion that society should be organized on the basis of merit (e.g., talent, effort, and skill) rather than privilege or status (Bell, 1973). The meritocratic ideal gave rise to the development of intelligence tests that were used in the early 20th century to identify the capabilities of individuals and rationalize promotions and ranks within the military, admissions to colleges and universities, and in some cases, job placements (Fischer, 1996).

In many respects, the concept of meritocracy was an advance over the beliefs and practices of the 19th century that rationalized slavery, the subordination of women, and other forms of discrimination. This is because it was well-aligned to the emerging notion of the American dream: the idea that in this country, intelligence, hard work, and natural talent would be rewarded and have greater value than inherited privilege. As the concept of meritocracy gained currency during the 20th century, it became easier to challenge discriminatory practices and to call for barriers to opportunity, especially those that were related to education, to be removed (Carnoy & Levin, 1985). Of course, the concept of meritocracy is undermined by the fact that those with inherited wealth and privilege still retain considerable advantage over others. Affluent parents are less dependent on schools. They typically have access to a wide variety of resources that make it possible for their children to keep ahead. Nonetheless, the emergence of the ideal of meritocracy was an important step forward because it introduced the notion that achievement should serve as the basis for organizing social hierarchies rather than race, class, religion, or other inherited forms of privilege.

Yet, despite the advances achieved under the meritocracy paradigm, it has clearly outlived its usefulness. In most schools throughout the United States, a child's race, socioeconomic status, and zip code continues to predict not only how well he or she will do in school but also the quality of school he or she will attend. While it is certainly good to reward talent and effort, it is also important to recognize that some children are denied the opportunity to have their talents developed because their families lack the time and resources to invest in them, and the schools they attend are often unable to develop their latent abilities. Too many students possess talents and potential that are unrecognized in school, especially when their parents lack the ability to advocate for their educational needs. The current approach to educating children has left us with millions who leave school disinterested in learning and unprepared for work, college, or the challenges of life in the 21st century. If we truly seek to ensure that all children have the opportunity to develop their potential, we will need a new approach to teaching and learning, one that matches what we now know about the nature of intelligence.

We need a new paradigm in order to move beyond the fear and trepidation that keeps us clinging to the idea that there must be winners and losers and that allows us to accept the failure of so many children in so many schools. High drop-out rates and pervasive failure, particularly in schools serving poor children, are by-products of the meritocracy paradigm that allowed us to believe that individual talent and grit are all that's needed to overcome society's obstacles. In order to free ourselves from the traditions and practices that keep us locked in predictable patterns of success and failure, we must embrace a new paradigm, one that makes it possible to pursue excellence through equity for all.

If we want to create schools where all students have the opportunity to be challenged and stimulated, and where their talents can be cultivated, we need a different paradigm to guide our schools. It could be argued that No Child Left Behind (NCLB) took us a step in that direction. When the law was enacted in 2001, for the first time in U.S. history schools were required to produce evidence that *all children*, regardless of race, class, or status, were learning. It was a bold idea except the only evidence schools were required to look for was how well students performed on standardized tests. While testing, and assessment generally, is an important tool that can be used to monitor learning (and even more beneficial when used to diagnose learning needs), NCLB has actually reinforced the notion that students can or should be judged based on how well they perform on tests. In many schools it has also led to a narrowing of the curriculum. Art, music, and even physical education are not tested subjects, so in many schools they are treated as extras that can be cut when resources are scarce or to create more time for subjects that will be tested. Sadly, rather than moving us forward, NCLB has reinforced the tendency to make premature and often inaccurate judgments about the abilities of children and has left the so-called achievement gap, which it was designed to ameliorate, largely untouched.

FOUNDATIONS OF THE NEW PARADIGM
FOR EXCELLENCE THROUGH EQUITY

The new paradigm we are offering for achieving excellence through equity is grounded in knowledge derived from three important areas of research: (1) child development, (2) neuroscience, and (3) environmental influences on child development and learning. While awareness about the importance of these three sources of knowledge to education has been around for many years, what we think is new is a recognition of how the three interact and can be used to meet the needs of individual students and guide the development of educational policy and practice. As we briefly spell out the specific aspects of what we think of as the three pillars of the paradigm, throughout the book we pay particular attention to their interaction and application.

Child Development

For the longest time, educational theory and practice has been guided by research in child development. The early architects of formal education (e.g., Froebel) recognized that that the cognitive, emotional, psychological, and physical development of children were interrelated, and that the capacity of children to undertake different learning tasks was related to their progression on different stages of the life cycle (Wood, 1998). Research from child development has influenced the development of school curricula (Connor, Morrison, & Petrella, 2004), learning strategies that have been applied within schools (Chatterji, 2006), and most importantly, the training of teachers (Ames, 1990, 1992). A central theme in the literature that has guided this work is the recognition that while child development followed typical patterns that correspond to age, there are also significant variations in how and when children acquire skills during different stages. Individual differences, differences in social context, and differences in culture have all been recognized as having bearing on the development process. For example, while it is common for most children to learn to walk sometime between 8 and 15 months, or to learn to use the potty independently sometime between age 2 and 4, the range for what is considered normal in acquiring these skills is quite broad. Furthermore, most developmental psychologists and pediatricians recognize that if a child is more advanced or delayed in acquiring these skills it does not necessarily mean that they are gifted or abnormal (Brooks-Gunn, Fuligni, & Berlin, 2003).

In recent years, educational practice has been less aligned with knowledge and research derived from child development. As policy makers have become more focused on holding schools accountable for producing evidence of student achievement as measured by performance on standardized tests, recognition of how variations in child development relate to reaching milestones such as learning to read has increasingly been ignored. Since the adoption of NCLB and its accompanying mandate for schools to produce evidence that students were achieving "average yearly progress" in math and literacy (Brooks-Gunn, et al., 2003), recognition of variations in child development have been replaced by the assumption that all children of the same age or grade should be able to acquire similar skills at a similar pace, regardless of who they are, whether or not their first language is English, the types of schools in which they are educated, or their life circumstances (Paris & Newman, 1990).

As we will show in the pages ahead, schools and academic programs that are committed to the principle of pursuing excellence through equity strive to address the developmental needs of each student. In fact, many attempt to *personalize learning* for their students in order to ensure that their needs are met. While personalized learning plans may seem beyond the skills and resources of most schools, a number of new innovations in the field of education are making it possible.

However, even when schools and academic programs that are committed to excellence and equity do not have access to such resources, some are still devising creative strategies to meet student needs. For example, rather than assuming that all students should read with proficiency by the third grade, some of the educators we feature in these chapters have developed practices grounded in an understanding of child development that make it possible for English language learners and children who learn differently (e.g., those who are dyslexic) to receive more support and take more time as they are learning to read in English. This is not a matter of lowering expectations or accepting that some children won't learn to read; it is simply an approach rooted in the recognition that not all children learn to read at the same pace. Similarly, while it might be a good thing to encourage high school students to take rigorous math courses such as Algebra and Geometry, some schools have figured out that if a student's literacy skills are not strong enough to comprehend complex word problems, it might not make sense to require such courses unless additional literacy support can be provided. As we will show, when such an approach was implemented at Brockton High School, it not only benefited the large number of English language learners at the school; it also helped the large number of students that entered high school with limited literacy skills. In each of the examples that will be shared in the pages ahead, the educators, schools, and programs demonstrate a profound recognition that understanding and responding to the developmental needs of each student is the only way to ensure that they will receive the education they need.

Neuroscience

In recent years, neuroscientists have gone from regarding the brain as a static organ that undergoes few changes after early childhood, to understanding that the neural pathways and synapses that wire the brain go through ongoing changes in response to behavior, the environment, and neural processes. The term *neuroplasticity* has been used to describe the ability of the brain to continue developing through neuronal activation in response to stimulation and experience. A growing body of neuroscientific research suggests that experience can actually change both the brain's physical structure and its functional organization well into adulthood (Pascual-Leone, Amedi, Fregni, & Merabet, 2005).

Research on the brain has significant implications for how we think about how children learn. For years, schools have relied on testing to sort students into groups or tracks, presumably for the purpose of efficiently meeting their learning needs. These practices have persisted despite evidence from research on tracking that has shown that such practices almost always result in separating students by race and SES. When this occurs, invariably low-income and minority students are consistently more likely to be placed in slow and remedial groups, while the most affluent and privileged children are generally placed in the advanced groups (Oakes, 2005). Given what we know about the elasticity of the brain, these practices are not only outdated and uninformed by the latest research; they also deny numerous children the right and opportunity to have their learning needs met. According to Fischer and Bidell (2006), "The brain is remarkably plastic, even in middle or old age, it's still adapting very actively to its environment" (p. 27). Several researchers have shown that when students are encouraged to view academic success as a product of hard work rather than an outgrowth of natural intelligence, they are more likely to perform at higher levels (Dweck, 1999; Boykin & Noguera, 2011). Research has also shown that when students learn about the malleability of the brain it can actually improve their performance in school (Trzesniewski & Dweck, 2007). Furthermore, when teachers understand that learning is facilitated by the formation of new or stronger neural connections, they are able to prioritize activities that help students tap into already-existing pathways by integrating academic subjects or devising class projects that are relevant to their students' lives.

As we will show in the pages ahead, a number of schools and districts are drawing upon research from neuroscience to provide students with the instructional supports needed to advance academically. Their success, and the research that supports it, provides further evidence that we can do much more to cultivate talent and ability in children.

Environmental Influences

For many years, educators have understood that environmental influences, including family, peer groups, and neighborhood environmental factors, have an influence upon child development and student learning (Rothstein, 2004). Neighborhood environmental factors may include air quality, interpersonal and institutional violence, the quality of housing, and even the level of noise or quality of water a child is exposed to on a regular basis (Jackson, Johnson, & Persico, 2014). In more recent times, awareness about how the environment impacts children has been extended to include recognition that even less direct environmental influences such as media, video games, music, and other forms of popular culture also have tremendous influence on the development of children (Syme, 2004).

Psychologist Urie Bronfenbrenner theorized that there were five layers to the environmental context that impact an individual's growth and development: the microsystem, the mesosystem, the exosystem, the macrosystem, and the chronosystem (1975). Bronfenbrenner's theory focused on the impact that environment played on the growth and development of the individual. Bronfenbrenner's work is important because it draws attention to the various layers of environment, from the interpersonal to even broader societal trends such as de-industrialization and immigration, and how they impact the individual.

As poverty rates have risen in recent years, a growing number of researchers have drawn attention to the ways in which food insecurity, poor heath, lack of safety, housing instability, violence, and poor nutrition negatively influence the welfare and well-being of children (Eccles & Gootman, 2002). Similarly, for immigrant children who often remain connected to families and relatives abroad even as they settle in the United States, war, famine, and natural disasters can all have tremendous bearing on their well-being and their academic performance (Suárez-Orozco, Suárez-Orozco, & Todorova, 2009).

While the relationship between the environment and student learning may seem obvious, in recent years, education policy has increasingly ignored the influence of environmental factors on children. Rather than devising or even recommending strategies that might make it possible for schools to respond to and mitigate harmful environment factors, policies at the federal and state level have adopted a context-blind approach and largely failed to acknowledge the ways in which the environment affects schools and children.

As an alternative, we suggest that schools must take time to deliberately understand the environmental factors that influence the children they serve. Plant closures, toxic waste sites, gangs, housing foreclosures, the absence of healthy food, and other conditions can have significant influence on children and learning. While schools may not be able to counter the harmful effects that arise from such conditions, they are more likely to be able to create strategies to counter and even mitigate these conditions if they understand how they may be influencing their students. For example, some of the schools that will be described in the following chapters developed partnerships with health clinics and after-school programs to address needs that they could not respond to on their own. While such strategies do not eliminate environmental obstacles, these examples show that when such strategies are pursued, which we describe as a more integrated and holistic approach, the ability of schools to meet the needs of their students is increased.

When these three pillars of the excellence through equity paradigm are used together in a coherent system for responding to and addressing the needs of children, the ability of schools to meet the developmental and academic needs of students increases significantly. When this occurs, the pursuit of excellence through equity becomes possible and attainable, but of course, never easy. We are under no illusion that the forces responsible for growing inequality can be easily abated through the adoption of a few strategies. That is why we describe the approach we are calling for as a new paradigm because we think it represents a very different way of thinking about how schools can serve the learning needs of students. Our hope is that readers will be inspired by these examples to think about how the paradigm can be applied in more classrooms, schools, cities, states, and beyond. While all elements of this paradigm are not necessarily reflected in the examples that will be presented in the pages ahead, we think the paradigm itself serves as a useful framework for thinking about how schools can effectively pursue excellence through equity.

PRINCIPLES OF ACTION

It is very important that our readers understand that we do not envision the pursuit of excellence through equity as a set of strategies that can be followed in a formulaic manner. On the contrary, we believe it is important to acknowledge that because children are different with respect to their interests, temperament, and needs, the strategies employed to serve their needs must vary. *Equity is not about treating all children the same.* However, schools and educators that use the three pillars of this paradigm—child development, neuroscience, and recognition of environmental influences—to guide their action will undoubtedly rely upon strategies that are similar. For example, some of the schools and districts we feature rely upon performance-based assessment to gauge student learning and personalized learning plans to monitor their progress and ensure that their needs are being met. Many of the educators also recognize that a key feature of equity is providing disadvantaged students with more learning time through high quality after school and summer learning experiences and increased exposure to the world outside the communities where their students reside to expand their horizons. These and other strategies will be described in detail in the pages ahead.

Second, the pursuit of excellence through equity invariably involves forging *collaborative relationships among adult stakeholders*—parents (or guardians), teachers, and administrators. When these adults begin working together to support the success of every student, possibilities for breaking predictable patterns of achievement increase. Of course, getting adult stakeholders to work together is challenging and sometimes involves conflict. As we will show, establishing shared goals for every student requires willingness and an ability to deliberate thoughtfully about what is in the best interests of the child. There must also be shared responsibility for ensuring that all students are equipped with the skills they will need for the future. Providing teachers with the social skills to have candid conversations with parents across race, class, and language differences, and supporting principals and superintendents so that they can handle the resistance mounted by affluent parents when they protest a decision to detrack a college prep course or expand access to advanced placement classes, is challenging to say the least. Yet, as we will show in the pages ahead, creating a sense of shared accountability for the long-term outcomes of students is a common characteristic of schools and programs that are committed to these values.

We realize that one of the most complicated issues at the center of this work is *defining what success means* for every student. When administrators do not pledge to get all students into college or promise that all students will graduate proficient in core subjects like literacy and math, it may seem like a step backward and open those individuals to attacks. However, we have already seen that grand promises like those associated with NCLB have not resulted in success for every student. In fact, because NCLB largely ignored the conditions under which children are educated and focused narrowly on test score results, it did relatively little to improve educational outcomes for the most disadvantaged students, the very students its advocates claimed it would help (Darling-Hammond, 2011). As we will show, calling for schools to set high but realistic goals for every student need not result in a drift back to the time when we assumed children from poor and working-class backgrounds were not college material and should instead be prepared for a trade. If we remain vigilant and focused on outcomes, if we examine achievement patterns to make sure that they don't become predictable with respect to the race and class of students, and if we genuinely hold all stakeholders—educators, policy makers, parents, community leaders, and students—responsible for their role in promoting academic success, it should be possible to create schools where a child's background does not predict how well he or she will do academically and that serve all children in significantly better ways than the ones we have now.

When there is *mutual accountability* and a shared commitment to the common goal of meeting the needs of all students among all stakeholders, schools can begin to realize the goal of excellence through equity. As our authors show in the pages ahead, some schools are doing this now by aiming for mastery in learning rather than settling for passing or even proficiency in critical subjects. They are doing it by ensuring that the support systems are in place for teachers so that they are clear about what effective teaching is and so that they can deliver high quality learning experiences to their students. When these principles are reflected in our work, the most important question that educators ask of themselves is this: Have we created learning environments that make it possible to serve the needs of every student? By focusing on the conditions within schools, the climate and the culture of the learning environment, it is easier to shift learning outcomes for students. Because they are not preoccupied with blaming students, parents, or the neighborhoods they live in for poor academic outcomes, the schools, programs, and educators we feature are able to ensure that the futures of the students they serve are not determined by demographics. These are the challenges that educators in various parts of the country and throughout the world are actively pursuing when they commit to the goal of excellence through equity.

Finally, the reader will undoubtedly be struck by the fact that the starting point for working toward the goal of excellence through equity is creating a community where the needs of each student are thoroughly known, and each member understands his or her role. By knowing our children—how they learn, what motivates them, what challenges they face, and so on—we are better able to create an environment in which all students can get what they need to succeed. We will also show that students can be part of this process, and spaces can be provided so that they can tell us what they need to be successful. No one, including children, should be expected to passively accept what others provide for them, even when presumably it is done in their interests. We want learning environments where students are invested in seeking out knowledge and information, where they are willing participants and collaborators in their education.

The central argument of this book is that if we can use this paradigm for excellence through equity to guide larger numbers of schools and districts, we can create a system that will do much more than simply espouse slogans about the ability of all children to learn. We have such schools and slogans already. Our deep and pervasive disparities in learning outcomes, disparities that mirror larger patterns of inequality in our society, are the clearest evidence that a new approach is needed. We offer the examples in this book because they show that pursuing excellence through equity can be achieved through the adoption of practices and procedures that are significantly different from those we rely upon now. In the final section of this chapter, we describe the five principles of Courageous Leadership, which serve as the organizational framework of this book.

COURAGEOUS LEADERSHIP: THE ENGINE THAT DRIVES THE PARADIGM SHIFT

The subsequent chapters demonstrate how excellence through equity is being achieved through the courageous action of educators who have taken decisive steps to make this ideal a reality. Each chapter presents concrete examples of educators, schools, districts, communities, provinces, states, and even nations that have successfully pursued this agenda. We also point out the common obstacles that can hinder success and ways to move forward and circumvent these barriers.

  We conceived of this book as a resource that could provide a framework and practical guide so that educators, parents, and advocates who are committed to going beyond moral suasion can root their calls for excellence through equity in evidence. In order for the concept of excellence through equity to be widely embraced, we need not only the vision for our new paradigm (described in the preceding section) but also specific strategies that will make it possible for the affluent to overcome their fears of loss when questions of equity are raised. We want to show them how *their* children can benefit from being part of an equitable school community. Likewise, the vision must be robust enough to support the aspirations and needs of children who come to school needing more; socially, economically, psychologically, and academically. We need a win-win strategy for all involved if our society is to make real progress. We offer this book, and the ideas, strategies, and experiences presented within it, as the starting place for this new vision, one that is bold enough to erase the fear of losing privilege among the "haves" and uplifting enough to counter the resignation and helplessness that too often characterizes the "have nots." In the chapters ahead, we present concrete examples to show with cognitive and visceral certainty that the best possible road to excellence is one that is paved with equity.

COURAGE TO ACT

Leaders across disciplines and throughout time have seen courage as the essential human virtue. Consider this small sampling:

Courage is the mother of all virtues because without it, you cannot consistently perform the others.

—Aristotle

Without courage, all other virtues lose their meaning. Courage is, rightly esteemed, the first of all human qualities (that) guarantees all others.

—Sir Winston Churchill

Courage may be the most important of all virtues, because without it one cannot practice any other virtue with consistency.

—Maya Angelou

Courage, the footstool of the virtues, upon which they stand.

—Robert Louis Stevenson

Leadership has for centuries been closely associated with courage. King Richard I, who reigned from 1189 to 1199, was dubbed "Richard the Lionhearted" for his prowess in battle. Likewise, Western interpretations have associated courage with war, battle, and physical feats of life-saving or life-taking heroes. Yet the word comes from the French root *coeur*, or heart, and the concept traditionally corresponds to acts of the heart.

Native American societies systematically developed courage in young braves by encouraging sacrifice for the greater good. "The greatest brave was he who could part with his cherished belongings and at the same time sing songs of praise" (Standing Bear, as cited in Agonito, 2011, p. 235). Developing young leaders' ability to face inner fears associated with loss strengthened their ability to sacrifice for the safety and well-being of the weakest in their village, invariably elders and children.

Likewise, we see the need to return to the roots of *courage* in our quest to defend and advance the well-being of the weakest in *our* community. As Natives of this land understood, *courage*, or acting from the heart, can be developed and is the most powerful virtue we can all tap. In this quest for equity for the weakest members of our society, and ergo for *all* of us, we use courage both as our source of strength and as the framework for this book.

While the research and practice point clearly to the need for a new and better approach than the one we are currently using to educate our children, making such a shift will require commitment and courage.

Advocates of policies like NCLB defend the policy based on the fear that schools can't be trusted unless they are held accountable for student outcomes (i.e., high-stakes testing). As an alternative, we describe systems that are based on mutual accountability among all stakeholders and show that positive changes in academic outcomes can be achieved when there is accountability in the state legislature and governor's office for adequate funding, in the classroom and the schoolhouse when educators are provided with adequate resources and guidance, and in communities and homes when trust and engagement are promoted. Advancing a new paradigm, especially one addressing one of the most charged issues of our time, requires courageous leadership at all levels. Our chapter contributors demonstrate a path forward, and we use the core principles of Courageous Leadership outlined in *Failure Is Not an Option* (Blankstein, 2004, 2010, 2013) to frame this work.

The principles are not discrete, and indeed acting on one advances the others, and collectively they build leadership capacity to advance equitable outcomes for every student. Although we have grouped the chapters under specific principles, the majority of chapters encapsulate more than one of these principles. A common narrative that emerges in many of the chapters is that a catalytic event or striking new data underscore glaring disparities in student performance along racial or SES lines. A courageous leader or leadership team "faces these facts" and their own related fears by tapping into their core values in order to derive strength to commit to specific, high-leverage goals and actions to change the situation. Once a strategy is set, those in leadership work to achieve buy-in from teachers, parents, and students so that together they can relentlessly pursue them while developing organizational cohesion through supportive relationships. The Courageous Leadership cycle is a common refrain throughout the book and is exemplified in our first chapter. We present the case of Brockton High School, the largest school in America's highest performing state (Massachusetts), and show how they moved from being among the worst schools to one of the best. (Using equity as a driver for change and overall success is another common theme that is further articulated by the former commissioner of that same state in Chapter 10). In Chapter 2, author Michael Fullan states, "It is crucial to declare that the moral imperative of all students learning is a core goal of the system." His case study of Garden Grove points to five success factors that overlap with the five principles of Courageous Leadership, including bringing "coherence" to educational efforts within the district.

Chapters 3 through 15 are framed by these principles of Courageous Leadership. They include the following:

Getting to Your Core

A new initiative may be undertaken initially through external mandate (e.g., due to a desegregation order), and the practical strategies in this book can assist in advancing the work. Yet to sustain the initiative, there will invariably need to be clarity around how it ties in with the moral purpose of its leadership and a majority of the stakeholders. People need to know *why* what they are doing is worth the effort and *how* it connects to their personal and collective mission and values, or the endeavor will soon be stalled. We show that morality is often reflected in the work and used as a means to inspire others. Virtually every author in this book describes a deep and personal connection to assuring equity for all students.

Carol Corbett Burris, in Chapter 3, sounds the theme of lifting all students to excellence through an equity agenda in her chapter describing how detracking occurred in a large suburban high school and then throughout the system. Catalyzed by dramatic data on school fights and academic failure, the Rockville Centre Schools' leadership connected to their core mission and values to bring about a dramatic and sustained turn-around in an inequitable school system.

The Chapter 4 example presented by Linda Harper at the Oak Hill School demonstrates how her personal reflections on inequity became a catalyst for initiating collective action in the larger school community. We also feature in Chapter 5 the work of Avram Barlowe and Ann Cook, who have responded to their core values in addressing the inequities foisted upon children in states and schools that use high-stakes testing to rank academic performance. Together with other educators, they have created a highly successful network of schools that use student-focused performance assessments throughout New York City.

Making Organizational Meaning

Bringing cohesion to schools and systems that are otherwise fragmented is critical for galvanizing and unifying all stakeholders toward common visions and goals. The gains in bringing this about in systems where clarity is lacking can be significant and notable early on. In Chapter 6, Ann Blakeney Clark writes about how using one simple, yet strategically important concept—"talent development"—made it possible to deploy talent that was desperately needed in low-performing schools. The results achieved through the courageous implementation of this strategy in the Charlotte-Mecklenburg Public Schools contributed to the district receiving the Broad Prize for excellence in urban education last year.

At the level of curriculum and assessment, Allison Zmuda, the author of Chapter 7, introduces an approach to personalized learning that helps students make meaning, prior connections, and relevance of their school work. Dennis Littky, in Chapter 8, organizes the entire approach of Big Picture Schools around the idea of finding and building individualized curriculum based on student interests. Similarly, Estrella Olivares-Orellana, a bilingual science teacher, describes in Chapter 9 how drawing upon culture as a resource in teaching can help in making classroom lessons relevant to English language learners (ELLs). In each of the cases presented, the authors provide a clear and compelling rationale for their efforts and how *meaning* for students who are often marginalized brought about unprecedented results for young people who previously were disconnected and had minimal hope of success in school or life.

Ensuring Constancy and Consistency of Purpose

Any new initiative is vulnerable to derailment, especially those that challenge the status quo. Courageous leadership is required to mitigate this common pitfall. The author of Chapter 10, former education commissioner Paul Reville, writes forcefully about six reasons for the "uncommon success" experienced by the state of Massachusetts. This includes "long-term commitment by various partners." Moreover, he further exemplifies this principle of assuring constancy and consistency of purpose by courageously concluding that even despite their extraordinary successes they still have further to go in providing additional supports to impoverished schools and communities. Reville provides eight recommendations for designing a "New Engine" in policy to take us to higher levels of success, pointing out that "we've gone as far as we can" get by simply "*reforming*" our current K–12 system.

Facing the Facts and Your Fears

It is typically easier to maintain the status quo than it is to change; yet this is not always the right or best thing to do. Several authors used the facts of glaring student disparities as the catalyst for their efforts to promote change, while successfully helping others to overcome their fears. Chapter 11, by Amy E. Sichel and Ann H. Bacon, chronicles the experiences of Superintendent Amy Sichel, who was running a school district that was widely regarded as successful, but when faced with the data that clearly showed low-income students and students of color were doing poorly, she and her team used that information to catalyze the school community to go from good to great. Likewise, Darlene Berg, author of Chapter 12, became aware of the disparity between high- and low-SES students in math outcomes. Rather than accepting disparities as inevitable, she challenged elementary school teams not to be complacent about the predictable results, while simultaneously providing them with the support they needed to rise to that challenge.

Building Sustainable Relationships

All of the courageous actions and advances described in the coming chapters occurred within the context of myriad relationships. Wise leaders understand the importance of fostering trust and buy-in to create common ground with key stakeholders, even with and among those of differing viewpoints. Marcus J. Newsome, in Chapter 13, provides a case study in advancing an agenda aligned with his "core" in a manner that builds and sustains relations. In Chapter 14, Lucy N. Friedman and Saskia Traill write about how to create these sustainable relationships on an organizational level to support both the launch and the continuity of successful after-school programs. Similarly, other authors remind us that building relationships rooted in respect, trust, and mutual responsibility is essential to advancing excellence through equity.

The closing Chapter 15 by Andy Hargreaves, in fact, draws on all five of these principles in an analysis of the variables—including a focus on equity—influencing the rise and fall of educational attainment in three European countries vis-à-vis one another and the United States and Canada. He closes this book as we began, with a call to action for courageous leaders to advance the economic, educational, and overall quality of life for all of our citizenry by using the facts to reevaluate our current reality and advance our future prospects. The lessons learned are summarized in eight recommendations for policy makers who are challenged to abandon failed policies and pursue those that *uplift* our children:

> Equity also requires uplifting leadership as a process—to inspire multitudes, not just a few individuals, to have the courage, commitment, and tenacity to lift up those around them.

The practices, policies, and purpose of courageous leaders described in the following pages are connected by our new and more powerful paradigm described in the preceding section of this chapter. By embracing its core tenets, we will advance the possibility of achieving excellence through equity. As we pointed out earlier, this is the manner in which progress has been achieved throughout the centuries. Our current approaches are holding too many back and preventing others from even envisioning a brighter, more equitable future. By embracing this paradigm, we believe that you, the reader, can begin taking steps toward a brighter future for *all* of our children.

REFERENCES

Ames, C. A. (1990). Motivation: What teachers need to know. *Teacher's College Record, 91*(3).

Ames, C. (1992). Classrooms: Goals, structures, and student motivation. *Journal of Educational Psychology, 84*, 261–271.

Barton, P., & Coley, R. (2010). *The black-white achievement gap: When progress stopped.* Princeton, NJ: Education Testing Service.

Bell, D. (1973). *The coming of post-industrial society: A venture in social forecasting.* New York, NY: Basic Books.

Blankstein, A. (2004, 2010, 2013). *Failure is not an option.* Thousand Oaks, CA: Corwin.

Boykin, A. W., & Noguera, P. (2011). *Creating the opportunity to learn: Moving from research to practice to close the achievement gap.* Washington, DC: ASCD.

Bronfenbrenner, U. (1975). *The ecology of human development in retrospect and prospect.* Invited address at the final plenary session of the Conference on Ecological Factors in Human Development held by the International Society for the Study of Behavioral Development, University of Surrey, Guildford, England, July 13–17.

Brooks-Gunn, J., Fuligni, A. S., & Berlin, L. J. (2003). *Early child development in the 21st century: Profiles of current research initiatives.* New York, NY: Teachers College, Columbia University.

Carnoy, M., & Levin, H. (1985). *Schooling and work in the democratic state.* Palo Alto, CA: Stanford University Press.

Chatterji, M. (2006). Reading achievement gaps, correlates, and moderators of early reading achievement: Evidence from the early childhood longitudinal study (ECLS) kindergarten to first grade sample. *Journal of Educational Psychology, 98*(3), 489–507.

Connor, C. M., Morrison, F. J., & Petrella, J. N. (2004). Effective reading comprehension instruction: Examining child × instruction interactions. *Journal of Educational Psychology, 96*, 682–698.

Darling-Hammond, L. (2011). *The flat world and education.* New York, NY: Teachers College Press.

Dweck, C. S. (1999). *Self-theories: Their role in motivation, personality and development.* Philadelphia, PA: Psychology Press.

Eccles, J. S., & Gootman, J. (2002). *Community programs to promote youth development.* Washington, DC: National Academy Press.

Equity and Excellence Commission. (2013). *For each and every child: A strategy for education equity and excellence.* Washington, DC: Author. Retrieved from http://www.foreachandeverychild.org/The_Report.html

Fischer, C. (1996). *Inequality by design: Cracking the bell curve myth.* Princeton, NJ: Princeton University Press.

Fischer, K. W., & Bidell, T. R. (2006). Dynamic development of action, thought, and emotion. In R. M. Lerner (Ed.), *Handbook of child psychology: Vol 1. Theoretical models of human development* (6th ed., pp. 313–399). New York, NY: Wiley.

Frey, W. (2013). *Shift to majority-minority population happening faster than expected.* Washington, DC: Bookings Institute.

Fullan, M., & Boyle, A. (2014). *Big city school reforms: Lessons from New York, Toronto and London.* New York, NY: Teachers College Press.

Harris, D. (2008). Educational outcomes of disadvantaged students: From desegregation to accountability. In H. F. Ladd & E. B. Fiske (Eds.), *Handbook of research in education finance and policy.* New York, NY: Routledge.

Jackson, C. K., Johnson, R. C., & Persico, C. (2014). *The effect of school finance reforms on the distribution of spending, academic achievement & adult outcomes.* NBER working paper #20118, May 2014.

Kahlenberg, R. (2012). *The future of school integration: Socioeconomic diversity as an education reform strategy.* New York, NY: Century Foundation Press.

Katznelson, I., & Weir, M. (1985). *Schooling for all.* Berkeley: University of California Press.

Kuhn, T. (1962). *The structure of scientific revolutions.* Chicago, IL: University of Chicago Press.

Lehman, N. (1996). *The big test.* New York, NY: Ferrar, Straus, and Giroux.

Mickelson, R., & Bottia, M. (2010, April). What we know about school integration, college attendance, and the reduction of poverty. *Spotlight on Poverty.*

National Center for Education Statistics. (2013). *Digest of education statistics* (Table 203.50). Retrieved from http://nces.ed.gov/programs/digest/d13/tables/dt13_203.50.asp

National Center for Learning Disabilities. (2014). *What you should know about the law.* Retrieved from http://www.ncld.org/

Oakes, J. (2005). *Keeping track.* New Haven, CT: Yale University Press.

Organisation for Economic Co-operation and Development. (2012). *Programme for international student assessment.* Retrieved from http://www.oecd.org/pisa/keyfindings/pisa-2012-results.htm

Paris, S., & Newman, R. (1990). Developmental aspects of self-regulated learning. *Educational Psychologist, 25,* 87–102.

Pascual-Leone, A., Amedi, A., Fregni, F., & Merabet, L. B. (2005). The plastic human brain cortex. *Annual Review of Neuroscience, 28,* 377–401. doi: 10.1146/annurev.neuro.27.070203.144216

Resmovitz, J. (2014, August 20). ACT scores paint troubling picture for students of color. *Huffington Post.*

Rothstein, R. (2004). *Class and schools: Using social, economic, and educational reform to close the black-white achievement gap.* Washington, DC: Economic Policy Institute.

Sahlberg, P. (2011). *Finnish lessons: What can the world learn from educational change in Finland?* New York, NY: Teachers College Press.

Standing Bear, L. (2011). My people the Sioux. In J. Agonito (Ed.), *Lakota portraits: Lives of the legendary plains people*. Kearney, NE: Morris.

Suárez-Orozco, C., Suárez-Orozco, M. M., & Todorova, I. (2009). *Learning a new land: Immigrant students in American society*. Cambridge, MA: Harvard University Press.

Syme, S. L. (2004). Social determinants of health: The community as empowered partner. *Preventing Chronic Disease: Public Health Research, Practice, and Policy, 1*(1), 1–4.

Trzesniewski, K., & Dweck, C. (2007). Implicit theories of intelligence predict achievement across an adolescent transition: A longitudinal study and an intervention. *Child Development, 78*(1), 246–263.

Tyack, D. B., & Cuban, L. (1995). *Tinkering toward utopia: A century of public school reform*. Cambridge, MA: Harvard University Press.

Tzu, S. (2007). *The art of war*. Minneapolis, MN: Filiquarian Press.

Wagner, T. (2008). *The global achievement gap: Why even our best schools don't teach the new survival skills our children need—and what we can do about it*. New York, NY: Basic Books.

Wood, D. (1998). *How children think and learn* (2nd ed.). Oxford, UK: Blackwell.

Brockton High School, Brockton, Massachusetts

1

Susan Szachowicz

Excellence through equity describes the culture at Brockton High School, but it was not always that way. For decades the leadership of the school had a philosophy that educational programs were made available to the students, but it was up to the students to take advantage of them. A culture of failure was pervasive. One longtime principal of Brockton High stated often to the faculty that "the students have a right to fail," and sadly that was a "right" that large numbers of our students exercised. Academic rigor and achievement took a backseat to athletic championships.

With 4,200 students in Grades 9 through 12, Brockton High is the largest high school in the Commonwealth of Massachusetts. The student population is diverse racially, ethnically, and socioeconomically. The demographics demonstrate the challenges we face: 60% of our students are Black, which includes African Americans, Cape Verdeans, Haitians, and many students from countries around the world; 22% percent are White; 12% are Hispanic; 2% are multirace; and 2% are Asian. Further, 17% are classified as Limited English Proficient, and approximately 40% do not speak English as their first language. A majority, 76% of our students, live in poverty and receive free or reduced-price lunch. The Massachusetts Department of Elementary and Secondary Education has classified greater than 80% of our students as "high needs," and 11% of our students receive special education services. Many of our students are the first in their families to graduate from high school, and most are the first in their families to attend college.

In 1998, Massachusetts introduced the Massachusetts Comprehensive Assessment System (MCAS), which was a high-stakes exam for sophomores; students had to pass both the English language arts and math exams to earn a diploma. When the results of the first MCAS administration were released, Brockton High was ranked as one of the lowest performing schools in the Commonwealth with a 44% failure rate in English with only 22% reaching proficiency, and a 75% failure rate in math with only 7% reaching proficiency. Hundreds of Brockton High students were at risk of not graduating. When the next year saw no improvement, Brockton High found itself featured on the front page of the Boston Globe, identified as one of the worst schools in Massachusetts. Our school was being labeled as a failure because of the statewide assessment, and it prompted a call to action. No longer could the "students have a right to fail" philosophy continue; it was time to embrace excellence for all at Brockton High School.

And embrace excellence we did! Almost exactly a decade later, Brockton High was back on the front page of the Boston Globe as a turnaround success story. On October 9, 2009, Globe reporter James Vaznis began his article entitled *"Turn Around at Brockton High"* with the following statement:

> BROCKTON—Brockton High School has every excuse for failure, serving a city plagued by crime, poverty, housing foreclosures, and homelessness. . . . But Brockton High, by far the state's largest public high school with 4,200 students, has found a success in recent years that has eluded many of the state's urban schools: MCAS scores are soaring, earning the school state recognition as a symbol of urban hope.

Imagine the pride of our students, our faculty, our parents, and our community as Brockton High received local, state, and national recognition for the academic achievements of our students. We went from being called a "cesspool" in our local media to being featured on the front page of the New York Times. We have been selected as a National Model School by the International Center for Leadership in Education for 11 consecutive years, as a Secondary School Showcase School by the Center for Secondary School Redesign, for a National School Change Award by Fordham, and for 4 years as a Bronze Medal recipient by U.S. News and World Report as one of America's Best High Schools, featured by Harvard University's Achievement Gap Institute for closing the gap, and highlighted by Governor Deval Patrick in his State of the Commonwealth Address. We transformed ourselves from being a school accepting every excuse for failure to a school with high standards, high expectations, and no excuses. While the MCAS scores demonstrated our students' academic improvement, our culture shift was much more than just test scores. We became a school where it is cool to be smart.

Excellence through equity; but how did we get there? Here is the secret we discovered about improving our students' performance—it was not about the students, it was about the adults. When we started teaching differently with a tenacious focus on literacy, the students' performance improved and the culture of the school changed.

CHANGING OUR MINDSET

The turnaround at Brockton High started with a team of teachers who were distressed by the failure rate and determined to do something. Calling ourselves the Restructuring Committee, we began our first meeting by posting the MCAS scores with a question under them: Is this the best we can be? And with our resounding "NO," we took our first steps toward improvement.

Initially we learned a hard lesson about trying to focus solely on the test. When we noticed that in the first 3 years of testing there were always Shakespearean readings and questions, we launched a "Shakespearean offensive" across the school. Our "Shakespearean offensive" turned quickly into the Great Shakespearean fiasco when that year there was not even one mention of Shakespeare on the MCAS. Our Restructuring Committee realized that school improvement could never be about outguessing a test. An examination of our data illustrated that our students were struggling in reading, problem solving, vocabulary, thinking, and reasoning skills, and the failure was not limited to any one group. We could not think solely about remediating particular students who were failing because our data clearly illustrated that the failure was widespread.

Instead of thinking about test preparation, we asked ourselves a series of questions that helped us frame our literacy initiative. Our discussions around these pivotal questions changed our thinking:

- **What are we teaching, how are we teaching it, and how do we know the students are actually learning it?** We determined that we were focusing primarily on content, compartmentalized into highly structured departments. While many of our teachers were highly skilled in instruction, many others struggled and relied primarily on lecture and teacher-directed activities. And in response to the question about how we knew the students had learned the material, we came to the difficult realization that we were not doing a good enough job with that. Our look in the mirror revealed to us that at Brockton High the quality of a student's education totally depended upon the teachers he or she had. We really did not have any schoolwide standards.

- **What do our students need to know and be able to do to be successful on the MCAS, in their classes, and in their lives beyond school?** That was perhaps one of the richest discussions we had, and it led directly to the development of our literacy initiative. Essentially we defined literacy and how our students would demonstrate mastery of these literacy skills.

- **We are not likely to get any additional staffing or resources, so what resources do we have now that we can use more effectively?** The resource of time was our area of focus. A great deal of time in the day was not instructional. Study halls could no more be on any students' program—students needed to be engaged, focused, and directed. We had some work to do with our schedule. But it wasn't only about the students' use of time. Our faculty meetings typically were used for administrative announcements, preparing for safety drills, or discussions of union business but not regarding educational issues. With the support of the principal and superintendent, we began using our two contractual faculty meetings per month for improving instruction. These faculty meetings now became Literacy Workshops during which we trained our faculty to teach the literacy skills we identified.

- **What can we control, and what can't we control?** We knew that we couldn't control the challenges our students face every day of their lives: poverty, homelessness, violence, family turmoil, transiency, language acquisition—we could make lots of excuses for failure. But instead of wringing our hands and feeling sorry for our students and ourselves, we decided to take a hard look at the 7 hours a day we had our students with us, and we knew we needed to ask ourselves how we could best use that time for their academic achievement.

The rich discussions our Restructuring Committee had as we wrestled with these questions led us to our tenacious focus on improving all of our students' literacy skills. We recognized that helping our students acquire these literacy skills needed to be the responsibility of every teacher in the school, not just the English or math departments. *All* meant *all*. The implementation of the Literacy Initiative provided a model of schoolwide focus on clearly defined literacy skills and the commitment that every teacher would be a teacher of literacy with their content serving as the context for teaching those literacy skills. That tenacious schoolwide commitment was the key to our improvement. No longer would the quality of a student's education be totally dependent upon the luck of the draw with teachers. Now all students would have the opportunity to master a set of skills and thinking routines that would help them succeed not only in school but in their lives beyond Brockton High School.

OUR FOCUS ON LITERACY FOR ALL

As our Restructuring Committee discussed what our students needed to know and be able to do, we began creating lists of skills, and soon we classified them into four areas: reading, writing, speaking, and reasoning. Within each of those areas, we detailed a series of objectives, or literacy skills, that every student at Brockton High would be expected to master. These essentially defined the school's academic expectations for student learning in specific, measurable ways. Essentially we defined literacy for our students, and we were determined to teach our students these literacy skills.

Drafts of these literacy charts were presented to faculty in small interdisciplinary discussion groups facilitated by members of the Restructuring Committee as well as to the School Council, including parents and students, and even to the Chamber of Commerce in the city to seek input. It was essential that these literacy skills were clearly stated so that all teachers, students, and parents understood them. Also, each of these skills needed to be applicable in every content area so that any teacher, no matter what the class, would feel that students would be more successful in his or her class if they mastered these skills. Teachers' voices were important in this process, and after months of discussion, revisions, more discussion, and more revisions, we established a set of literacy objectives in reading, writing, speaking, and reasoning (see Figure 1.1).

Once the literacy charts were finalized, they were posted in every classroom. But simply posting them in classrooms would not change instruction. Our challenge was again about the adults—how could we change instruction so that every teacher, no matter what the discipline, taught these literacy skills in the same way? Every student deserved to learn these skills; they needed to learn them to be successful. It was about equity.

So where to begin? Our Restructuring Committee knew that it was essential to focus. If we tried to attack every skill on our literacy charts, it would be overwhelming for teachers and students. One teacher on the Restructuring Committee argued passionately for beginning with writing,

Figure 1.1 Literacy Charts: Reading, Writing, Speaking, and Reasoning

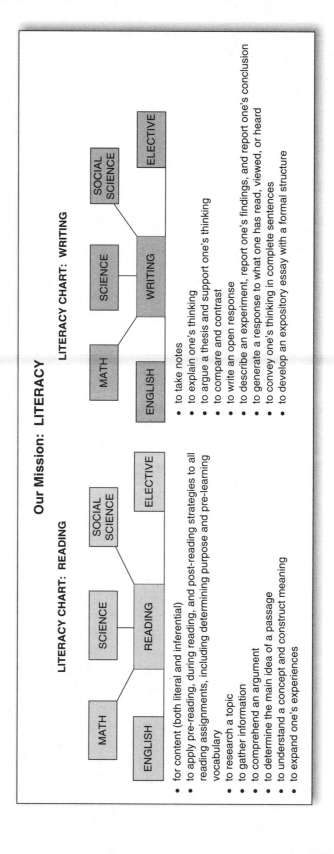

Our Mission: LITERACY

LITERACY CHART: READING

MATH · SCIENCE · SOCIAL SCIENCE

ENGLISH · READING · ELECTIVE

- for content (both literal and inferential)
- to apply pre-reading, during reading, and post-reading strategies to all reading assignments, including determining purpose and pre-learning vocabulary
- to research a topic
- to gather information
- to comprehend an argument
- to determine the main idea of a passage
- to understand a concept and construct meaning
- to expand one's experiences

LITERACY CHART: WRITING

MATH · SCIENCE · SOCIAL SCIENCE

ENGLISH · WRITING · ELECTIVE

- to take notes
- to explain one's thinking
- to argue a thesis and support one's thinking
- to compare and contrast
- to write an open response
- to describe an experiment, report one's findings, and report one's conclusion
- to generate a response to what one has read, viewed, or heard
- to convey one's thinking in complete sentences
- to develop an expository essay with a formal structure

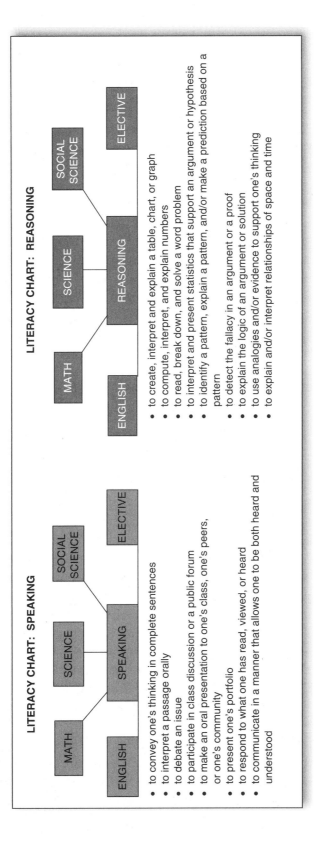

LITERACY CHART: REASONING

MATH	SCIENCE	SOCIAL SCIENCE
	REASONING	
ENGLISH		**ELECTIVE**

- to create, interpret and explain a table, chart, or graph
- to compute, interpret, and explain numbers
- to read, break down, and solve a word problem
- to interpret and present statistics that support an argument or hypothesis
- to identify a pattern, explain a pattern, and/or make a prediction based on a pattern
- to detect the fallacy in an argument or a proof
- to explain the logic of an argument or solution
- to use analogies and/or evidence to support one's thinking
- to explain and/or interpret relationships of space and time

LITERACY CHART: SPEAKING

MATH	SCIENCE	SOCIAL SCIENCE
	SPEAKING	
ENGLISH		**ELECTIVE**

- to convey one's thinking in complete sentences
- to interpret a passage orally
- to debate an issue
- to participate in class discussion or a public forum
- to make an oral presentation to one's class, one's peers, or one's community
- to present one's portfolio
- to respond to what one has read, viewed, or heard
- to communicate in a manner that allows one to be both heard and understood

stating, "Writing is thinking. If students can articulate their thoughts clearly in writing, we can better assess their mastery of the skill and their mastery of our subject area." That discussion convinced us all, and we began training our entire faculty, in every discipline, to teach writing.

HOW WE IMPLEMENTED AND MONITORED THIS LITERACY INITIATIVE: WE ALL DO IT THIS WAY!

The first step for our Restructuring Committee was to develop a clear writing process that would be implemented across the school. Once we settled on our 10-step process, we had to figure out how to model the process for every teacher in a scripted training that was the first of our literacy workshops. In our Restructuring Committee discussions, many of us admitted that we had not been trained ourselves in how to teach reading or writing. One teacher stated she thought she was teaching reading by saying to the students, "Just read it again!" At the high school level, our teacher preparation programs focused heavily on learning the content. Our literacy initiative would train every teacher at Brockton High in how to teach these literacy skills using a common process, common vocabulary, and a common assessment. This was almost revolutionary at Brockton High. We had never before focused the entire faculty like this.

Using our contractual faculty meeting time, we trained the entire faculty in our open response writing process that was developed by the Restructuring Committee. Teachers used readings in their own content areas to provide the context for the writing. The key to success was that the same process and same skills were being taught and applied school-wide to ensure consistency.

Once every teacher was trained in the open response writing process, the Restructuring Committee developed a calendar that was distributed by the principal and associate principal to set the dates for the implementation. Teachers in specific departments were assigned a week during which they would teach the writing process to the students using their own subject area content. For example, if you were a history teacher and during your assigned week you were teaching the Revolutionary War, you would create a writing assignment based upon a reading you selected about the Revolutionary War. The content provided the context, but the writing standards across the school were the same.

The implementation calendar was developed for two reasons. First, it ensured that every teacher was involved and provided a clear schedule for administrative monitoring. This structured implementation left nothing to chance and demonstrated our commitment to teaching all of our students crucial literacy skills. Our literacy initiative would not be the one-shot deal professional development that so many of us had previously experienced. Secondly, and more importantly, the implementation calendar provided for repeated practice of the skill for every student, and that deliberate practice is an essential ingredient for mastery.

Establishing schoolwide standards was a new endeavor for us at Brockton High, and ensuring a consistency in the assessment process was a challenge. Because our Restructuring Committee believed strongly that what gets monitored is what gets done, and *all* means *all*, we monitored both the implementation process of the faculty and the quality of student work across the school. An essential component in teaching the writing process to the students was introducing a schoolwide rubric that maintained a level of consistency in the assessment of student writing. But perhaps the most powerful piece of this process was the collection and review of student work by the faculty. As faculty met in interdisciplinary groups to review the work of the students, some powerful discussions ensued. Only by actually comparing student work were we able to see the inconsistencies of expectations for our students we had in our school. In a faculty of more than 300 teachers, there were many who doubted that our students could reach the rigorous standards we were now demanding. When these doubting teachers were able to see the quality of writing that students were producing in some classes, they began to understand that our instruction could directly impact the quality of our students' work.

We maintained a tenacious, unwavering focus in implementing this in every classroom, with no exceptions: the same objective, same process, and same assessment in every class. The students started to recognize that something different was happening in the school; there was a focus on reading and writing that they had never seen before, and they were learning valuable skills that they started applying not only to state assessments but in all of their classes.

WHAT ABOUT FACULTY BUY-IN?

Frankly, if we waited for buy-in from everyone, we would still be waiting. Instead, we forged ahead. At Brockton High, we had too often developed plan after plan with far too many goals, discussed them endlessly, but never really got off the mark and started implementing. This time we pushed the literacy agenda forward. We had been labeled across the Commonwealth of Massachusetts as a failing school; there was no more time for discussion. We had to do something. With more than 300 members on our faculty, of course there were resisters. But the Restructuring

Committee and the administration worked hard to support the teachers as they began implementing these literacy lessons. Our teachers' union was engaged in the process from the beginning, so that they were on board, and we were careful not to violate the contract in any way. We heard comments such as "I was hired to teach art, not English," and "Don't worry, this too shall pass," and "What can we really expect from kids from these backgrounds." But we faced the dissention head-on with clear guidelines and processes, lots of training and support, and strong monitoring. True buy-in really only comes with results, and fortunately we saw dramatic improvement immediately.

In the first year of our literacy initiative, we cut our failure rate in half and doubled our proficiency percentage. In the second year, we did it again. The voices of the few dissenters were silenced by the performance of our students.

LITERACY FOR ALL, SUPPORTS AND SAFETY NETS FOR STRUGGLING LEARNERS

This meticulous process of monitoring, which involved direct observation of the instruction of the literacy skill and the collection and review of student work, revealed to us that we had raised the standards across the school and provided our students with literacy skills that would help them succeed beyond their Brockton High years. It was working! However, it also revealed to us that some of our students needed more support, direct instruction, and feedback.

Teachers began identifying students who needed more assistance and direction and provided a great deal of one-on-one support during the day when time was available and after school. Students' Individualized Educational Plans (IEPs) were revised to include literacy goals and the supports they would need to reach the standards. A portfolio for every student with an IEP and every English language learner was created to ensure careful progress monitoring.

A tutorial center, called the Access Center, was created for students throughout the day and after school. Teachers who were willing to provide tutoring assistance to the students were recruited to work in the Access Center. Juniors and seniors were also recruited to serve as peer tutors, and they were well-trained on the writing process so that their tutoring was consistent with the schoolwide process. Initially, teacher referral was really the main reason a student reported to the Access Center. But over time, word spread among the students that this was a positive, safe, and supportive atmosphere to receive assistance, and the

Access Center soon became a bustling place. A Boxer-2-Boxer mentoring program was also put in place, which paired seniors with teachers of freshmen to provide student leadership and assistance. Our literacy initiative involved total schoolwide commitment.

SUCCESS BRINGS MORE SUCCESS, AND MORE LITERACY

Waiting for the results of the MCAS after a tough year of implementing our literacy initiative was excruciating. While we knew that our students had improved their reading and writing skills, it would be the state assessments that would validate our efforts. Imagine our joy when we received a call from the Massachusetts Commissioner of Education that we were the most improved school in the Commonwealth. Not only had we cut the failure rate in half, but we had also dramatically improved our proficiency ranking. And we have continued this trajectory of improvement for over a decade.

Even those initially reticent about the literacy initiative were now ready to move forward. Comments such as "This is working; what else can we do?" have replaced the groans about "teaching English." There is an understanding among the faculty at Brockton High that when we learn to teach these skills and provide our students with the thinking routines they need, they achieve.

We have continued to train our faculty in a number of literacy skills using the same format. Once the faculty has been trained, we then teach these skills to the students. Workshops have included Using Active Reading Strategies; Analyzing Difficult Reading; Reading and Analyzing Visuals; Analyzing Graphs and Charts Across the Curriculum; Developing Speaking Skills; Checking for Understanding; Problem Solving Strategies; Helping English Language Learners Achieve; and Teaching Vocabulary in Context.

RECAP: THE STEPS IN BROCKTON HIGH'S TURNAROUND

It is important to realize that the turnaround at Brockton High was no easy pirouette. Rather, it was about a tenacious focus on literacy, deliberate practice, and hard work. Too often turnaround efforts are neither sustained nor replicable; our literacy initiative is both. The improvement has been sustained now for over a decade, and the process has been replicated by schools and districts in many states as the Brockton model has been presented at national conferences.

Essentially, there were four steps in the development of our literacy initiative:

1. **Empower a team.** Our Restructuring Committee has become the think tank for our school. What started as a mission to improve test scores evolved into a powerful force in our school's improvement. Members of the Restructuring Committee target the skill, develop the training, train the faculty in teaching the skill to the students, and lead the discussions about student work. It is true instructional leadership.

2. **Focus on literacy.** Too often school improvement efforts embrace too many goals, include lofty educational jargon, and shift from year to year.

3. **Implement with fidelity.** Faculty were trained and required to implement the literacy skills according to a calendar so that students received the deliberate practice they needed to master a skill.

4. **Monitor, monitor, monitor.** Our meticulous process of monitoring helped both our faculty and our students. By establishing schoolwide standards, students knew what excellence looked like. And by collecting and reviewing student work, our faculty began to establish consistent standards for all students.

LESSONS LEARNED

At Brockton High, it was not lofty vision statements or educational platitudes that helped us achieve excellence through equity. Excellence has resulted from our tenacious focus on teaching ALL of our students the literacy skills they need in life, no matter what subject we teach. That process has taught us all a few lessons to keep in mind.

To achieve excellence through equity, high expectations for ALL is essential; however, it is not enough. Along with high expectations, the students need to be taught the skills necessary to reach those expectations. Teaching all students the literacy skills in reading, writing, speaking, and reasoning prepared them for success on assessments and in their classes, for college, for work, and for their lives beyond school.

To achieve excellence through equity, the focus needs to be on adult learning, not just student learning. Too often the quality of a student's education depends on the selection of teachers he or she has.

Was the student lucky enough to get the best teachers? Improving our school meant that we needed to improve instruction across the school. Quality instruction was the driver of our improvement. When we learned to teach differently, and focus on teaching our students the literacy skills they needed, the students learned the material better.

To achieve excellence through equity, you cannot wait for everyone to buy in before you take action. In education, we are experts in writing plans, but we sometimes falter when it comes to implementing them. At Brockton High we had to move our agenda forward; *all* meant *all.*

Brockton High has transformed itself from a school labeled as a failure to one recognized as a national turnaround model. The Massachusetts commissioner of education, Mitchell Chester, told the *Boston Globe,*

> To me, Brockton High is evidence that schools that serve diverse populations can be high achieving schools. It's just very graphically ingrained in my mind after having walked through the building and gone into classes that there's a culture of respect among students and adults. You don't see that in every school. (Vaznis, 2009)

Yet, our belief is that our work is far from complete. We are proud of the culture change in the school but mindful that the hard work is never ending. Our students deserve our best.

REFERENCE

Vaznis, J. (2009, October 12). Turnaround at Brockton High. *The Boston Globe.* Retrieved from http://www.boston.com/news/education/k_12/mcas/articles/2009/10/12/turnaround_at_brockton_high/

The Path to Equity 2

Whole System Change

Michael Fullan

Thehe pursuit of equity in education systems was launched in the United States in 1983 with *A Nation at Risk.* Despite enormous fanfare and expenditure there has been almost no progress in raising the bar and closing the gap in the more than 30 years since that time. There was no specificity and no strategy in the 1983 call for action. What action, you might ask? It took almost 20 years to get started, and all we got in 2001 with No Child Left Behind (NCLB) was a strong declaration with no strategy to get there. Then, a decade later, we got Race to the Top with its equity emphasis on improving the bottom 5% of schools. Arising in parallel with Race to the Top are the Common Core State Standards (CCSS) that have both content and strategy and include equity goals. How likely is CCSS to make system gains in improving the learning of all students? My answer is, not very likely. Despite some good things within CCSS, it is too unwieldy and too fraught with complexities to make much progress. What is involved is a massive overhaul of standards, pedagogy, and assessment systems, all while operating under alienating conditions.

In this chapter I will step back from the cacophony of education reform to identify what we know about what does work. I will do this in two ways: first to list the basic ingredients and then to provide some big examples of what this looks like in practice.

WHOLE SYSTEM REFORM

In our work in a number of large systems in North America, and in a careful reading of the research, it is possible to identify a small number of key factors that *in combination* make a difference. Before discussing the particular components of success there are three overriding orientations that stand out. First, strangely enough, if you want to change the system you have to declare that it is the *whole system* that is implicated in getting better—not the bottom 5% or 20% but all of the schools. In a kind of rising tide lifts all boats, every school must be held accountable for improvement. Only if the whole system—district, state, province—is on the move will there be any chance of sustainable gains. Furthermore, no matter how well a given school or district is performing there are always sub-pockets of failure and upcoming changes in the environment that will challenge even the best systems.

Second, you can't make the solution overly complicated. There is a big difference between complicatedness and complexity. The former is when you add layers of coordination, and you increase the number of initiatives under way. These responses only add to the confusion and overload. By contrast, complexity involves enabling key factors to converge and cohere. We use the term *simplexity* for this process, which is identifying the smallest number of key factors that will make a difference (typically six to eight)—this is the simple part; and then orchestrating these factors to work in interaction—this is the complex part.

Third, you have to integrate what Andy Hargreaves and I have come to call the push and pull forces (Hargreaves & Fullan, 2012). You can't force (push) change or people will rebel; but you can't just leave it to chance or nothing will happen. Leadership then that combines push and pull forces is of the utmost importance. The difficulty with the concept of change is that you need to end up with new ideas *and* ownership of these ideas by large numbers of people in the system. Here is my definition of this phenomenon: an effective change process shapes and reshapes good ideas while it builds capacity and ownership among members in the group. The sophistication of leadership is that it must manage such a process with all the issues therein.

In sum, a whole system perspective (everyone is implicated), simplexity (a small number of factors that everyone can grasp), and the dynamics of push and pull (innovation and ownership) are necessary for fundamentally addressing equity-driven performance.

Let's look more closely. For the past 15 years, my colleagues and I have been working with systems (districts, states, provinces, countries) to help bring about and understand the dynamics of system success. All of this work examines specific factors linked to measurable student results targeted to raising the bar and closing the gap. Joanne Quinn, Eleanor Adam, and I have worked out a recent version that contains eight (interactive) factors (see Table 2.1).

Table 2.1	Whole System Change

1. Foster deep commitment to the moral imperative.

2. A small number of ambitious goals relentlessly pursued.

3. Establish a developmental culture and invest in capacity building.

4. Build leadership at all levels.

5. Cultivate districtwide engagement.

6. Learn from the work.

7. Use transparent data to improve practice.

8. Monitor for innovation and improvement.

These eight factors interact to produce cultures that focus on, and persist in, system improvement. In many ways, each factor is good in its own right and positively affects and is affected by each other factor. I give some examples in the next section but will provide brief commentary here. It is crucial to declare that the moral imperative of all students learning is a core goal of the system. But unlike NCLB, which makes such a declaration, whole system change advocates actually develop specific strategies that are directed at this goal. I titled one of my books *Moral Imperative Realized,* noting that it wasn't really a moral imperative if you could not explicitly identify what progress you were making. I wanted to put the feet to the fire by emphasizing that only realization counts—authentic measures of progress.

The other seven factors increase the chance that realization will indeed happen. One is working on a small number of ambitious goals—usually three or four. Again, we will see examples in the next section, but successful systems know when to say no to overload. They know how to cluster core goals and connect the dots. They know how to pursue and preserve the emphasis on the core. They figure out how to remove or blunt the impact of diversions pertaining to bureaucratic demands, initiatives that do not, and so on.

One of the biggest blocks to change is that people do not know what to do or do not know how to do it. They need, in other words, *capacity*—the competencies and skills to deal with the problems at hand. Because people typically fear change, that is, they fear the unknown, leaders must establish a learning culture. This means a culture where mistakes are seen as a normal part of learning something new, where trust is developed, and where the positive pressure of getting better at something is established. A developmental culture is not laissez-faire. By definition it expects some actual development in the skills and performance of people relative to selected goals. What helps this very development are the capacity-building skills (e.g., more effective pedagogy) that are part of the professional learning of individuals and groups. New capacities have multiple payoffs: by definition they increase efficacy, but they also generate greater clarity and greater ownership.

Leadership at all levels is also key. In a recent book on the "principalship," I documented how the role was being submerged in the minutiae of micromanagement, and that greater progress—on the equity agenda, for example—is made when principals are proactively "lead learners" (Fullan, 2014). By participating as learners with staff in moving the school ahead, the principal becomes more knowledgeable about problems to be solved and at the same time fosters leadership in others. Leaders developing other leaders at all levels of the system is central to short-term efficacy and longer-term sustainability in systems.

The factors five and six go together. Cultivating districtwide engagement also serves a multipurpose. The biggest problem districts have is coherence, which we use as a subjective concept. It is the mindset coherence that matters. Moreover, this coherence must be shared and deep. This shared depth of understanding about the nature of the work among staff is powerful on a day-to-day basis. It develops by defining the culture "as learning is the work." What is likely to be the most powerful form of learning for teachers and principals? It won't be teacher appraisal (too superficial and episodic). It won't be professional development (too disconnected from implementation). It will be collaborative cultures because they have the day-after-day learning built into purposeful interaction. Andy Hargreaves and I have detailed "professional capital" cultures as consisting of three parts—human capital (the quality of the individual), social capital (the quality of the group), and decisional capital (expertise at making decisions based on evidence). Districts that expect and develop collaborative cultures within schools, that use network strategies for schools to learn from each other, and that form two-way partnerships between schools and the central district are in effect mobilizing the power and identity of districtwide engagement.

Factors seven and eight also work in tandem. Education systems are inundated with data. Two things have to happen for data to play an effective role in equity improvement. One is that the data have to be positioned *primarily* as a force for improvement, not judgment. In fact, diagnostic data and improved teaching *are* pedagogy. To focus on instruction is to integrate data and teaching. The second aspect is transparency. In order for a culture to be developmental, it has to have easy access to data about both practices and outcomes. Who is getting results, and what teaching practices are they employing to get those results? Transparency is an essential part of learning from each other, as well as serving an effective "internal accountability" role—having the group account to itself how well it is doing.

When all eight of these components are in place, the district is in a position to effectively relate to the external accountability requirements. For one thing, districts with these qualities perform better. There is nothing like success to gain credibility and power. For another thing, such districts can articulate what they are doing. They can in their works "talk the walk." Because they are doing things concretely, and because there is constant processing of how well they are progressing, they become "accountability literate." They become the best examples of districts on the move.

EXAMPLES IN ACTION

Three examples show clearly how whole-system change strategies serve equity effectively and deeply. Two are school districts in California— Garden Grove (GG) in the Anaheim area and Sanger near Fresno in the central valley. The other involves the provincewide turnaround strategy for the province of Ontario.

Garden Grove has just under 50 elementary schools and about 20 intermediate and high schools. The increasingly diverse student population is 47,600 with 86% Latino and Asian and an average poverty rate of 72%. In 2004, the percentage of high school graduates meeting state standards, at 24%, was well below the state and Orange County average; by 2012, it reached 50%, well above the state (38%) and Orange County average (43%). In elementary English Language and Math proficiency, Garden Grove moved steadily up over the decade, eventually outperforming at or above its highest performing urban peers. Within this overall performance, the gap for all groups was reduced. In short, the focus was on the system and all its schools. We only have space to comment briefly on some of the details, which are based mainly on the report from an external researcher, Joel Knudson of the American Institute (2013).

Laura Schwalm was superintendent during this entire period and built what is quintessentially a "stay focused culture." As Knudson describes it, Garden Grove's success boils down to six interrelated elements that have become part of its deep culture—the Garden Grove way— as it is often described by its members:

1. The centrality of students and teachers

2. Coherence

3. Emphasis on relationships

4. Central office service mentality

5. Trust and empowerment

6. Orientation to continuous improvement

Overall focus does not come from doing one or two things in isolation. It comes from a set—albeit a reasonable small set, given the complexity of change—of, in this case, six key factors. First, GG is relentlessly committed to student success and to the success of its teachers. They realize that you cannot have one without the other. In our own workshops, we sometimes will say: Almost everyone will agree that all students can learn, but not as many will readily agree that all teachers can learn. The first step is that student and teacher learning is a two-way street. Once you say this, you know that you must make it come true on the ground. Because GG holds the learning of students and adults as central, they know that you can't just focus on test results. You must focus on quality instruction, in fact, on *shared quality instruction.* The hard part of focus is that it must become shared across a very large number of teachers, in this case in some 70 highly diverse schools. The question then becomes, what else must be done to ensure widespread and deep quality instruction?

Embracing the first factor does not amount to much unless you have accompanying strategies to deepen it. *Coherence* is a good word for our purpose. It is not just alignment where the elements of curriculum, instruction, assessment, professional development, finance, and so on are abstractly aligned but rather how these components are experienced day after day by individuals and groups. In this regard, GG leaders are focused on identifying and spreading the best (with evidence) ideas and practices across the system. The issue is not where the ideas come from—top, bottom, sideways—but what are the effective ideas and how can they become widespread. In many ways, coherence is at the heart of the change process, and we do not underestimate the difficulty in achieving it. For one thing, the other five factors in the culture all contribute to reinforcing a growing coherence in the culture about quality instructional practices. The bottom line is, as Superintendent Laura Schwalm explains, "if you want to move something that's difficult to move, everyone needs to be pushing in the same direction[; otherwise,] very good people can build very effective silos" (Knudson, 2013, p. 10).

Another in the culture is the emphasis on relationships. The first aspect is the care paid to hiring people and the personal attention they receive on many fronts welcoming them to the GG culture. From day one, people feel valued by the organization and by peers and district leaders. But note this personal touch plays itself out in the context of the other five factors that link personal valuing with the content of the work.

The problem in most districts is that instructional practices are all over the map—so many silos. Attempts to rein in practice by tightening supervision or by prescribing instructional solutions lead either to resistance or to superficial compliance. By contrast, we have seen in GG that focus is a *process of interrelated forces at work.* GG starts with a vision of quality instruction, pursues it by building the individual and collective capacity of teachers and administrators to do the work that best gets results, reinforces this by the teachers and administrators that they hire and develop on the job, and always assesses how well students are faring on indicators of performance, self-correcting as they go.

After a decade of success, it is no accident that the new superintendent, Gabriela Mafi, comes from within the culture, having been Schwalm's superintendent of secondary school instruction. Focus does not mean more of the same. It is a process quality more than a content quality. Thus, it can serve continuous improvement as well as innovation that will be necessary in the more uncertain times in the next years arising from CCSS, local funding and accountability in California's new laws, digital ubiquity, socioemotional needs of students, and much more.

Located in California's Central Valley, Sanger Unified is about a quarter of the size of GG with 10,800 students and 20 schools. The demographics are similar: 73% low income and 84% minority (mostly Latino with a growing group of Asians). In 1999, the local union took out a billboard advertisement that blared, "Welcome to the home of 400 unhappy teachers." In 2004, it was named as one of the 98 (out of 100) lowest performance districts in the state and put on notice as a program improvement district.

Less than a decade later, Sanger students outpaced the state performance for English Language Learners on the State's API index, 770 versus 718. On the overall state index, where a score of 800 is the state goal, Sanger rapidly moved up to 820 compared with a state average of 788. A union leader observed that "there is not a principal in this town that I would not work for" (David & Talbert, 2013, p. 3). How did they do it?

Marc Johnson was appointed superintendent in 2004 and set the tone by saying to school principals that being on the watch list was a wake-up call that they could use to their benefit. The story is similar in essence to what Garden Grove did. Once again, success boils down to persistent focus on a small number of key interrelated elements. David and Talbert (2013) note: "District leaders have stuck to a vision of what their learning organization would look like and a few principles for moving the system in that direction" (p. 5).

David and Talbert (2013) identify three key principles that underpinned the Sanger journey:

1. Take a developmental approach to change (change takes time; select a few complementary strategies and stay focused year after year).

2. Ground decisions in evidence (look closely at student data to define priorities; use feedback loops to test out and improve approaches; use evidence to identify and spread effective practices.

3. Build shared commitments and relationships to sustain change (communicate purpose, build trust, foster ownership around effective practices).

As with GG, what we see in Sanger is a combination of an intense commitment to the moral imperative that all kids can learn and tight focus on execution through building relationships in order to get results. David and Talbert (2013) pinpoint the shift in district culture in four dimensions:

From professional isolation to collaboration and shared responsibility

From following the textbook to diagnosing student needs

From principals as managers to principals as leaders of adult learning

From top-down mandates to reciprocal accountability (p. 7)

The Sanger case is also instructive about how effective accountability works. There is a deep student-centered commitment, nonpunitive climate (data are used to focus on improvement), and transparency of results and practice that serves to leverage further improvement. Schools are held accountable for using evidence more for literal results (of course using evidence contributes to better, more valid results). The district holds itself accountable for providing principals and schools what they need to become successful. This reciprocal accountability is the bond we also saw in GG (central office service mentality in exchange for high expectations that performance will increase in quality and impact). Progress is continually reviewed in an open climate with corrective action built in.

The third example is the school turnaround strategy in Ontario, called the Ontario Focused Intervention Partnership (OFIP). Consistent with the themes of this chapter, Ontario took a whole-system approach.

They declared that 100% of their districts (72) and their schools (4,900) were part and parcel of the goal to improve all schools in the province. We won't talk about the overall strategy, which is focused on raising the bar and closing the gap in literacy, numeracy, and high school gradua- tion. I take only the OFIP component. Using assessment data from the independent provincewide agency, schools were identified that were con- sistently low or stuck in performance. These schools were then supported explicitly in building instructional capacity with staff with a strong developmental (as distinct from judgmental) emphasis. School staff members were supported by external resource teachers who provided direct training; as well they linked OFIP schools with other schools with similar demographics that had had some success.

The first wave of schools involved those that had high percentages of students with low performance. The second wave included schools that had middling but unimpressive results. These schools were called "schools in the middle," and the strategy clearly conveyed that schools that were doing aver- age were also implicated in deliberate improvement interventions. Overall, more than 800 (of the 4,000) elementary schools have been engaged in OFIP, signaling that this is a systemwide effort. As of 2014, there are now 69 schools remaining in the OFIP group. The combination of the across-the- board strategy of raising the bar and closing the gap and the targeted OFIP have significantly reduced the gap for key subgroups: English language learners (there are large numbers of non-English-speaking immigrants con- tinually entering Ontario), special education students, and schools in pov- erty. What we see in Ontario is a large provincewide entity that took a deliberate systemwide equity strategy and moved the whole system.

CONCLUSION

My main conclusion is that achieving greater equity requires a systemwide focus that consists of three components. First, the goal must be declared that all schools in the system are part of the improvement effort. Second, a small number of core strategic elements must be in place to guide the effort (I provided a set of eight core factors; see Table 2.1). Third, systemwide results must be monitored and used as developmental levers for interven- tion. This does not rule out strong intervention (to replace a principal, for example), but the overall emphasis must be on moving the whole system. If you follow these principles, you increase the chances of not only achiev- ing greater equity but also, as in the case of our three examples, establish- ing the conditions for sustainable continuing improvements. In short, if you want success, equity must be a whole system responsibility.

REFERENCES

David, J., & Talbert, J. (2013). *You'll never be better than your teachers.* San Francisco, CA: Cowell Foundation.

Fullan, M. (2014). *The principal: Three keys for maximizing impact.* San Francisco, CA: Jossey-Bass.

Hargreaves, A., & Fullan, M. (2012). *Professional capital.* New York, NY: Teachers College Press.

Knudson, J. (2013). *You'll never be better than your teachers.* Washington, DC: American Institutes for Research.

PART II

Getting
to Your Core

Navigating the rolling tide of initiatives and balancing the interests of varying groups of stakeholders are delicate and daunting tasks. Leaders must have a solid core (an understanding of one's purpose, beliefs, and intentions) in order to sustain efforts, especially when challenged by opposing forces (Blankstein, 2004). The authors in this book have a strong sense of their core. They understand that stakeholders will buy into the "why" of their actions, not merely their actions. However, getting to your core requires an intense, reflective process. Time and critical analysis of one's answers to questions such as "What do I value most?," "What is my purpose in life?," and "What are my intentions relative to my work?" provide leaders with a solid core. The complexity of this task is reason enough for some to avoid pursuing it. Other factors, such as lack of time or the impression that this type of introspection is soft or unnecessary for leaders, add to the difficulty that leaders may experience when confronted with making difficult decisions related to equity.

Moreover, leadership is occasionally a lonely role. At times, educational leaders may feel it is not safe to include their staff and others in important, controversial decisions. However, recognizing and owning one's core as an individual and a leader, and drawing on the advice of those you trust (as well as listening to those you may disagree with), is possibly the most valuable and important thing that a leader can do (Bennis, 1989).

In the following section, our authors illustrate how drawing upon their core values has helped them to navigate obstacles and move forward when confronted with opposition. Carol Burris, a highly acclaimed principal, uses her chapter to illustrate how she and her colleagues drew upon their core values to take on the bold task of detracking their school. As a high school teacher, she understood that tracking was denying many students, especially low-income, minority students, the opportunity to excel. Her commitment to putting equity first and her willingness to evaluate the reforms as they were implemented made it possible for them to overcome concerted opposition. Burris navigated the rocky waters of the school board and parents by holding firmly to her core. Drawing upon her practical knowledge as a teacher and her understanding of her students' needs made it possible to create buy-in from the stakeholders around her and to move forward despite significant challenges and opposition.

Similarly, Linda Harper uses her chapter to provide readers with valuable insights on how to develop resilience in students who have been cast off as less able. Through her highly reflective process, we learn how she drew upon personal experience and professional learning opportunities to affirm the development of her core. Leading a school that services a wide spectrum of students, including students with disabilities and students with severe behavior infractions, Harper has developed a moral culture that nurtures these students and fosters their academic success. Her belief that all students should be provided access to a powerful academic program and support to graduate fostered the enhancements and accomplishments of the Success Prep Academy at Oak Hill School.

In the final chapter in this section, Avram Barlowe and Ann Cook pose this question: "Isn't it time to consider a fundamental shift in our thinking?" They make their beliefs, sense of purpose, and intentions crystal clear as they describe their efforts to challenge all students with an intellectually rigorous curriculum. Through the use of performance-based assessments they show that by focusing on what students know and can do it is possible to provide a broad range of students with equitable learning opportunities. Their work focuses on shifting from traditional state accountability testing to performance-based assessment methods. The leaders here are successful because they know who they are. It is this factor that gives them the credibility and moral influence to lead great change.

In each of these chapters, elements of the new paradigm we describe in the Introduction can be gleaned. All four authors are focused on the developmental needs of their students, and they recognize their enormous capacity to learn in ways that defy how they have previously been tracked, measured, and assessed. They also demonstrate a keen understanding of the challenges their students face outside of school, and rather than making excuses for these, they find ways to mitigate them so that a greater number of students can achieve excellence through their commitment to equity.

REFERENCES

Bennis, W. G. (1989). *On becoming a leader.* New York, NY: Addison-Wesley.

Blankstein, A. (2004). *Failure is not an option: Six principles that guide student achievement in high-performing schools.* Thousand Oaks, CA: Corwin.

Building a School of Opportunity Begins With Detracking

3

Carol Corbett Burris

When Finnish scholar Pasi Sahlberg speaks of his nation's reforms, he describes how equity was the driver of change. In *Finnish Lessons* (Sahlberg, 2010), he explains that

> It [equity] means more than just opening access to equal education for all. Equity in education is the principle that aims at guaranteeing high quality education for all in different places and circumstances. In the Finnish context equity is about having a socially fair and inclusive education system that is based on equality of educational opportunities. (p. 45)

On international student achievement measures, such as the Program for International Student Assessment (PISA), Finland is one of the highest performers in the world.

Sahlberg is right. If schools try to achieve excellence without minding equity, the attempt is doomed to fail. If, however, educators put equity first and create a school of opportunity for all, excellence will surely emerge. Not only did the achievement gap between the country's highest and lowest achievers decrease; the gaps among Finnish schools shrunk as well. While there were many equity initiatives in Finnish school reform, one stands out the most. Finland eliminated the country's tracking practice known as streaming.

Excellence emerging from leading with equity is what happened in the Rockville Centre Schools when they engaged in the systematic detracking of students. As the doors of opportunity were opened for all students, the schools engaged in decades of continual improvement. The achievement gap in the earning of the New York State Regents diploma closed. All students, including special education students, take International Baccalaureate English for 2 years prior to graduation. Self-contained special education classes disappeared. The curriculum that used to be for "the best" is now the "best curriculum for all."

The Rockville Centre School District is a racially and socioeconomically diverse district on Long Island, a place where racial and socioeconomic separation by community is the norm. Although the majority of students in Rockville Centre schools are White and come from middle- and upper-middle-class homes, the village also has low-income federal housing as well as apartments subsidized by Section 8 housing. About 21% of the student body is Black or Latino, and 15% of all students receive free or reduced-price lunch.

Rockville Centre Schools were not always the equitable places that they are today. In the 1970s, the schools were under a desegregation order, which resulted in the closing of one elementary school and the rezoning of others. In 1981, racial tensions erupted at the district's one high school, South Side. Fights between Black and White students occurred again in 1991—tension was so bad that the school was closed for several days.

The racial tension at the high school was an important wake-up call to a school community that had designed very different educational experiences because of the way it tracked students. The tracking system resulted in separate and unequal educational experiences for students. When fights occurred, they were nearly always in the school's low-track classes. The upper tracks were filled with middle-class White students, while Black, Latino, and White students from blue-collar homes were in the low-track classes. School Superintendent William H. Johnson and then-principal Robin Calitri recognized that low-track classes had to go. They methodically began untangling and undoing the tracking system.

REDUCING THE TRACKS

Tracking was not limited to the high school. As is typically the case, tracking began in the middle school. In 1988, the middle school had five tracks. Slowly, those five tracks became one. Reducing middle school tracking resulted in improved achievement—the number of students failing courses decreased, although it was the easier, low-track courses that were cut.

Detracking by getting rid of the lowest track was the strategy used at South Side Middle School. The principal, Larry Vandewater, phased out the lower track with students leveling up to the higher-track classes. Larry placed the reform within the context of middle school philosophy. He reminded parents that the former junior high school was a middle school, not a mini high school. He talked about the importance of developing the social and emotional needs of middle school children. Vandewater made it clear that Grades 6 through 8 were the time to open up opportunities and help students believe in their capacity to learn, not the time to close the door to high expectations, while labeling some young learners as less capable than others.

In 5 years' time, the tracks in all subjects, with the exception of math and science, had been eliminated. Those two courses had two tracks, beginning in Grade 6, from which students could choose. From 1992 until 1995, between 33% and 42% of students chose to accelerate and take high-track mathematics and science—and while that was a good improvement, there was still work to be done. Although acceleration in math was now available to all students, in practice, White, Black, Asian, and Latino students were not choosing to accelerate at the same rates. For example, during the 1996 to 1997 school year, only 11% of Black students and 15% of Latino students opted into accelerated eighth-grade math, compared with a 50% acceleration rate for white and Asian students.

This stratification was not in the best interest of students—especially those in the low-track class. The nonaccelerated, eighth-grade math classes began to assume the classic characteristics of low-track classes. Minority students, poor students, and special education students were overrepresented in the classes, and the failure rate for the lower track was much higher than in the accelerated classes.

Clearly, choice was not the solution to bring equity and excellence to the school given that accelerated math is the key to taking advanced math courses, like Calculus, later on. There was only one strategy that would work to truly bring equitable learning experiences to all students and close the achievement gap—every student had to be accelerated[1] in math and all student tracking in science had to be eliminated as well.

Cognizant of the importance of preparing all students, the middle school and the superintendent developed a multiyear plan to accelerate all students in detracked classes. In 1995, all sixth-grade math classes were detracked, and all students started down the road to math acceleration.

Detracking is never an easy reform to accomplish. Scholars such as Jeannie Oakes, Kevin Welner, and Amy Stuart Wells have extensively documented the politically treacherous environment that surrounds detracking efforts (Oakes, Wells, Jones, & Datnow, 1997; Welner, 2001).

There are also real challenges that must be addressed to make sure that all students are successful. When math acceleration for all began, parents and teachers worried that there would not be enough support for struggling math students. Parents of high achievers worried that their children would be shortchanged by the presence of students who were less adept at math in the class. These concerns cannot be dismissed. The district needed a plan to make sure that this initiative worked for all students.

Every other day math classes called "workshops" were added to the schedules of students who needed or wanted extra help. The typical math teacher's schedule changed so that they taught four accelerated classes and two math workshops that met every other day. The school established a common planning period so that teachers could dialogue and create common plans and assessments. It also gave teachers time to discuss how to meet the needs of struggling learners.

As noted above, the parents of students who traditionally would have been accelerated were concerned that the level of challenge might be diminished. The administration assured them that the curriculum would not be watered down, and teachers provided voluntary enrichment activities, such as Mathletes, both during and after school. The assistant principal, Delia Garrity, who supervised math in the middle school, and four of the five Board of Education members had high-achieving children in the first cohort of students who were detracked in mathematics. Their presence in the class sent a message of confidence in the more equitable math program to the community at large.

Professional development was also an important part of the process. The teachers and the assistant principal directed the staff development and regularly met to evaluate and tweak the program. Teachers wrote curriculum, developed lessons, chose materials, and evaluated student progress.

Assistant principal Delia Garrity, who was a former math teacher, was key to implementation success. Garrity analyzed the pass/fail rate of the students each quarter and made a point of sharing that information with the teachers, especially those who were resistant to the change. This ensured that those who were opposed could not dominate discussions with impressions rather than facts. Whenever the discussion moved to subjective discussions of problems, she skillfully steered the conversation back "to the data." Although it was assumed that failure rates would increase, that was not the case. Low-achieving students were more successful in heterogeneously grouped, accelerated classes with a more demanding curriculum. Despite these results, a few teachers continued to doubt that all students could do the accelerated work.

Vandewater and Garrity carefully listened to faculty members who were critical of the new math program. They would respond to complaints by asking, "What more do you need for student success?" With this question they moved the discussion from "is this reform working?" to "what do we need to make it work?"

When schools detrack, it is not unusual for dissenting teachers to align themselves with dissenting parents in whispering campaigns. That is what occurred at South Side Middle School, just prior to the Regents exam. All of a sudden, the passing rate dropped. The Board of Education told the superintendent that parents had informed them that more students were failing the course and that large numbers of students would fail the Regents examination. The superintendent told the middle school administration that he would like to speak directly with the teachers.

After complimenting the math faculty on their work with students, he told them of the rumor his Board had heard. He asked the teachers what resources or help they needed to make sure that students would be successful. The teacher who started the rumors was never directly confronted—she did not need to be. Needless to say, the rumors stopped. She received the message that her efforts to undermine were known.

When it came time to take the test, the students did well. The eighth-grade passing rate on the Regents was higher than the teacher-assigned passing rates for the marking periods. Over 84% of students passed the exam, and 52% were at the mastery level with a score of 85% or above (Burris, Heubert, & Levin, 2008). The passing rate continued to improve, even as the state algebra curriculum changed, with the passing rate increasing. In June 2014, 97% of all eighth graders passed this high school course, which is a New York State graduation standard. It is now commonplace that over 60% of all of the district's students take AP Calculus prior to graduation each year.

After detracking math, the middle school moved to science—first giving all students a life science course, and then accelerating science study even further. For the past 6 years, all eighth-grade students have taken Earth Science, a high school science course that ends with a New York State exam. This has also been a great success. Not only do students enter the high school with a high school credit in science, but the challenge of taking a laboratory-based state course has resulted in improved results in high school biology, a course known as *The Living Environment*.

DETRACKING SOUTH SIDE HIGH SCHOOL

Even as the middle school was detracking, the high school was slowly reducing its tracks as well. When I arrived at South Side High School in the spring of 1997 as an assistant principal, there were two or three tracks in the academic areas. As in the middle school, track choices were now made by parent choice, allowing families to make the decision about which courses the student would take. The one exception was foreign language, in which there was only one level in Grades 9 through 12.

The commitment to detracking was the reason I wanted to be part of the leadership team of the school. The high school where I was teaching was heavily tracked, and the tracks were identifiable by the race and socioeconomic status (SES) of the students in the class. As diversity increased in that high school, so did tracking. When I interviewed for the assistant principal position, I met other educators who believed in putting equity first, and luckily, I was offered the position.

In addition to supervising the high school math and science department, I was in charge of the review of the school's exams. As I reviewed the school's English and social studies midterm and final exams for ninth graders, I noticed that the tests were the same, although the scores would be weighted for honors students. In addition to the inequity of weighting, I questioned why we needed two levels—honors and school level—in the first place. If the cumulative exams were identical, how different could the courses be? I discussed my observations with teacher leaders and the rest of the administrative team, and, to my delight, we all agreed that there was no need for two courses. The following year, there was no tracking in ninth-grade English and social studies. All students studied an enriched, "honors" curriculum together with great success. As in math, every-other-day support classes in English Language Arts were put in place to help all students who needed more instruction.

Robin Calitri retired in 2000, after over a decade of reducing tracking. I was appointed principal, a position I still enjoy today. It was time to bring detracking forward (Burris & Garrity, 2008).

TURNING SOUTH SIDE HIGH SCHOOL INTO A SCHOOL OF OPPORTUNITY

Despite the reduction of multiple tracks, there was still a big gap in the earning of the Regents diploma at South Side High School in the year 2000 when I assumed the principalship. For those students who began South Side High School in 1996 (the graduating class of 2000), only 32% of all African American or Hispanic students earned a Regents diploma. The percentage of White or Asian graduates who earned it was far higher at 88%. Getting rid of the lowest track and putting in choice clearly were not enough. Minority students were not passing the tests required for earning the Regents diploma at the same rate as the majority students.

Furthermore, as in the middle school, the two tracks were identifiable by race, ethnicity, and SES.

We knew that our efforts with detracking Grade 9 English and social studies were successful. The heterogeneous classes had fewer discipline problems than the low-track classes of the past, and the tone and culture of the classes were similar to the former honors classes. Teachers now taught the same literature at the same time so that support classes could truly help struggling students. In support classes, teachers no longer focused on skills, but rather they helped students master the higher level curriculum.

In the fall of 2000, the New York State science course in biology was changed to a new course called *The Living Environment*. We used that change as an opportunity to detrack. The following year we detracked mathematics. We wrote a support curriculum along with the class curriculum. Although teachers still had their own style and lesson plans, they taught the same topics at the same time so that the support classes could work for all students regardless of which teacher they had. As mentioned earlier, there were no tracks in foreign language. Beginning in 2001, all freshmen studied the same curriculum in detracked classes.

Each time we moved forward with detracking, students were more successful, and so we discussed with central administration moving detracking into Grade 10. As in Grade 9, we thought it best to start with English and social studies first.

There was some hesitation among the social studies faculty, but they recognized the inequities that were associated with tracking, and they were not resistant to the change. The English department was enthusiastic in its support. When it came time, however, to make a presentation to the Board of Education, we met with unexpected resistance. A parent-teacher association president, who quietly opposed detracking, had e-mailed parents asking them to attend the Board meeting and oppose the change. For hours, the teachers and I answered question after question posed by parents who feared that challenge would be eliminated, or that the course would be too difficult for some students. We heard a few coded comments that disguised racial or class prejudice. One parent argued that some students were destined to work in the mailroom and that being in an honors class was just not for them. I received a call that complained that tenth grade should be the year that we "weed those children out." Parents suggested that we should leave the top track alone and just "raise the ceiling in the low-track class."

Our presentation lasted several hours. We showed data that demonstrated how results had always gone up with detracking, and that students still received excellent scores. We described how support classes would fill the learning gaps for struggling students. We explained the new grading system based on both progress and process, which was designed to reward student effort, so that every student could be successful.

The teachers and I left the meeting exhausted and unsure if the Board would support the change in the face of such opposition. After the meeting, the Board engaged in an internal debate. Superintendent Johnson and Assistant Superintendent Garrity reassured the Board that the program would be successful and said that to turn back now would not only be difficult but would put the high school administration in an untenable position. To their great credit, the Board of Education supported the recommendation and detracking moved to Grade 10. They did insist that the district curriculum committee, which is made up primarily of parents, be kept up to date by the high school principal.

The resistance of parents was an important wake-up call. We realized that detracking is not only a technical change but also a normative one. Traditional beliefs about intelligence and merit must change to win parent support. It was up to us to ensure that the curricula for the new tenth-grade courses would be everything we promised. We could not allow it to be watered down for our traditional honors kids, nor could we allow struggling students to flounder.

In order to make sure that challenge was a hallmark of the course, we used the curriculum rewrite to set the stage for preparing more students for our International Baccalaureate program in Grade 11. Teachers wrote a curriculum that integrated the use of the "IB Commentary" (a detailed, coherent literary interpretation of a brief passage or poem). The tenth-grade social studies curriculum included the beginnings of the "IB Historical Investigation" (an internally assessed component of the course whereby students create an annotated bibliography based on a research question of their own making). As promised, we made sure that process, as well as assessments, were part of grading. Teachers developed process rubrics to assess individual student growth.

The process rubrics were key to the success of struggling students. They rewarded students for the academic behaviors that would ensure success in the class. They also embedded a process for teacher feedback and how students should respond to that feedback to improve their writing.

Every-other-day support classes were equally as important to the success of students who struggled. These classes were not remedial. Rather, instruction in support focused on the enriched content learned by all students, using a pre- and postteaching approach for students who needed more assistance. Special education teachers were trained to support the curriculum as well. By implementing a sound and transparent model that worked for all students, we won over our critics and eradicated the fears expressed during the contentious Board of Education meeting. Detracking in tenth-grade English and social studies was a great success—former critics became supporters, and the move to one enriched curriculum for all was never questioned again.

In 2004, our tenth-grade math course, advanced algebra and trigonometry, was detracked, with an every-other-day support or enrichment (advanced topics) option available to students upon request. In September 2006, the last vestige of tracking in the tenth grade was eliminated, when chemistry was detracked, at the request of the chemistry teachers. Finally, in Grades 9 and 10, there was one course of rigorous study for all students.

We were not done. In 2011, we detracked IB English 11, putting all students in the first year of a 2-year course for which they could receive college credit upon successful completion,[2] and 2 years later (2013) we detracked the second year so that all seniors take the course as well. Further detracking is occurring next year when we eliminate American History 11, and instead have only one course of study—IB History of the Americas. Once again, we are carefully rewriting curriculum and putting in support classes for students who need them. We are proud that our classrooms as well as our halls are integrated by race, ethnicity, and SES, and that all students are studying the best curriculum we offer.

EFFECTS ON STUDENT ACHIEVEMENT

As in Finland, by leading with equity our learning outcomes improved. By the time the detracked classes moved through the school, the gap between the rate at which our majority and minority students earned the Regents diploma had closed. In 2000, there was a 66-point gap in the earning of the Regents diploma. For the Class of 2013, there was no gap at all—every graduate earned the Regents diploma.

Although Regents diploma rates across the state had risen, the rates for South Side High School students clearly exceeded the average rates for New York State students. For the past 2 years we are proud of our 100% Regents diploma rate. In addition, nearly 50% of our minority students graduate with the more challenging Regents diploma with Advanced Designation,[3] which is about the same rate as the cohort rate for White students in the State of New York. Clearly, detracking was having a positive effect on closing the school's gap in achievement.

DETRACKING AND THE
INTERNATIONAL BACCALAUREATE

If a school wishes to provide an excellent curriculum to all, it is important that it use a proven model to guide the development of that curriculum. We looked to the International Baccalaureate with its world-class curriculum and high quality assessments embedded throughout the course. We had reason to believe that our choice was a good one. Our graduates consistently reported that the IB prepared them well for college. In addition, we followed up by surveying two cohorts of graduates. From those surveys we learned that if students took two IB courses—one in English and one in Math, regardless of scores—the chances of graduating from college in 4 years dramatically increased. The 4-year college graduation rate for such students was 90%.

The International Baccalaureate Program believes that "student capability . . . is not a static, invariant quality, such as a student's height would be, but is something more dynamic and variable in nature" (IBO, 2004). That philosophy dovetails with the beliefs of our detracking reform—that given the opportunity to study challenging curriculum that develops higher order thinking skills, student capacity to learn can grow and expand. We understand that student talents, experiences, and efforts vary, and so learning outcomes will vary as well. Although everyone may not get high scores, students can learn far more in detracked classes with challenging and interesting curricula than they can when they are isolated in the low-track class, with low expectations.

As we progressively detracked, enrollment in courses grew, as did the percentage of students pursuing the full IB diploma. In 2001, even though any student who wanted to take IB courses could, only 27% of students were IB diploma candidates. In contrast, 50% of the students in the Class of 2014 are full diploma candidates, and 55% of the Class of 2015 is committed to earning the full diploma. In June 2014, 88% of our Black or Latino students graduated having taken one IB exam—a far cry from a decade ago when only a handful of minority students participated.

Even as greater numbers of students participate, school IB scores have remained stable, and there is no evidence that performance of our highest achievers has declined. The school has successfully leveled up without watering down.

LESSONS LEARNED

The detracking reform of the Rockville Centre Schools is a remarkable story of what can be accomplished given commitment, resources, time, and patience. Like the reforms of Finland, which also included extensive detracking, it is important to keep in mind that such reforms are far more than a mechanical process of eliminating tracks and rewriting curriculum. They require schools to move from a mindset of competition and exclusion to one of cooperation and inclusion, guided by a belief that the success of some need not come at the expense of others.

In a 2006 article in *Theory Into Practice*, Kevin Welner and I discussed key components of Rockville Centre's success in detracking (Welner & Burris, 2006). Those components, along with others that have emerged since then (Burris, 2014), are listed below.

• **Stable and committed leadership:** William H. Johnson has served as Superintendent of Schools since 1986. His beliefs in equity and opportunity not only guided the reform; they also led to the selection of principals and assistant superintendents who shared his beliefs and remained in the district. I have served as principal for 15 years. Knowing that you are making a profound difference is a powerful motivator to stay and lead, even when other opportunities arise. Most important, a vision that is consistent and stable allows a school to overcome challenges and resistance. As success grows, trust grows.

• **Elimination of the lowest track first:** The research is clear—low-track classes depress student achievement and rather than help students catch up, students in low-track classes fall further behind (Peterson, 1989). When low tracks are eliminated, student achievement rises, there is an improvement of school culture, and, in demographically diverse schools, racial isolation decreases.

• **Struggling learners must be supported:** Schools cannot expect students who struggle to learn high-track curriculum without the proper support. Every-other-day support classes, morning extra help, after-school tutoring and peer tutoring were all important parts of student success in Rockville Centre. It is import that districts work with their unions to find the time to provide such support. Community resources can help fill the gaps as well. The support that is provided must be carefully linked to the courses supported. Remedial skills models are not effective for supporting challenging curriculum.

• **Teachers were eased into teaching heterogeneous classes:** Prior to the abolishment of tracking, we engaged in a period of allowing students to choose their track, rather than be assigned to one. As more families chose the upper track, the class became more heterogeneous, allowing teachers to adjust their teaching methodology. By the time we moved to heterogeneous grouping, our teachers were ready.

• It is critical that schools remember that track choice is an interim step, not the final goal. The research is clear—choice results in the same stratification as systems that assign students to tracks.

• **Steady determined progress:** The school did not wait for everyone to agree that detracking was important. When middle school math teachers said that accelerated math needed to begin in kindergarten, the district wisely said "no," and saw the entry point at sixth grade where tracking began. At the same time, the process of detracking was gradual and thoughtful. For example, only after IB English 11 for all students in detracked classes had a 2-year success record did we detrack Grade 12.

Careful and deliberate rollout is critical for the success of any reform. Many of the problems associated with the implementation of the Common Core State Standards in New York State exist because of the insistence that the new standards and curriculum be rapidly put in place in K–8 rather than with a thoughtful, cohort phase-in approach.

• **Ongoing professional development:** Professional development is key to reform success. In our case, every teacher went through 6 hours of training in differentiated instruction taught by two members of the faculty and me. Teachers were trained in the use of jigsaw techniques, how to use the multiple intelligences of our students to differentiate instruction, and how to differentiate the kinds of assessments so that students could show what they know in a variety of ways. Special education teachers received professional development in coteaching and in taking field notes on student learning. Such notes provide evidence of student learning and help guide instruction in special education support classes. Teachers, both general and special education, also participate in the excellent professional development of the International Baccalaureate.

Since 2005, teachers participate each year in lesson study so that they can collegially practice their teaching—always with a specific purpose and always focusing on the learner. Lesson study has been an excellent way to embed professional development so that it moves from staff development to professional practice.

• **Careful selection and retention of staff:** If a teacher is convinced that all students cannot succeed in detracked classes, it is difficult to change that belief. Although we have seen the belief systems of experienced teachers change based on successful experience with detracking, it is important to make sure that new teachers support the ideals of equitable schooling and are willing to take on the challenge of teaching in a detracked school. In other words, during interviews it is critical that school leaders not only focus on the experience and skill of the teacher but also probe the teacher's belief system.

• **Make sure that classes are truly heterogeneous classes:** There is a lot of defacto tracking that occurs in high schools during the creation of the master schedule. Students at South Side who were high achievers clustered in classes because they chose French and played in the orchestra. Low achievers clustered when they chose support classes or when they have English language learner or special education supports in their schedules. This must be addressed. At South Side, much of my time in the summer is given to the review of class rosters and the hand balancing of classes. It is well worth the effort.

• **Earnest responses to parental concerns:** Parent concerns cannot be dismissed out of hand—even the ones that you find to be offensive or elitist. Parents love their children, and it is their obligation to put their child's needs first, even as it is a school's obligation to put the needs of all students front and center. Teachers need strategies to challenge high achievers and strategies to support lower achievers. It is the obligation of school leaders to provide the professional development and support to make this happen. It is also the obligation of the district to make sure that schools have the resources to provide support.

• **Don't forget the socioemotional needs of students:** Finnish schools ensure that students have access to health and emotional support. There are ample counselors for students, even in the earliest grades. I have come to appreciate the important role that guidance counselors, social workers, and psychologists play in supporting students. Students who are suffering emotionally cannot keep their mind on challenging curriculum. Students who are hungry, afraid, or without appropriate role models will not have the energy to excel in school. Drug addiction or addiction to alcohol impairs the ability of a teenager to do his or her work. Even the best teacher cannot teach an empty seat.

Mentoring programs, school to home connections, and support personnel (social workers, nurses, psychologists, etc.) play an important, though often unacknowledged, role in student achievement. Schools also need the support of the courts and social services when truancy and criminal behavior enter the schoolhouse door.

If we ever hope to close the achievement gap, we must address the opportunity gap—both between and within schools (Carter & Welner, 2013). One of the first steps in closing that gap is the dismantling of tracking. It cannot, however, happen in a vacuum. It is a reform worth doing, but like all reforms, it must be done well.

NOTES

1. New York State required schools to provide highly proficient math students with the opportunity to take algebra, normally a ninth-grade course, in the eighth grade. If the school were to detrack math, it had to provide that opportunity to all students

2. Students who score well on the IB exam often receive college credit. The required scores vary from university to university, even as AP scores that result in college credit vary.

3. In order to graduate with Advanced Designation, students have to pass additional math Regents exams in Geometry and Advanced Algebra and Trigonometry, as well as in an additional science.

REFERENCES

Burris, C. C. (2014). *On the same track: How schools can join the 21st century struggle against desegregation*. Boston, MA: Beacon Press.

Burris, C. C., & Garrity, D. T. (2008). *Detracking for excellence and equity*. Alexandria, VA: ASCD.

Burris, C. C., Heubert, J., & Levin, H. (2006). Accelerating mathematics achievement using heterogeneous grouping. *American Educational Research Journal, 43*(1), 103–134.

Carter, P., & Welner, K. G. (2013). *Closing the opportunity gap: What America must do to give every child an even chance*. Oxford, England: Oxford University Press.

International Baccalaureate Organization (IBO). (2004). *Diploma programme assessments: Principles and practice*. Retrieved October 30, 2005, from http://web3.ibo.org/ibis/documents/dp/d_x_dpyyy_ass_0409_1_e.pdf

Oakes, J., Wells, A. S., Jones, M., & Datnow, A. (1997). Tracking: The social construction of ability, cultural politics and resistance to reform. *Teachers College Record, 98*, 482–510.

Peterson, J. M. (1989). Remediation is no remedy. *Educational Leadership, 46*(6), 24–25.

Sahlberg, P. (2010). *Finnish lessons: What can the world learn from educational change in Finland?* New York, NY: Teachers College Press.

Welner, K. G. (2001). *Legal rights, local wrongs: When community control collides with educational equity*. Albany, NY: SUNY Press.

Welner, K., & Burris, C. C. (2006). Alternative approaches to the politics of detracking. *Theory Into Practice, 45*(1).

The Voices and Hearts of Youth

4

Transformative Power of Equity in Action

Linda Harper

As an educator, I am aware that the professional decisions I make each day are serious and consequential. Some have the potential to have a dramatic impact on the future lives of young people. I know well that my actions as an educator have the potential of giving hope or stripping it away. I have never taken this responsibility or power lightly.

The education of children is a profession like none other. Because of its potential to impact the lives of children and families positively or negatively our roles as educators seem similar to the roles of health care professionals. Like health care, it is one of the most important if not *the* most important careers that an individual can choose because of the impact we can have upon the lives of the children we serve. Consequently, as an educator and school principal, I reflect constantly on how I can be better professionally. As I reflect, I relate many of my personal, everyday life experiences to my profession. Often, I am taken back to a traumatic experience involving my brother, Anthony.

I will not provide an extensive detail on his childhood or character, since these issues are not germane to the story. I will simply say that Anthony loved motorcycles, particularly crotch rocket style bikes. Even as a young child, Anthony loved motorcycles; the louder the sound, the greater his love for the bike. Like some bike lovers, he also loved speed. Someone described motorcycles as being highly addictive—their openness to the air, sound, and speed, freeing and exhilarating. Although my bike riding experience is limited to nonmotorized vehicles, I could certainly understand the appeal. My mother hated his passion and regarded his love of motorcycles as a terribly dangerous habit. As mothers often do, she would frequently remind him of the perils that were associated with speeding. However, to Anthony the combination of crotch rocket motorcycles and leisurely rides through neighborhoods seemed oxymoronic. He wanted to burn the open highway. He wanted freedom. He wanted exhilaration.

At the time of the incident, my family had been grieving the imminent loss of our dear Uncle Bennie. His illness was very difficult for our family and especially for Anthony. In the past, you would always find them playing checkers and hanging out together like father and son. I recall Anthony sitting at the end of Uncle Bennie's bed in tears and much pain before leaving the hospital. It was difficult for me to watch this image. They were both strong family men, but now, against their will, they were both reduced to their weakest state, one more so than the other. We both knew that this would be the last time that we would see and talk to our Uncle Bennie. Anthony especially knew this as he left to take the long ride home, with much pain in his heart and mind.

Just days after Uncle Bennie's death, my mother recounts the day she heard the ambulance that seemed to aimlessly and frantically rush through her neighborhood. Her home is located in the center of a very steep, blinding hill. The ambulance driver appeared to be lost, desperately looking for someone. She surmised this when she continued to hear the loud siren as it repeatedly passed her home. They were looking for someone. She had no idea that they were looking for her son. When they found my brother, he was near death. Allegedly, he hit the side of a moving vehicle or was hit by a moving vehicle as he approached the area. We still do not know what truly happened. On the passenger side of the vehicle sat a young child being driven by his grandfather. With the impact, Anthony and his bike traveled over the vehicle. His physical damage was critical. We just didn't know how critical. Our dear uncle had passed away the day before this accident. We did not expect to be praying for the recovery of our brother as my aunt planned for my uncle's memorial service.

I remember receiving the call about Anthony's accident. I then had to take the hour ride to my mother's hometown. While driving, I received a call from my sister who explained that Anthony had been transported to the University of Alabama at Birmingham's (UAB) Hospital and was in the trauma unit. It was late in the evening, and I, like my other siblings, was very afraid. You can never know what to expect. He was my younger brother, and I wasn't prepared to say goodbye to him. We cannot lose him, I prayed. The drive to my mother's home was difficult and seemed endless.

Upon my arrival at UAB, my cousin met me to explain what had taken place. She received the preliminary details of his injuries. I was told that my mother was also en route to the hospital. As I sat in the emergency room waiting to see the doctors, I could not have imagined what I would hear. My mother then arrived. My younger brother Arthur could not be present in the waiting room area and was not doing well after hearing about the accident. He stood with friends in a nearby parking lot. The doctor eventually arrived to speak with my mother and me. That is when I saw the doctor's white coat as what it truly is, an understandable distractor. Wearing a knee-length white coat, I looked down as he spoke. As I peered downward, I noticed a failed attempt by the white coat to camouflage my brother's blood that covered his lower pants legs and boots. The doctor began to explain that my brother was in a very critical condition, and that he was still in surgery and would be there for several more hours. He went on to describe his extensive injuries and dire condition. He was described as being in trauma due to a motor vehicle accident.

After describing a litany of ailments that they were trying to address, he concluded with the phrase "and he may die." My mother dropped her head. She appeared strong during this conversation, but I knew better. When the doctor finished speaking, in disbelief and confusion, I could only ask, "Is he in pain?" I was afraid and wanted assurance that he was not suffering. I am typically emotional and have been known to cry and even scream when I am upset or confused. However, I knew that I could not show my fear at this time, for my heart told me that I needed to show strength for my mother and family. The doctor assured me that they had induced a coma that would allow him to rest peacefully as his thin frame attempted to heal and repair from the damage that had been done.

He was in surgery for more than 12 hours. His femoral artery ruptured on the operating table; this required multiple blood transfusions in one night. The doctor's words of assurance provided me with a sense of calm although I continued to ask myself if he was really talking about *my* brother. There was no time to react since my parents would now face something that no parent should face—the loss of a child. Throughout what seemed like an endless evening, my mother's attempts to rest were interrupted by her fear and disbelief. She was visibly worried. She was frail, and I knew that the loss of her son would be too much for her to sustain. The next morning she agreed that she should return home. I would keep her posted. Later, my mother asked as I walked her to my aunt's car, "Will he be ok?" She asked this in a way that beckoned for a reassuring response; it was not a confident question rooted in a religious claim or belief in a higher being. "Of course, he will," I replied. But at that point, I knew that no one could be certain. As they drove away, I hurt for them both. I knew that they were both struggling to find strength from each other—one with the loss of a husband that she had known for more than 40 years and the other with the potential loss of her son. I knew they would find comfort and support in each other.

Through many weeks spent in the trauma department, I saw amazing professionals committed to life-saving work. The very best physicians came together to determine the best treatment for my brother. They did not bring in the interns or the neophytes, only the best specialists, who worked collaboratively to save his life. They reviewed his medical records closely and monitored his progress around the clock. The ICU nurses provided minute-to-minute data collection and immediately applied their findings to improve his health. They provided briefings during shift changes to the nurses who were responsible for his care. Daily, ongoing briefings were provided to our family as well.

Data that was not relevant to his health care was not discussed. In our presence, there was no discussion of his presumed socioeconomic status. Our mother, whose address was in the western part of town, an area known to be predominately low income and of color, was not relevant since it had nothing to do with the medical treatment that he would receive. These issues were simply not a factor. Hospital records indicated that my brother had been at UAB before. He had been shot twice, once by an unknown assailant and once due to an accidental self-infliction. In determining the quality of care, this too was deemed irrelevant. They did not review the police report that recorded this most recent incident. If they had, they may have wrongly judged him and labeled him irresponsible and quickly surmised that the life of a small child could have been taken because of what they may have presumed were his reckless actions. They had no knowledge of the history where my mother had warned him several times about his risky behavior. This too was not considered relevant. There was no pity or excuses given for the pain he felt for his dying uncle. What mattered to these doctors and nurses were the results of his daily tests and ongoing reports. They reviewed the records and did not base his medical care on any of the background issues: African American male, low-income, possibly engaging in risky behavior. Only the best medical practitioners came to the room to attend to my brother and save his life. For 6 weeks they worked with focus and commitment, and they never wavered in providing the very best care.

Although my brother's accident was not about education, I often reflect on what my family's life would have been like if the doctors at UAB had done what so many of my colleagues do today as they interact with "at-risk" students. What if the doctors looked at the police reports and assumed that my brother was irresponsible and to blame for what had occurred? What if they contended that "this is an adult who should have known better, plus he almost took the life of a grandfather and his grandson"? Though such judgments might seem reasonable, they did not engage in them. Instead, he received the very best care.

What would have happened if the hospital administrators had assigned the least skilled surgeons to his case and allowed nurses who had fewer qualifications to monitor his care because they didn't value him as a patient? What if only newly trained interns came to assist my brother, without the support of the seasoned veterans?

As I think about the excellent care my brother received, I feel compelled to recognize that in education we often do not follow this example. Instead of the best in professionalism, our "high need" students often get the worst. I do not blame my colleagues for the incarceration or death of students who slip through the cracks and drop out of school. Clearly, such an assertion would be irresponsible and unfair because there are so many factors that contribute to a student's failure. However, I will say that the combined efforts and resources that are available to educators can change the life trajectory of many young people if we act as though we have their fate in our hands, just like the doctors who saved my brother. As an experienced educator, I know the power of strong adult-student relationships and the need for professional educators to provide equitable, research-based practices, resources, and opportunities to all students, without judgment about their worthiness.

Critical care units are generally staffed with the best medical problem solvers. Triage units are trained to quickly review the symptoms; the most critical patients are seen first and immediately shifted to available, skilled physicians. If a patient is too ill, like my brother, he or she may bypass much of the standard protocol. The process for caring for patients is purposefully differentiated. Certainly, the medical field is imperfect, and there are numerous examples of inefficiency and improper care given to patients in need. Clearly, doctors lose patients, even some who might have been saved if care had been provided in a different manner. However, I have never seen a *good* doctor limit or deny a patient high-quality care because he or she has refused to change his or her diet or shun bad habits. Even if death is imminent, *good* doctors generally do their best to make their patients comfortable. Such decisions are made after all efforts have been exhausted, and time has literally run out. In my brother's case, they worked tirelessly to provide the best quality of care, and as a result, he survived.

Unfortunately, some educators may review a student's data and make quick recommendations without carefully considering the long-term consequences for the student. Placing a student in special education placement or remedial class, or not allowing a student to be promoted to the next grade, must be done with a thorough review of the student data and an awareness of how it will affect him or her over the long term. To rush to judgment with pronouncements such as "He can't read in the third grade, so we must retain" can have detrimental consequences, particularly if we never ask why and search for the root cause.

Over the course of my career, I have seen cases where recommendations are made about a student that do more to exacerbate his or her deficiencies than treat them. Too often, we apply interventions with no intent or possibility of correcting or improving the *ailment*. Good medical professionals review data that are relevant before making a decision about a patient's care and so should *good* educators. All students should receive the best educational care to address and target their specific needs. It should not matter who their parents are or what their family's socioeconomic status is. It should not matter if there is a lack of parent involvement. Moreover, it should not be an issue if a parent or child has made poor choices in the past. We should expect the highest form of professionalism, just as my family did as we waited to see what would happen to my brother after the accident. Educators should serve as advocates for all children regardless of whether or not their parents are involved.

During our visit at UAB, my sister, who is a nurse, traveled from New York City to support our family. She was able to offer a great deal of feedback to the medical staff, and her voice was not silenced when her suggestions differed with those of the medical staff. When she recommended an inferior vena cava filter for my brother, the nurses listened politely. Her voice was not silenced because she was not a staff member, nor was she perceived as a "know-it-all."

As I thought about how the medical staff responded to our questions, I wondered: Do educators truly value parent involvement and the knowledge that our parents bring about their children to the educational table? Some educators regard the input of parents as a nuisance. When parents raise questions about the curriculum or challenge practices that they feel may negatively impact their child, how do we respond? Do they truly have a voice? Some educators want to restrict parent involvement to bake sales and other fund-raising activities. I have noticed over the years that many educational colleagues are threatened by the input of parents and student advocates. There have been occasions when I have sat in on conferences for the purpose of supporting families as a recommendation is being made about a child. As soon as I introduce myself and provide information about the child based on my experience and credentials, I have been dismissed because "according to our school policy, we are only obligated to communicate with the legal guardian." When this occurs, I know that the desire to remove me from the process is nothing more than a tactic to limit the ability of family members to get the assistance a student may need.

Many students enter school excited about learning but later become discouraged and despondent due to the effects of educational policies and practices that stifle curiosity and crush their enthusiasm. I am convinced that we have a push-out problem in education and not a drop-out problem. For example, in many of the schools I have worked with, some educators attempt to limit access to the advanced classes to the very best students and attempt to make sure that they are taught by the very best teachers. This is why even in racially diverse schools, honors and advanced placement classes are often comprised of White middle-class students, while poor children of color are excluded. As an administrator, I have often encountered resistance from students who oppose taking these classes because there is an unwritten message that only certain students are welcome. In my experience, when students enter our schools ready to learn, full of hope and possibility, we must nurture their enthusiasm with quality opportunities to learn.

As principal of Oak Hill School, engaging in one of my daily classroom walk-throughs, I frequently reflect on my personal life and my classroom experiences. I observe extraordinary moments as Oak Hill staff work to inspire and motivate new students. I also reflect on the students who have left our school and died, leaving the earth with untapped potential.

The students that arrive at Oak Hill School and enter our Success Prep Academy particularly move me. Many of them enter high school behind academically, but they commit to the goal of getting on grade level or graduating with their ninth-grade cohort. The expertise and dedication of the teachers, combined with their caring hearts and willingness to be advocates for students who have agreed to take on the challenge of completing what seems like an overwhelming, unthinkable feat, inspires me. I am moved by my students' determination to take on extra work and endure whatever is necessary to get their lives on track. As the principal, I am simultaneously driven to think about what I can do to support these students and their teachers as they pursue this arduous journey together.

Together, we have found a way to create a culture in the Success Prep Academy that has been extremely effective in supporting students. It has become a positive and extraordinarily special place. Its dedicated educators have demonstrated the capability and compassion to transform minds and hearts of children. As I see them at work, I am reminded of the triage unit at the UAB hospital that saved my brother. I feel strongly that this is how it should be for all students. But it wasn't always this way. In the following pages I share how we transformed the Success Prep Academy into the powerful institution that it is today.

THREE SCHOOLS IN ONE: SUPPORTING SUCCESS PREP ACADEMY IN A NONTRADITIONAL SETTING

I became principal of Oak Hill School in the summer of 2008. While I would love to claim credit for all of the wonderful educational accomplishments that the school has achieved for children and families with exceptional needs, I cannot. Decades before my arrival, the school had long been an extraordinarily positive place for children to learn and for educators to teach, grow their capabilities, and continuously improve. In 1976, pressured by parent and community advocates, leaders of Tuscaloosa City Schools System made a decision to build Oak Hill School. Over the decades since the school's foundation was laid, the school's students, parents, and teachers collectively proved to be among the most dedicated, hardworking, and passionate people I have ever worked with.

In addition to the Success Academy, the school served students with severe to profound disabilities. Oak Hill is known for its superb, award-winning Special Olympics program, and its students have competed in sporting events at the national and international levels. The students also participate in transition job training, partnering with local businesses and the University of Alabama at Tuscaloosa. These transition programs have been key in helping the students to transition into postsecondary job opportunities as well as independent living. Its award-winning exceptional student programs are unmatched in their determination to reach for and achieve high goals—personally, athletically, and academically. Its parents are some of the most determined advocates for their children and for all children that any educational leader could face and that any child could ever wish for. Its educators are among the most knowledgeable, capable, dedicated, and hardworking, not just in our state but in our nation, and I appreciate them all.

Prior to the 2008 school year, Oak Hill was designated to serve students with severe behavior infractions in specialized classes. Teachers in this program came from all over the county to be placed at the Oak Hill location. Students that were assigned to the alternative school had committed offenses that the state considered Level III offenses. These were the most severe and included assault and battery, drug possession, and weapon possession. Students that were returning from the Juvenile Detention Center would also transition through the system's alternative program.

To ensure the program's success, the teachers knew that that the image of this program could not be as it was in the past: a place where students with poor behavior were held until released to their home schools. One of the first items addressed was the need to stop referring to the program as the "alternative school." To change its image, the teachers worked all summer to change the program's name to STARS Academy. They also worked to solicit support for students from outside agencies and businesses. They worked to secure partnerships with the University of Alabama at Tuscaloosa's Computer Science Department to enhance the curriculum.

Understandably, the original families of students from Oak Hill were apprehensive about combining the two programs. We understood and respected the parents' concerns, but we knew something that most would fail to consider when combining the programs. Admittedly, students in STARS Academy would have conflicts with each other. On more than a few occasions I even found myself on the floor of a classroom or hall, safely restraining female students during a "cat fight."

Interestingly enough, the special needs teachers and students were not aware of our initial travails in STARS Academy. It was our goal to protect the STARS students' images because I soon found that they were all great kids that lacked appropriate peer conflict resolution strategies. We also knew that these students had amazing hearts and would be more protective of the students living with disabilities. Knowing this, we began to schedule events that allowed STARS Academy students into the special needs classrooms to read to the students or play with them in the playground. Later, the number of events and projects that we did together increased. These activities were designed to support students living with severe disabilities, and even more so, they served to merge the two programs. STARS Academy students planned sporting events and assisted with Special Olympics competitions. It was a remarkable sight to see the two groups of marginalized students working together, with clear benefits to both groups of students.

During the 2009 to 2010 school year, the second year of combining the Oak Hill School special needs and STARS Academy programs, the Council for Leaders of Alabama Schools (CLAS) awarded the programs with the distinction of CLAS Banner School. This honor is bestowed upon schools or programs in Alabama that offer exceptional services for students. These groups of students worked well to break down barriers. Both programs would only continue to grow and evolve into services that would create additional opportunities for all students.

It was not until 2011 that Success Prep Academy was added to this already rich and thriving school. During the 2011 school year, the Success Prep Academy concept grew from STARS Academy teachers' ongoing concerns regarding students that were typically being served from the system's centralized alternative education program. These students were in need of additional academic and socioemotional support. To increase the likelihood of their success, we knew that a major component of the program would be the counseling and other wraparound services that were present in the alternative program. We then expanded these services to students in the new academy. The teachers understood that if we were going to prepare our students with college courses, we would have to do more than merely focus narrowly on academics.

Based on the middle school math grade distribution of alternative education students assigned to Algebra I or I A/B during the 2009 to 2011 school years, 41% of the students enrolled in past years of the alternative program had received the grade of D, 53% received the grade of F, and only 6% received a grade of C. There were no students that received grades of A or B in Algebra. Geometry and middle school system benchmark assessment scores also revealed, overwhelmingly, that most students were failing or nonproficient in math. A further review of the Alabama Reading and Math Test (ARMT) revealed that on average, students in the alternative program were scoring at a Level 2 or below or were nonproficient. In reviewing the students' individual National Percentile Rank (Middle School SAT-Based), students were ranking at the 7th to 48th percentile in math performance. The Otis-Lennon School Ability Test (OLSAT) is a group assessment measuring certain cognitive skills deemed important for successful learning. With 100 being the mean or average score on the test, scores below 100 are considered below average. The alternative school students scored from 66 to 82, significantly below average. Based on results of these assessments, the students in STARS Academy scored within the bottom quartile of test takers.

The system leaders knew the importance of ensuring that students be given equitable opportunities, even if the program is located in a nontraditional learning environment. A team of professionals supported by our school board and Superintendent Paul McKendrick understood that providing equitable opportunities was vital to the students' success. Rooted in what is best for students, the team of professionals began to closely review student data to develop a program that would serve students that were in danger of discontinuing their educational services. They found that school years' data demonstrated that the alternative education students lacked a readiness and success in Algebra I.

After a close review of the data, the faculty and staff then began to research highly effective alternative or nontraditional academic programs that served students with similar demographics. They found and became intrigued with the success of a high school located in a midwestern community that was open to all ethnic groups. Under the leadership and support of Dr. Mike Daria, assistant superintendent of general administration, a visionary and courageous leader, an expanded Success Prep Academy was developed to support more students at risk of discontinuing their educational services. Dr. Daria has always been a focused leader with a clear vision and a belief system rooted in doing what is best for all students. His leadership and courage to support us proved to be essential to ensure the success of our students.

During the first year of Success Prep, the program limited its enrollment to eighth graders in danger of being retained or who had been retained one to two grade levels. These students were placed in a ninth-grade cluster and offered a compressed eighth/ninth-grade curriculum to prepare them for Grade 10. Community activities were put in place to address attendance and discipline issues as they occurred. They were also given rigorous course offerings, Algebra I, Honors History, and Advanced English, with additional layers of support in Algebra and writing.

At the conclusion of the first year, 93% of students had completed the program and received all of their ninth-grade credits. Remarkably, these were the courses that ensure high school completion and college readiness. Had they not been placed in Success Academy, these students would not have been placed in such courses because of their deficiencies in reading and math. By the end of the first year, assessment results revealed that the students were proficient in select Algebra I standards. Monthly monitoring of this assessment revealed a 7% average increase in performance.

When reviewing individual strands, students in Success Prep increased performance, for example, from 30.5 in Linear Equations and Inequalities to 53.9 from August to December. Considerable growth was noted also in Operations and Real Numbers from 12.7 to 48.6. Additional Algebra I strand results revealed considerable group growth. The additional Algebra I class period as well as the after-school tutoring was instrumental in the growth achieved. Students were also allowed to retake until mastery was achieved. No excuses were allowed or given!

During the visit to the midwestern high school, the Oak Hill team was able to understand and appreciate the power of strong student-adult relationships and how this could impact a student's future. Our team's visit validated what we knew about reaching and teaching at-risk populations. We knew that the academic rigor along with educator and student expectations must first increase. Our educators courageously jumped the high hurdle of low expectations knowing that this was the first barrier that could impede student progress.

In our system, we were challenged with taking our lessons learned and enhancing our current program options for our students. With a sense of urgency, high school graduation coaches, central office administrators, and the school leadership team reviewed the system's Graduation Tracking Reports as well as additional risk factors when identifying students that should be considered for the expanded Success Prep Academy. The following candidate criteria were established:

- Incoming Grade 6 through 8 students who have been retained twice in their school careers **OR** have been retained once but strongly considered for a second retention **AND** have a Tier III RtI Plan with limited progress
- Incoming freshmen who are the most at risk for not graduating from high school
- High school students who are 17 or older with 10 or fewer credits **OR** will turn 17 prior to the end of the school year and are not on track to earn more than 10 credits

   Note: If a student has an IEP, regulations involving placement in a program must be considered, Least Restrictive Environment for the student must be consistent with Success Prep, and the IEP must be able to be followed within the restrictions of Success Prep. The local school IEP committee has to meet to review the placement every 45 days if the student is accepted in the program.

Teams met to develop program components that specifically targeted improving graduation and drop-out rates. The criteria were based on Tier III students that would potentially leave school due to a lack of credits, students that typically experience attendance issues, and students that have received excessive discipline referrals. These priorities were addressed in the program. Students that fell into these categories required and received specialized educational and social services.

The goal of the expanded program was to support our students' academic, socioemotional, and behavioral needs. Students had the opportunity to receive additional credits toward graduation. This required an extended day program as well as a curriculum design that allowed students to obtain more than the traditional amount of credits usually received by their classmates, all within one school year.

At Success Prep Academy, there is no school-to-prison or school-to-poverty pipeline. This is our commitment to our students and to the Oak Hill School community.

PACTS TO SUCCESS

Many of the students arrive at Success Prep Academy with very low academic self-esteem. They are not convinced that they are capable of achieving at the same or higher levels than their peers, and many have not learned the basics: how to study, how to plan, and how to organize themselves to get work done. However, the teachers in Success Prep Academy believe in them. They know that they are truly some of the most innovative thinkers, and they are confident that with the right support, these students can excel. The teachers are also advocates for their students and have on many occasions courageously challenged procedures that they felt were not equitable. This level of courage was not seen until the faculty began a campaign to stamp out the low academic self-images of their students. Although many of them do not know it themselves, the students already possess many qualities that separate them from most students their own age. I would see their confidence come to the surface as they stood before judges, our city mayor, and other government officials, speaking on matters of importance to their community. The faculty and staff understood the importance of building on their students' belief system as part of the academic strategy to raise their achievement. Before an instructional program would ever be introduced, the teachers, with support from community members and mentors, would tackle the formidable challenge of improving our students' self-esteem and raising their academic self-images.

Many of our students enter our program having experienced very little success in school in the past. Unfortunately, what has happened is that they enter elementary school with excitement and willingness to learn, but that vanishes over time. By the time they leave elementary school, they have become despondent, stricken with a deep and profound estrangement from learning. If our staff were to blame their parents, communities, or prior schools, it would make us complicit in their continued failure. The blame game has never been part of our work. The Success Prep teachers and community teams work to undo what has been done to these children in the past. We build them up to get them eager and ready to return to being engaged as learners.

We all agreed and understood the value and importance of strong adult-student relationships. To cement this belief, we began our year with a program retreat. The purpose was to improve student-student and teacher-student relationships. We were engaged in "deprogramming" work and knew there would be challenges. Many of the students arriving in our program did not see themselves as confident, smart, or physically beautiful. They had been convinced that they were simply regular or below average or as one student lamented, "I am just slow." We saw quickly that many of the students internalized the labels that had plagued them for much of their school careers. They never saw themselves as anything but these labels. We had to counter these beliefs that infiltrated their daily thoughts. During the retreat week, our students engaged in activities with their community mentors, classmates, and teachers that emphasized the importance of teamwork, proper uniform presentation, community relations, and professional etiquette. Students learned that the language of success includes eye contact, firm handshakes, and improved oral communication. The retreat was designed in a conference or workshop style format. During this first week of school, students rotated to different sessions that had a specific goal of changing their perception of themselves and of their communities.

During this week, the students did not wear their required uniforms. There were sessions specifically developed to help them value the school uniform and the power of their appearance. They had to earn the *privilege* of wearing our blazers and neckties. During this time, they also learned the program creed, participated in team building activities, reviewed school policies and procedures, and learned the importance and powerful meaning of one's mental and physical image.

For example, the students participated in a workshop entitled "Ties to Success." Here the students learned how to properly tie their scarves and neckties. Several professional organizations, university professors, and community members hosted these sessions. Our mayor donated one of his neckties. It was amazing to watch the interaction between the students and the adults. You could already see a transformation occurring with many of the students. I recall Michael as he began to learn to tie a necktie for the first time. He requested Mayor Walt Maddox's tie and meticulously tied it around his oversized T-shirt. Once he finished, he held his chin, tilting his head to the side with distinction, and stated, "Yes, I am the mayor. May I help you?" The confidence was amazing to watch. This very important workshop assisted with establishing the school culture, a culture that is rooted in being your best in the classroom and in your communities.

The students also learned the importance of coming together as a family unit. We briefed them on the daily procedures that take place during our program's community meetings. These meetings were the most powerful tools for building strong relationships. There were daily morning assemblies designed to motivate and inspire. We used the power of music to cue and engage the students. The music that was selected was intentional, purposeful, and powerful in tone and message. For example, as our students entered the community meetings, we played their popular music, full of energy. We didn't worry about them bouncing off of the wall, because it actually served to energize the teens who were typically tired in the morning. Each day was filled with its own share of fun and exciting music. Depending on the day, the music was aligned with the day's theme. For example, on Wednesdays it was not uncommon for students to enter listening to songs about "hump day." The Geico commercial with the famous hump day camel was their favorite.

Students were encouraged to facilitate the daily morning meetings. It was important that they developed the confidence needed to stand before any group by practicing their oral communication skills. It was always amazing to watch the students conduct these meetings. We were all proud of their transformation. When the students were all settled in, the adult leader would begin to play The Script's *Hall of Fame*. At that time, this cue signaled all other students to become quiet, stand, and remain quiet. During this time, they were often seen checking their attire and that of the other students, serving as their brothers' keepers. After about 30 seconds the song would stop. The students would be seated, and the morning meeting would begin. Student leaders would recite the program's creed. Students who were members of clubs would also make announcements. It was their time to serve as the facilitator. Each morning, new students would take the lead during our community meetings. The teachers called the selection of music and the repetitive play a positive use of the term *brainwashing*. Daily, the songs reminded them that they *could be the greatest, be the best*, and that *the world's going to know your name*. There were only music cues used during these meetings to move students; there were no yelling adults or unruly students. The students were expected to comply with the procedures and did just so. All of these expectations were taught during the retreat gatherings. More importantly, the students were taught these expectations during our retreat week.

Since we knew that labels can be damaging to students, we took away their negative impact and grouped the students according to student pacts. This was based on the book called *The Pact* by the three Black doctors from Newark. Pacts would remain together and be required to support each other. The students were always identified by their pact name. When they were dismissed from our community meetings or competed during academic activities, the following labels would be used: The Pact of Resilience (seniors only) . . . Empowerment, Courage, Determination, Success, Excellence, Solidarity, Relentless.

For example, if an individual student won an award, this statement would be a part of the teacher's presentation: "Ms. Jackson, from the Pact of Courage . . . " To add to the goal of boosting their self-esteem, students were only referred to by their surnames. This practice seemed to do wonders to their self-esteem. We observed a similar practice at the midwestern high school we visited, and we thank them for allowing us to adopt strategies that quickly boosted students' self-esteem.

The faculty and staff developed words that they wanted the students to see and say daily. It was important for the program creed to depict the teachers' beliefs in the students as well as the students' internal beliefs. The students would begin the meeting by reciting the following words:

> What is our limit?
>
> There is no limit.
>
> We are the young men and women of Success Prep.
>
> For us, there is no limit!
>
> There is no limit to what we can achieve through hard work, endurance, and determination.
>
> There is no limit to our potential for success, which is governed by our choices, not stereotypes or the beliefs of others . . .

A focus on improving their confidence meant that they would be better equipped to meet the many academic challenges that they would face as participants in our program. Many of the challenges would seem insurmountable to them and observers. It was always remarkable to watch the teachers reminding their students of their value and potential.

The community meetings are daily reminders of their beauty and their self-worth. Students are reminded daily by the administration and teachers that they are needed and must all aim for their optimal potential; nothing less will ever do. This is also a time to express disappointment but with love. This is their daily morning message. They hear it, internalize it, and become empowered by it.

The weekly morning assembly schedule is listed below:

Motivate Me Monday: Speaker Series. The *Motivate Me* speakers start at 8:30 a.m. and speak for 5 to 10 minutes. Speakers often focus their discussions on the importance of staying in school and meeting academic and career goals as well as the pitfalls of discontinuing your high school education.

The schedule of speakers is designed to specifically merge our school with community leaders. It is important for our students to see successful people that have a vested interest in their community. It is equally important for our students to understand that they too can aspire to become whatever they choose to become. These are powerful experiences for our students. Our speakers graciously tell their personal stories. A few even venture to discuss times when they were teens and had engaged in behaviors that were not so pleasing. The speakers at times chronicle their struggles in school and at home.

I will never forget a group of girls that confidently approached one of our speakers following her presentation. One of the young ladies simply stated, "I want to be a lawyer, too. I can do it." This is what we hoped would happen by inviting these very inspiring individuals to our campus. Various stakeholders from the community were invited to the school to provide inspirational morning messages to our students.

Dialogue between the guest speakers and students is encouraged. Some of the speakers have included our superintendent, Paul McKendrick, school board members, city council members, Tuscaloosa mayor Walt Maddox, Tuscaloosa chief of police Steven D. Anderson, the president of our local chapter of the NAACP, Jerry Carter, our state representative, Chris England, our vice chancellor for academic and student affairs, Dr. Charles Nash, and other local entrepreneurs. All of the speakers have continued to display an amazing level of support for our young people. Because of our Mayor's leadership and forward thinking, when our staff has called upon city employees and leaders to support Success Prep, they have been available and present to do whatever it takes to ensure that our students are successful. I think this is the mark of what sets great cities apart from the mediocre ones. We thank him for his commitment to our wonderful city.

With the empowerment of the entire Tuscaloosa community, these professionals do an amazing job and they do, in fact, care, capture, and inspire our young people.

Testify Tuesday. This activity permits the students to share with their peers and their teachers positive or not so positive experiences that they have experienced during the previous week. It is our opportunity to listen to our students. In addition, the activity addresses any concerns students, teachers, and the administrators might have regarding any situations that may have arisen during the week, and the team works to resolve anything deemed problematic to the success of the students. We discuss our observations in the classroom and in the halls. We use this time to connect to our students.

I will never forget when we were discussing the importance of being respectful, Devonte raised his hand to question me about a concern that he had. "Dr. Harper, you are telling us to listen and not talk while our teachers are talking, and that it important to listen and value the opinions of others before speaking; you are asking us to be respectful of others as they speak, not talking above them?" "Correct," I responded. He then added, "Well, you have several teachers behind me that do not get that message and have been talking the entire time during your presentation." His response was not in a reprimanding or *gottcha* to the teachers. He wanted to express his sincere concerns and the importance of our community meetings. He valued this time together and confidently and courageously expressed his concerns.

Mental Math Wednesday. We recognize that most of our students do not have the confidence to be successful in their math classes. It is the lack of confidence and past poor instructional practices that impede their math progress; we know that they can do it. Their standardized test scores and previous course grades are outward indicators that our students struggled in this area. Again, this is what we already knew. During the hiring process, it is important to look for teachers that are not only skilled in their core area of certification but have done very well in their college math courses. For example, our history teacher took pre-Calculus and other higher level math courses and had done very well. Our math teacher had to lead her team in skills and pedagogy. Mental math, math team, and other math-related competitions were her projects. Mental math competitions for example allowed our students to build their confidence in their ability and improve their attitudes toward math. Seeing its importance, each Success Prep Academy homeroom studied various mental math calculations daily. On Wednesday during our community meetings, each homeroom designates a representative from their homeroom pact to serve on its team. Students are not permitted to work the problem on paper. During the morning assembly, pacts stand before their peers and compete. Not only does this activity provide students with the opportunity to become more proficient and confident with their math skills, but it also promotes healthy competition.

Gold Tie Ceremony Thursday. This ceremony was featured in the *Tuscaloosa News* under the title of "The Gold Standard." This program activity celebrates the epitome of excellence among the Success Prep students. Its purpose is to acknowledge and reward excellent student behavior, academic performance, and daily attendance at school. Teachers vote on the recipients of the Gold Tie Award. A recipient must be present at school for the entire week. The students have to be free of all disciplinary referrals, assist their "brothers" and their teachers, and be great community members. They are rated on their uniform presence; our students do not let their pants sag. They are instructed on the importance of their image and take their appearance seriously. Uniform expectations are set in the very beginning stages of the program.

I recall a young man rushing into my office upset because he had left his necktie at home. He pleaded to borrow one because he felt "naked." "Absolutely," I responded. During a music-filled ceremony, with personal accolades being read in the presence of their peers, selected students trade their standard crimson and gold uniform necktie or scarf with a gold necktie or scarf. Students' attendance and discipline referrals are closely tied to this honor. This is a highly competitive program. I recall a student that had become very upset because he felt that he had worked very hard to obtain this honor but was wrongly denied the opportunity. I rushed into the hall to observe an uproar that I thought was tied to typical student issues; maybe an argument over a girlfriend? No, he felt that the teacher had overlooked him for the gold necktie. With his ongoing efforts, he felt that he was not being recognized. The teacher was able to calm the student down and assist him through his emotions. Eventually, at a later time, the student went on to earn this honor. He did not give up. During this interchange, I saw the importance of strong adult-student relationships. I also saw what I and so many other students and teachers at Success Prep Academy know and believe. All students want to do well in school. The students in this program felt valued and did not have a need to create a disruptive subculture to gain attention.

Each Thursday, this ceremony brings many community dignitaries to our campus. Members of the 100 Black Men of West Alabama, led by President Chief Steven D. Anderson, as well as university and city government officials, visit our campus to assist the young men and women with their neckties. I personally thank them and Chief Anderson for their weekly commitment to our students. These amazing professionals are clearly dedicated to our students, providing them with much needed hope.

Free-Style Friday. Students are given the opportunity to share original speeches, spoken word poetry, inspirational quotes, word-of-the-day, or rap songs with their classmates and teachers. These activities are designed to build their self-esteem and academic self-image. In the presence of their peers, it is always powerful to see members of the spoken word organization present their work. Many of the students use this time to sing and rap their appreciation for their teachers or just to be "cool." From the establishment of Free-Style Friday, other clubs and organizations began to form. Students formed a choir and called themselves "The Treble Makers." They formed praise dance groups as well as other student groups and organizations. They felt empowered.

These daily reminders are powerful. Students are often seen settling their disagreements using their words and avoiding the inclination to use physical violence. Each student stands before his or her peers daily challenging them to be their very best.

The effects of such support became obvious to all members of our community. Surprising to some, although the Academy is the home to students that may have had significant discipline and academic challenges, students in this program currently hold the title of Regional Robotics Champions in the Tuscaloosa area as well as second place in the University of Alabama State Robotics competition. They were seen as a force. During this competition, they completed complex computer programs and synced them to their robots that they worked to build. "I just never thought I would be here doing this," one student stated with great pride. To be there and to win was validation of what all of the adults that supported these students knew.

They also compete as members of their school's chess team. The University of Alabama has been an amazing partner. University students from the Center for Ethics and Social Responsibility meet with our students weekly to teach them the game of chess. Success Prep and STARS Academy students are often seen throughout the city and on the university campus participating in chess competitions. Robert, a former STARS Academy student, told me that he was unsure that he could "compete against those White and Chinese kids." I reminded him that chess, as with any competition, is about skill. You must learn the game, practice, and compete. Robert did compete at competitions and did extremely well. During a recent university-sponsored chess competition, a Success Prep student received the tournament MVP.

These students are taught the importance of contributing to and serving their communities. They have attended Tuscaloosa City Council meetings as well as supported special education students through their student-developed "Adopt-a-Buddy" program. Moreover, students participated in fundraisers to benefit local social service organizations such as the United Way and Temporary Emergency Services. These projects have served to show our students the importance of being good, productive citizens as well as emphasizing the importance of giving back to the community in which they reside.

Community members, mentors, and outside counseling and support agencies are all active participants in our program. There is a strong mentorship program for student participants. Students visit college and university campuses to experience the college life. The students receive weekly visits from students from Stillman College. These are usually members of local Greek sorority and fraternity organizations. Since many of the students have to obtain additional credits in a one-year period, with the support of local grants, the school generally opens daily 8:00 to 5:30 and Saturdays from 9:00 to 12:00.

Success Prep Academy will continue to improve secondary students' educational outcomes. At the program's core, the primary focus is to improve student high school graduation rates and create postgraduation and career opportunities for students. This student population, if not served with specialized services, could potentially leave school due to a lack of credits or attendance issues, or could have their services suspended due to excessive discipline infractions. Addressing these critical factors are priorities.

In 2013, students in Success Prep participated for the first time in their home school graduation ceremonies. The Pact of Resilience was made up of 15 students that began the program with significant challenges. None of the students were considered seniors at the beginning of their enrollment. In May, 13 of the 15 seniors from the Pact of Resilience graduated with their home school. The other two seniors will become summer graduates. We knew what challenges they had faced throughout the year. We knew that they initially may have viewed us as "all of the *others*" or simply as some "snake oil salesmen." We told them that they would graduate, and then we put the systems in place to make sure it happened. Since each student graduated with his or her home school, each ceremony was well attended by the Success Prep teachers. As each one of our students stood up to march across the stage, my heart was moved to tears of joy. They were told by so many that they would not make it to this day. With *resilience* they did. The other underclassmen that were assigned to Success Prep all made their promotion goals.

Many students have chosen to remain at the Academy while others are transitioning back to their home schools on track for graduation, with the confidence needed to compete with their classmates. They are back on track, and this is because of the committed teachers, system administrators, school board members, and community leaders. In journalism, brighteners are often used to cheer up the viewers, especially after viewing news that has been overwhelmingly tragic. These news clips are usually pleasing, light spirited, even funny, designed to make the viewers feel better about the mental torture they have had to endure. They are often found at the end of the news story, leaving the viewer with a feel-good spirit. I have no brightener. I end with a plea for educators to address the lack of equitable opportunities and to have the heart to listen to the voices of the young people that all have an innate desire to be successful.

FINAL THOUGHTS

I was reminded of the need for urgency when my family was faced with the tragic loss of my grandmother. Dorothy Mae Scott (known to us as Mother) was found raped and murdered outside of her home. She was a strikingly beautiful woman, and I will always remember arriving at her home after her death waiting on my other family members. It was difficult for me as I walked around in her yard after the murder. Although her body had been removed days before, I could still smell her remains. I did not understand why this was the case. I vividly recall seeing what appeared to be fine silver strings entangled in nearby brush on the side of her porch. I reached to pick it up and realized that it was Mother's hair. She had lain in the Mississippi sun for 2 days before her body was discovered. She had become nothing to the animals that she loved and cared for as they eventually began to feed on her body. I stood there thinking about how her loss would affect my mother and her siblings. At that time, there were no answers to what had happened to her. I was sick to my stomach thinking about the pain and suffering she endured.

As I stood at the end of Mother's porch, I watched the convoy of cars approaching her home. She lived in a very small town, Cleveland, Mississippi. She had returned to her native home to retire and care for her land and animals. As I watched the cars progress toward Mother's home, it appeared as if they were moving in slow motion down her long drive. We were all devastated by the latest event that had brought us together but clearly focused on finding answers. She was 80 years old and killed by a 31-year-old man who could barely write his name. Because of the devastation of this event, my sister and I had to take the lead in emotionally supporting my mother and her siblings during this difficult time.

My sister and I attended the court proceeding of the young man who had been accused of taking her life. As is typical in a small town courthouse, seating was very intimate. We found ourselves sitting very near her alleged killer. As my sister sat near his attorney, she noticed that the perpetrator wrote a note to his attorney that read the following: "me goig hom day." My sister rewrote this to me as I sat next to her. I knew exactly what she meant and why she rewrote this note. I was quickly drawn to the impact or consequences of poorly educating people. Could this be a factor that contributed to this tragic event? As with so much of my thinking, my intensity about the importance of being serious about what we do to serve our students had become a real-life example personified by my grandmother's murderer.

We may grow up and move away and live in our suburban communities and drive our pricy vehicles, but at some point we will all be affected by the consequences of poor education. This perpetrator could barely spell his name or write a simple sentence. He was unable to take care of his basic needs, so could this have contributed to his decision to choose crime? There is no way to know. What I did know was that his life's route would eventually crash and tear into mine. Against my will, he etched his way into my mind and life, forever. People like him did not live in my community, or at least I was not unaware of their presence. I did not hang out with people that behaved in such a manner, people that did drugs or settled disputes by fighting.

Perhaps my perspective is an overly simplistic view of what happens when a man or woman is unable to think and provide for himself or herself. Surely, there are so many factors to consider. I have never shared this with my family, but my heart ached not only for Mother but also for this sick individual that tragically took her life. I felt anger, hate, and pity at the same time. He could not read or write. He could not think and make lifesaving choices. I thought about how miserable it must have been to live in a world and not be able to obtain your basic needs. Did this push him to a life of crime and drugs? I can no way know what the precursors were that led us to be united for the rest of our lives.

I know from my life's work that teaching is the most serious and consequential career; it impacts all other careers and all areas of life. Delivering a high-quality education to all children cannot be taken lightly. If we do not provide equitable opportunities, will we miss the opportunity for individuals to step up and rise beyond the circumstances they are born into? We must find a cure for so many of the social ills that our society has grown to accept as natural.

The Success Prep faculty and staff, community members, and families are fully committed to ensuring that students graduate from high school as well as pursue postsecondary education. Graduation from high school is only the beginning for these brilliant young people. The teachers in this program understand clearly the seriousness of what they do. At Success Prep, failure is truly not an option. The teachers recognize that what they do daily impacts the lives of students daily and in the future. They know well that ineffective or poor practices could guarantee a life of poverty, incarceration, or death. They understand that they are also trying to save the lives of their own family members.

The teachers live by the Success Prep Creed they created:

There is no limit to what we can achieve through hard work, endurance, and determination.

There is no limit to our potential for success, which is governed by our choices, not stereotypes or the beliefs of others.

They are amazing professionals, simply put. Although, I have since left Oak Hill School, I have no doubt that the faculty and staff will continue to do their collective best each day to move in a clearly stated strategic direction: ***High Expectations, Motivation, Innovation—Every Child, Every***

Chance, Every Day. This strategic direction is the true North on our educational excellence compass.

Our students leave Success Prep Academy as confident learners and high school graduates. As a team, the educators in Success Prep Academy are not exceptional; they are extra-ordinary! The students have extraordinarily high potential. Knowing this, we realize and act on the understanding that our educational practice must also be extraordinary. By doing so, we achieve extraordinarily positive results!

Empowering Students and Teachers Through Performance-Based Assessment

5

Avram Barlowe and Ann Cook

A dangerous thing has happened to American education—predictable, but disturbing nonetheless.

We have lost sight of what education is for: why we send our kids to school; why people enter the teaching profession; indeed, what a school or classroom should look like or what a well-educated high school graduate should be able to do. The goal of leveling the playing field to enable all students to have access to opportunity has been lost. We have become so obsessed with *keeping track*—of holding accountable—of comparing and ranking and sorting—that we have little time or appetite left to question what we are keeping track OF . . . or WHY.

The United States Federal Department of Education and most state education departments rely heavily on high-stakes standardized tests to do the ranking and sorting. For well over half a century, these tests have determined which students succeed and move on and which students are held back and have future prospects seriously impaired. Their reach has been extended to teachers and schools as well, illegitimately defining success and failure with assessments not even their creators think are valid. Test scores often determine promotion, school admission and graduation, school closures, teachers' tenure, and principals' contracts (not to mention property values).

Standardized tests have become the main instrument for determining children's worth and teachers' competence. And, because test results have been tied to every aspect of instruction, testing and curriculum have become interchangeable.

This occurs despite the fact that, nationally, test results show that the same type of students who did poorly on standardized exams 40 or 50 years ago continue to do poorly on them today with even greater consequences. An analysis of this year's twelfth-grade National Assessment of Educational Progress (NAEP) test scores revealed that the last dozen years of test-based accountability have had virtually no effect on the test scores of high school seniors taking NAEP tests. There has been no improvement for high school seniors on NAEP tests in reading and math since 2009 and only minuscule progress in the last decade.

Poverty and segregation are at the heart of the matter; schools cannot, and must not, be held solely responsible for redressing society's deep-seated inequities resulting from poverty, nor for the impact of racism and segregation on children's psyches. What educators *should* be accountable for, however, is the excessive, and nearly obsessive, use of poorly designed instruments intended to capture children's educational achievement (along with politicians, policy makers, and billionaire philanthropists).

However, despite years of lackluster test results, no urgent demand for alternative measures of assessment has emerged—no acknowledgment that if learning is complex, assessment should be too—that short-answer, multiple-choice questions and formulaic essays on topics of little interest to the test-taker send all the wrong messages about what teachers should teach and what children should learn. Why is it that attempts to chart educational progress remain so stuck in the use of conventional and failed approaches?

Some would argue that one powerful reason for muted opposition is the influence of those who call themselves reformers but who favor a public education system that is "an unregulated, survival-of-the-fittest, business-first market" (Brazile, 2014). For such "reformers" testing represents an opportunity to subject public institutions to the laws and vicissitudes of the marketplace.

Others hold that educational achievement is mainly about competition anyway—that for every child who succeeds (most often, White middle- or upper-class children), one must fail (most often poor children of color). *That's the way it is.* In that scenario, results will always be separate and unequal.

The introduction of so-called "new standards," cast as promoting civil rights, was hailed by some as creating greater opportunity for equity. But, though the standards may have raised the bar, the resulting curriculum and assessment instruments have not. High-stakes testing is still regarded as the central measure of student achievement with the added twist that the new higher standards will be met if test-makers simply ratchet up the difficulty of test items to reflect a more challenging curriculum. Put another way, this approach argues that not the *idea* of standardized testing but rather the tests themselves are presumably misguided. Change those, and the problem will be fixed. So far, however, the goal of improved results has proven elusive. The one-size-fits-all approach has continued to yield unequal results, not to mention growing resistance from parents and teachers, and even students. (When was the last time you heard even successful test-takers extolling the virtues of standardized tests?)

So isn't it time to consider a fundamental shift in our **thinking**? Shouldn't we be asking ourselves whether all the attention and time, not to mention money and resources, spent on test development, test prep, and test analysis is actually resulting in better schools and better prepared students? Isn't it time to acknowledge that we need to rethink what we mean by achievement, student success, and quality education? Shouldn't we be disturbed by the unintended consequences of such tests . . . the drop-out rates, student accounts of classroom boredom, and the high rates of college failure?

Isn't it time to consider an alternative approach to assessing what students know and can do—a new paradigm in which all students can contribute, learning from and with each other in a process where a variety of academic, intellectual, and social skills **can** develop—an approach which results in greater equity?

This chapter describes an alternative: a different and more equitable way to build students' skills and assess progress in achieving them. While it certainly does not claim to solve all of the social issues connected to equity, the system of student-focused performance-based assessment developed and implemented by the New York Performance Standards Consortium presents compelling data in support of more equal educational opportunities. It captures and uses students' strengths, interests, and ideas in ways that create a different paradigm.

The Consortium, a coalition of public schools, has developed and implemented a system of performance-based assessment that is practitioner-developed, student focused, and externally assessed. The schools that have embraced this approach are committed to four central ideas:

- A pedagogy based on **inquiry** teaching and learning
- A respect for the **diversity** of ideas and experiences
- High **expectations** for all students
- The value of **community** and collaboration

Together these principles have resulted in schools that promote equity.
The Consortium's system of assessment includes these components:

- Practitioner-designed and student-focused assessment tasks in the major disciplines with additional school-designed tasks
- Educator-designed rubrics used in the assessment of student work
- Moderation studies in which student work is reassessed annually by practitioners and critical friends in order to maintain task and rubric validity
- Extensive professional development designed to support and develop teachers' ability to use inquiry, pedagogy, and performance assessment tasks
- Predictive validity studies based on graduates' college performance

A recent consortium school graduate explained the system's assessment components this way:

All consortium school students are expected to complete four Performance Based Assessment Tasks (PBATs): English, social studies, math, and science. Individual schools require additional PBATs. In my school, Urban Academy, I also did a creative arts PBAT, a PBAT in art criticism, a library PBAT, and an internship. With the exception of the library PBAT, students choose to pursue their own PBAT topics, which grow out of classroom work.

Consortium students are required to make an oral presentation for each PBAT, and there are rubrics, which a committee uses to assess their work.

The social studies PBAT requires us to do text-based research using primary source materials and then to write an analytical research paper. My paper grew out of a philosophy class I took. I wrote a paper on Hobbes's and Kropotkin's views on what is the right form of government. Although I started off convinced by Hobbes, I reread Kropotkin's writing a few times, read background material, and found that I actually agreed with many of his opinions. I revised, and in my paper I argued that neither of them was completely correct.

For the English PBAT, you have to write a well-developed literary analysis. I did an analysis of the religious views of the main character in *The Life of Pi*. Pi claims he's a part of three different religions, but I felt there were many contradictions to that claim and examined how successful the author was in conveying that idea.

For the science PBAT, students must develop an original science experiment about a question that requires developing a hypothesis, doing the experiment, writing a lab report on it, and then defending the project in a discussion with a team including a real scientist. My science PBAT grew out of work in a course on anatomy and physiology. I designed and carried out an experiment on the effect of stress on memory.

The math PBAT requires us to use what we have learned to solve problems in the real world. For example, I used what I had learned in trigonometry to calculate how far away the Empire State Building is from my school and then explained how you could solve this and other problems using trig.

RESULTS

The Consortium's system has demonstrated impressive results:

1. The Consortium has a documented record of improving skills in ways that standardized testing does not. In addition to maintaining a graduation rate that exceeds that of overall New York City public schools, a study conducted by Dr. Martha Foote shows that the Consortium has a proven record of producing graduates who go on to successful undergraduate careers. Results from the study have been impressive.

In the sample, 77% of consortium school graduates attended 4-year colleges, 19% attended 2-year colleges, and 4% attended vocational or technical programs. In the sample of students attending 4-year colleges, 7% enrolled in the most competitive colleges, 14% enrolled in highly competitive colleges, 30% enrolled in very competitive colleges, 32% enrolled in competitive colleges, 14% enrolled in less competitive colleges, 2% enrolled in noncompetitive colleges, and 1% enrolled in specialized colleges. These results, combined with the consortium's high school statistics, indicate that consortium schools are highly effective. They hold onto their students, teach them well, graduate them, and send them on to higher education prepared to accomplish college-level work and persist in their studies. (Foote, 2007, pp. 359–363)

2. Using National Student Clearinghouse data, the study further revealed that Consortium school graduates have a 93.3% 4-year and an 83.9% community college 2-year persistence rate compared with the 74.7% and 53.5% national rate. The Consortium's impact on minority males is equally telling: 86% and 90% of African American and Latino

male Consortium graduates, respectively, were accepted to college in 2011. In contrast, the national acceptance rate for African American and Latino male high school graduates was 37% and 42% nationally.

3. Consortium schools also have significantly lower student suspension and teacher turnover rates than both charter high schools nationally and New York City high schools as a whole.

All this was accomplished despite the fact that the Consortium's pool of students includes more students living at the poverty level, a higher percentage of Latinos and English Language Learners, and a higher percentage of students with lower English and math skills than the overall New York City public high school population (Performance Standards Consortium, 2012).

These outcomes were achieved by holding students to high standards through a performance-based system that emphasizes curriculum and instruction that challenges students to build on the skills they have to improve and by encouraging them to grapple with difficult questions. Performance-based assessment gives students ownership of the learning process—something standardized testing and conventional test prep cannot do. It says to the student: "We are asking you to develop and demonstrate skills by reading, writing, investigating, and problem solving topics and questions that you participate in choosing. The topics you choose should be something that interests you and about which you may have a strong opinion. You must support your viewpoint with evidence, do research, ask questions, and learn how to express your views while still respecting others." Through this process, the assessment itself becomes a vehicle of equity because it tells students that their ideas matter, and that the development of their ideas is a crucial component of the hard work they must do.

PERFORMANCE-BASED ASSESSMENT: NUTS AND BOLTS

The contrast to standardized testing could not be more striking. In test preparation, students are expected to work hard acquiring disparate concepts and pieces of information; motivation rests on a delayed gratification (i.e., the notion that their test score will open doors or catapult them into the next and higher phase of their life). The false assumption here is that working-class students, minority working-class students, in particular, will assimilate the middle-class value of doing well in school so as to enter the best universities and access the better paying jobs. Performance assessment, however, insists upon empowering all students, not through external motivation, and not as a one-day performance resulting from repetitive drills and test prep, but through the realization and expression of their ideas in more extensive and nuanced activities experienced over time.

In the following discussion, the Urban Academy Laboratory High School, a public transfer school and one of 39 Consortium schools in New York State, is used to illustrate the Consortium's performance assessment principles in practice.

INQUIRY PEDAGOGY AND THE ROLE OF DISCUSSION

Effective performance assessment cannot be standardized. It has to occur within the context of curriculum and instruction that empowers students in the learning process. The centerpiece of such an approach is the type of discussion that allows students to exchange and develop ideas within an inquiry framework. Whether students are interpreting historical documents to debate a question or offering different methods of solving a math problem, analyzing a poem, or considering the results of a science investigation, they will learn more effectively when they feel that their ideas are incorporated into instruction. Teachers introduce topics, themes, concepts, or materials, but in an inquiry classroom students are encouraged to make informed contributions reflecting their own point of view. Inquiry teachers become skilled at asking open-ended questions and maintaining a focus while mastering the art of exploring new, student-generated questions and arguments as they arise. The classroom agenda reflects an ongoing partnership between teachers and students.

Discussion of this kind is by nature more equitable, especially in diverse school settings. Critics will say that mixing students of different racial and economic backgrounds often has a negative impact on more skilled and privileged students since they will not be challenged as teachers seek a happy medium, while less skilled and privileged students will be intimidated and silenced as the academic bar is raised. Such a view assumes a competitive structure very different from that of a school community in which inquiry discussion is the foundation. In an inquiry discussion, students begin to look at differences between them in new ways and approach participation quite differently.

As Khalil, a student at one of the performance assessment schools, put it,

The school I came from before the Urban Academy, which was a very competitive school with all college bound students, was not a very diverse environment. So there weren't too many opportunities to hear ideas from kids who came from really different backgrounds and neighborhoods. It wasn't a place where your ideas really mattered in the classes. Discussions were pretty predictable leading to specific answers that we knew the teacher wanted us to give.

The first week I came here, I was in a class where students were having a lively discussion about the behavior of people during the Great Depression, and I hear a White girl—someone with dyed red hair—make a controversial point. I'm sitting there thinking, wow, I agree with her. . . . I didn't expect someone like her to say that. . . . And the next person who speaks is a Black guy in a hoodie, and he's agreeing with her! That was a very important moment for me, because I suddenly realized that in this school, in this class, in this discussion, kids could learn from one another— from what others say. School wasn't just a social place; it was academic. You could agree with kids and share something uncommon—the hoodie guy and the dyed redhead could agree on a topic . . . people who were not like one another could agree on a point . . . and the teacher could listen to the points being made without judging.

THE TEACHER'S ROLE IN DISCUSSION

As this student points out, the teacher's role in such discussions is crucial as all students must feel that the teacher is a neutral chair, a fair arbiter of debate, and a defender of their right to interpret and analyze through the prism of their perception and experience. Listening to students is therefore critical. This does not mean the teacher is passive. During the discussion, he or she is taking notes, asking for evidence when arguments are made, feeding back the threads of the discussion, managing digressions and diversions, and framing and reframing arguments as the discussion unfolds. And the teacher is maintaining order especially when disagreements enliven the proceedings.

Discussion and Privilege

In inquiry discussions at schools like the Urban Academy, privilege and the classroom behaviors traditionally associated with it are constrained, allowing everyone to participate on a more equal footing.

Commenting on his experience in a previous school, T.J. noted that in his former school,

> if you were a struggling student, and especially if you were a struggling Black student, you wouldn't feel comfortable speaking because you didn't have the *credentials*, meaning you were a low B or C student, and everyone in the class knew it.

A middle-class White girl who had attended a similarly competitive school before transferring to Urban Academy described the manner in which discussion in such places can frequently be gamed:

> Discussion in my school was very predictable. . . . There was a rigid formula. You made an argument, supported it with a small piece of evidence, and you could participate in class without even having read the book. The whole thing felt scripted because kids weren't asked for their own reaction to the text or to what others were saying.

In contrast, the realization that your ideas are an important part of the learning process, and that therefore your voice matters, is especially empowering for students who have previously been labeled disruptive or resistant. As James, an African American boy, put it,

> the kids who in another school you may have considered the bad kids—in this school, you'll see them participating. And they're not participating by (just) saying, "Shut up! You have to listen to what I have to say." They're participating by actually intelligently telling how they feel about a certain topic. They're not just blowing out answers for no good reason.

According to yet another student, this is because when students' ideas matter,

> it kind of leads to a real respect among students. The minute we stepped into this school we were told by teachers and students that you have to respect people here. You may really dislike another person, but you have to respect them, especially in discussion.

The constant exchanging of ideas in a setting where those ideas matter creates an environment in which students can feel they are on an equal footing. It is often argued that students must acquire fundamental school knowledge before they can engage in higher, conceptual thought. Yet most teachers who have worked in public schools know of many young people not regarded as academically skilled or sophisticated who often operate at a higher level conceptually than their skills would suggest. Providing a setting in which such students can demonstrate complex thinking helps them realize that they can be just as thoughtful as their classmates who may be better readers, writers, or calculators. It also encourages more conventionally skilled and privileged students to see the possibilities of learning from all of their classmates. Conducted well, with good questions and unbiased facilitation, an inquiry discussion lays the groundwork for other academic skills, building insight and confidence.

Without the pressure of having to articulate correct answers, students also feel free to change their minds. As Maritza put it,

> You have to stretch your thought . . . if someone has something to say that I disagree with, by the end of the class she might have changed my whole entire opinion on the subject just because she has stronger points or she's done more reading or she has more evidence for her point of view. Or I might have changed her mind because of something I know that she doesn't.

Listening, Not Talking

Observers of class discussions, particularly important now in the wake of teacher evaluation, often use formulaic measures of participation, keeping track of the numbers of speakers in a given class period, without ever considering the substance of what was said. Doing the math, they frequently note that this or that percentage of the students participated. In an inquiry classroom where answers require students to present and support their point of view, participation is not always verbal. Some prefer to participate at any given time by listening. In such situations, discussion works just as well for them as for those who speak.

As Nayisha put it,

> When I don't talk, it's not because I'm not interested or that I'm bored. I like to observe. Me personally, I just like to look at the people and listen to what they're saying because observation for me helps me get my thoughts together for my papers. And then I write my paper, and that's how I show the teacher that I'm thinking, that I've been paying attention in class. I've been listening even though I don't talk much there.

The talkers understand this insight. Alyssa, a more vocal student, put it this way:

> Even for the kids who don't talk—they're still taking in other opinions.

The teacher's job is to discover what quieter students are thinking through their written work, discussions in smaller groups, or conversations with them outside of the classroom, and then to bring their ideas in some form to the other students' attention.

In most cases, given enough time, even the most reticent students begin to contribute verbally. Juan, an extremely shy boy, barely spoke a word in any class for 2 years. His written work, however, showed serious thinking. Eventually, Juan began to offer his opinions in short snatches that were rarely sustained. Finally, in his last week of high school, he spoke up to offer a highly sophisticated analysis of performance artist Nick Cave's "sound suits" creations. He suggested that one of their possible functions was protection from overt racial profiling expressed within the cultural context of the African Diaspora. He not only explained his insight at length but also, and in response to others, raised related ideas about Cave's work. It was a very proud moment for him.

Discussion, Confidence, and Writing

Inquiry discussion lays the groundwork for other academic skills as it builds students' confidence. Cindy observed:

> In every class I did a PBAT in, there was discussion. The whole class had to work as a group to make discussions as good as possible. That meant participating and talking in front of a lot of people, which is nerve-racking a lot of the time, especially when I was speaking about something I cared a lot about. But it also meant creating room for those who were reluctant to speak. I was really embarrassed the first time someone disagreed with me during a discussion because I thought that instantly meant I was wrong, and that I had said something stupid in front of the whole class. But of course that wasn't true; the other person just had a different way of thinking about it. But no one attacked me, they criticized my idea, and no one thought or acted like I was stupid or inferior, so I learned that it was OK to be disagreed with and to have my own opinions, which was very important for writing papers and developing opinions, ideas, and solutions while doing PBATs.

Herb Mack, Urban Academy's founding principal, confirms Cindy's point:

> Over and over we see how discussion helps kids become better writers. They think through ideas in discussions with others, and then they write. They do a lot of writing so they get a lot of practice. They write in class. They're assigned research papers, analytic papers, narratives—across the disciplines. But they get their grounding in discussions.

In exit interviews conducted when they graduate, students often comment on how discussion connected to the writing process for them. As Denise recalled,

> I learned a lot about developing my ideas by expressing them to other people; that, in turn, has helped me learn about writing papers. I had an organization problem, and discussion helped me learn how to organize papers a lot better and not get lost.

And Dakota noted,

> If you don't focus in the discussions or sleep through the whole class, and then the written assignment comes due, you're not gonna write a very good paper, cause you haven't been thinking about the ideas we've been discussing.

Discussion can be particularly helpful to students with learning disabilities. Richard, a motivated, dyslexic student, explains how the Urban Academy prepared him for Hampshire College:

> I was very quiet in classes when I first got to Urban. I listened a lot and had ideas, but I preferred just to write about them. I always needed more time to do the reading and writing, but at Urban I realized that I also needed to plan my time better. I'd sit with my teacher and go over everything I had to do and decide when and where I was going to do it, how much time I would need, and who I could go to if I needed help. We also talked about the assignments, the class discussions, and what was going on in school. As I became more comfortable and confident, I began to speak more in classes and that helped me too. My ideas became clearer to me, and the reading and writing became more accessible.

Each of these remarks reflects an understanding that discussion in this context allows students to see and practice how a question or problem can be thought about or analyzed; how different viewpoints or solutions can be considered; how evidence can support or oppose an argument; how an argument can be defended, developed, or modified; and how this would be reflected in a PBAT.

A CURRICULUM EMPHASIZING
DEPTH OVER COVERAGE: ITS IMPACT ON EQUITY

In performance assessment schools, skills such as inquiry discussion and writing are linked to subject discipline courses that emphasize depth over coverage, which offer students a range of options based on their interests. The curriculum promotes equity by both grounding students in "the canon" (i.e., familiarizing them with great works of established literature, exposing them to key events in history, showing them how to conduct a proper experiment, teaching them how to approach math applications, etc.) while also encouraging them to formulate new questions and seek answers in different ways. This helps students plug in to the disciplines by matching them to their more specific concerns. To the extent that they want their students to have a wide range of choice with respect to PBAT topics, some Consortium schools construct their curriculum around what would ordinarily be considered electives. Other schools prefer to give individual teachers considerable leeway within the framework of required classes. Thus, one Consortium school offers courses ranging from the Civil War and Reconstruction to the French Revolution to Gender Identity to Contemporary Issues in Hip-Hop, while in another, teachers of freshmen and sophomores select the specific themes, to be covered within common topics such as colonialism, imperialism, and industrialization.

Courses in Consortium schools are less bound to cover specific information, remaining responsive to new ideas and questions which might take a course in unexpected directions, pushing both students and teachers to access new resources.

INQUIRY IN ACTION: PBATS IN FORMATION

Student Input

Inquiry discussions and classwork lead to questions that matter to students, which may become the basis for PBATs. Some of these may be questions the teacher has anticipated and planned for, but others may not.

For example, in a Civil Rights History class, discussion focused on a source that argued that the integration of baseball was negative, destroying both the Negro Leagues and a host of other Black-owned businesses connected to them. Several students disagreed, claiming that the gains made through Jackie Robinson's breakthrough were worth those losses. Others were not so sure. At this point one student asked,

> What if instead of Jackie Robinson coming in as an individual player, they had pushed for some of the best Negro League teams coming in to baseball and competing against the White teams and each other?

A fierce debate ensued generating a host of additional arguments and questions. Several of these provided a framework for students who chose to research and write about the integration of baseball for their performance assessments.

Genuine performance assessments create learning opportunities by using students' interests and curiosities as entry points. Joshua, for example, describes how a fondness for cookies opened doors:

> In a chemistry class I got interested in how the sugar content affects the dimensions and shape of a cookie. My question quickly became more complicated. I began looking at how the molecular structure of the butter fat in a cookie weakens the molecular structure of gluten, which contains proteins. And as I researched the role of proteins in the baking process, I discovered that when proteins are heated they *coagulate*. I didn't know what *coagulate* meant, so I had to look that up. Then I began to understand that heated proteins bunch up and thicken, which affects the cookie's height. And all this was happening even before I started setting up an actual experiment.

> In designing and completing the experiment, I learned a lot about molecular bonds and denaturation. But what really struck me was the fact that my school allowed me to choose something as minuscule as a cookie, and take it a lot further. It showed me how something that almost didn't seem serious could turn my mind to think about something so much more than cookie baking. You start thinking about things like what's going on with these molecules, what are different reactions, how can you change them, why do cookies bake differently on the top shelf of the oven than on the bottom shelf. You begin to think about really deep questions that you would've never thought about if you were just baking a cookie.

Joshua's comments demonstrate that the key to doing authentic PBAT work is helping students find an interesting angle—one that motivates them to construct authentic research questions, to read, revise, edit, tinker, and attend to details. In a genuine PBAT process, a student's thinking deepens as the exploration of a basic interest unfolds. The teacher often helps a student formulate his or her question, but the question itself develops from something in the classroom that has importance to the student. And, in a setting where all viewpoints and interests have validity, equity is part of this learning process. The problem with even those standardized tests that attempt to include presumably more relevant documents, problems, and questions is that students have little investment in them and certainly no ownership as one size does not fit all; they are simply not invested in what standardized tests select, and no attempt is made in them to start with their interests.

PBAT SKILLS DEVELOPED
THROUGH HIGH EXPECTATIONS

The same student ownership that pervades the classroom and allows students to formulate PBAT research questions guides the sustained work they put into the PBATs themselves. These analytical research papers, science experiments, literary essays, math applications, and the optional, additional assessments demand much more complex and sustained work than does a high-stakes test. They are student-focused and require students to revise, reorganize, reconsider, extend, or modify their work. As one student put it,

> One of the most important skills we learn while doing PBATs is problem solving. I was never told exactly what I needed to do every step of the way. I always knew what my assignment was, but I needed to figure out on my own how I was going to do it. I made a lot of mistakes along the way, and I rarely got things right the first time. But it wasn't about being right. I revised and eventually got where I needed to be. I did get frustrated a few times, but I developed a problem-solving attitude. If something went wrong, I could fix it. Things will definitely go wrong sometimes in the real world, but I'm not so afraid of that now, because I have the skills I need to try and fix whatever problems come up.

This process is facilitated by teachers' high expectations of students and themselves.

Consortium teachers created the performance assessment rubrics for evaluating the PBATs in the four major disciplines. These are used by teams of teachers and external evaluators to assess the quality of student work. Periodically, rubrics are adjusted by teachers. If a rubric lacks clarity or is found deficient in some other way, teacher committees have the power to change it. In addition, once a year, teachers across the Consortium come together to reassess work that has already been evaluated by individual schools—student papers, experiments, problems, essays; work submitted across the disciplines—is reevaluated, a process that leads to greater reliability for the PBATs across the member schools. Eventually, exemplar or anchor papers are produced and made available to the public.

In addition, moderation studies—involving the regrading of PBATs by groups of teachers to determine reliability—are conducted on the assignments themselves. Using both the Consortium rubrics and Norman Webb's *Depth of Knowledge,* teachers consider the quality of assignments and questions that students explored in their PBATs. Such activities are invaluable as teachers work to constantly improve the quality of these questions and their assignments.

Finally, an external group of educational experts known as the Performance Assessment Review (PAR) Board reviews how well Consortium schools are doing in fulfilling their responsibility to provide the scaffolding and documentation of student work.

This approach relies heavily on teacher trust, that is, on the belief that intelligent, well-trained teachers can teach effectively and, in conjunction with external evaluators, be relied on to assess the results of their teaching efforts. The current focus on standardized testing rests on the contrary assumption that teachers will generally be mediocre unless they are guided by the results of externally developed uniform exams. It supposes as well that mediocre or failing results on such exams and consequent job loss or diminished pay must be used as a threat to motivate better teaching. It is interesting to note the high Consortium teacher retention rates and Consortium graduates' retention rates in colleges that belie these claims.

HIGH EXPECTATION FOR ALL STUDENTS

Amber is an example of a student with uneven skills. When she came to the school, her math work demanded considerable teacher support. The skills she had acquired by her senior year were so newly formed that her ability to grasp and apply them seemed questionable. Teachers worried about her ability to explain the data that are an important component of the PBAT science experiment. The experiment's focus, however, reflected a personal interest, which helped her. It involved analyzing differences between the Disney and Nickelodeon TV stations' depiction of minority group characters and how these depictions impact young children.

A science PBAT requires the defense of the student's lab report before a panel of teachers and outside examiners (frequently scientists) and a revision of the report based on their questions and feedback. During Amber's defense, she demonstrated a grasp of mathematical concepts which, up to that moment, had seemingly eluded her. She had counted the number of minority group characters she and a small group of children had seen in both Disney and Nickelodeon TV shows airing in the same prime-time hours. She found the same number of Black characters on both channels but noticed that there was a difference in the number of times these characters appeared on-screen. Realizing that percentage of appearances was different, she calculated the percentages and included them in her data. She was able to explain this data to the examiners and respond well to nuanced questions about percentages, ratios, and other concepts she had used, demonstrating that she understood not just their operation but what they meant conceptually.

Audrey presented a similar challenge. She is intellectually curious and participates well in analytical discussion, but she had no confidence in herself as a student. Her basic math skills were reasonable, but the subject intimidated her, and her work habits were poor. She chose to do her math PBAT in a course called Proofs and Games, which included students of different skill levels.

She created an assessment based on dominoes, a game she had seen played many times but never understood. "I wanted to learn how to play it," she reflected, "but also learn what kind of strategies there were. I'd seen other games played in class, like Mastermind, where math helped kids win." She started by looking up the game's rules. With guidance from her teacher, she began to consider the different possible variations of domino tiles being distributed in a given player's hand. She learned that this is a probability concept and began to research that. As she struggled to grasp her findings, explain them to other students, and apply them to dominoes, she realized that success in the game involved a process of elimination: at the game's beginning there are many possibilities, but with each tile played there are fewer. Through the process of mathematical elimination, as well as intuitive logic, a player can anticipate possibility reductions and craft a winning strategy.

In Audrey's math assessment paper, she displayed a sample dominoes game showing the application of a "tile tracker" she created on the basis of her research. A student who once found math intimidating was able to work with it at a more conceptual level through her ownership of an interest. The work had a broader impact as well, prompting the following unsolicited observation in the concluding portion of her paper:

> One real world connection I discovered in dominoes is being able to think ahead and making decisions based on what's going on around you. Just like with games, there are goals in life you want to eventually reach, and if you play it randomly you might not end up where you want to be. That sounds cheesy, but the process I went through here really showed me that it's true.

A good performance assessment system also stretches students who arrive in Consortium schools with stronger academic skills. Zack comes from a highly educated family of academics and writers. He floundered in his first year at a predominantly middle-class public high school where the classes and work seemed dull. At the Consortium school, however, Zack thrived immediately. Engaged by discussions and assignments, he began to strengthen skills that had atrophied and pursue new interests:

> I started out taking the Civil War/Reconstruction class and got interested in different explanations of how and why the war ended slavery. Then I took a course that compared the Autobiography of Malcolm X to Marable's biography of him and another about American slavery. I wrote a prerequisite assessment paper on why Malcolm X left the Nation of Islam, and my PBAT on whether or not the Nat Turner Rebellion was successful. The Turner paper was based in the beginning on a lot of sources we used in class, but the more I dug into my question, the more I began to find other sources and new information and my argument became much more complex.

> At this point I said to myself, "This is sort of a trend in me. I guess I'm interested in the history of race in America." So I took a civil rights history course in my senior year. I really enjoyed the readings and documentaries and hearing how very different people in the class responded to the issues they raised.

> I also wrote a pretty extensive paper in this class that required me to do a lot of additional primary source reading, even though I had already fulfilled my social studies PBAT requirement.

Zack's experience belies the notion that diversity lowers standards for more privileged students. His PBAT work pushed him but so, too, did the exchanges he had with students from decidedly different backgrounds. He drew on their contributions in discussion in the conduct of his own research and analysis. Having done the minimum or less in an environment where his opinions were irrelevant, he developed intellectual hunger and a work ethic in the Urban Academy's more diverse setting. He enters college with better skills, focused interests, and a greater ability to relate to varied groups of people.

A student such as Ron faced a different challenge. He had difficulty with analysis. He struggled with discussions and assignments that required the development and explanation of his thinking. By senior year, however, exposure and persistence produced results. In the same civil rights history class as Zack, he became interested in the movement's nonviolent strategies and Malcolm X's criticisms of them. Deeper discussions of the tactics employed in important civil rights protests had him making more nuanced and sophisticated comments than before. In the wake of these discussions, Ron outlined a PBAT that compared Martin Luther King's defenses of nonviolence and Malcolm X's criticisms by applying them to the sit-ins, the Freedom Rides, the armed resistance of a local NAACP chapter to White mob violence, and the Harlem and Los Angeles riots of 1964. This demanded a level of complexity he had struggled with in the past and which the next level of his education will certainly require.

BUILDING COMMUNITY THROUGH CURRICULUM

Policy wonks are fond of evaluating schools on the basis of whether they provide their students with "21st century skills," which are typically defined as creativity, critical thinking, problem solving, decision making, communication, and collaboration. Yet, despite the rhetorical emphasis put on these skills, the focus in the current wave of educational reform is on the individual student in isolation from others. "Personalization" reinforces that isolation by emphasizing computer programs for individual instruction. In contrast, private schools—such as Sidwell Friends and the University of Chicago Lab School (the Dewey School)—extol the virtues of community, a concept that is completely absent in the test-driven environment of so-called school reformers. Consortium schools, guided by the philosophy of John Dewey, look to find ways to help students in the context of building an academic intellectual community, not unlike some of the most admired private schools in the country. True equity occurs when the nation's public school children can benefit from the same respected education philosophies as the private school child.

As Dewey (1916) wrote,

> The object of a democratic education is not merely to make an individual an intelligent participant in the life of his immediate group, but to bring the various groups into such constant interaction that no individual, no economic group, could presume to live independently of others.

At the Urban Academy and other Consortium schools, a key component of intellectual community building beyond the classroom is a schoolwide project, which can occur once or twice a year. These schoolwide projects are collaboratively conceived and planned by teachers (with student input) and conducted in the first 2 weeks of each semester before regular classes begin.

Projects are organized around a single theme or question, which is developed collectively by the teachers. Here are some examples: What is a good museum? Do elections matter? Is our environment doomed? Is New York changing for the better? What role does religion play in people's lives? and Do the subways work? Project subgroups of two teachers and 15 to 20 students investigate variations on that theme mainly by getting out into the metropolitan area to gather information, make observations, and interview people. Thus, a project whose theme was city parks contained a subgroup that spent 2 weeks researching the history and current state of Tompkins Square Park, a Lower East Side institution in New York, which has been the site of a sometimes hotly contested battle over gentrification. Students in this group decided to unpack the history and legacy of that battle with each of them writing an analysis of it.

Each subgroup ventures, with its own agenda, into different parts of New York, examines different texts, sounds, and images, and speaks to sometimes vastly different people. Periodically, the entire student body is reorganized into even smaller groups that spend a morning or afternoon investigating the general question in a different way. The project groups continue to meet for $2\frac{1}{2}$ to 3 weeks; on occasion, the entire school community convenes to interview someone who could bring a broad perspective to the question being considered. Thus, during the project focusing on *Do Elections Matter?*, politicians campaigning for city council came before the full school to make their pitch and answer student questions. During the project focusing on *What Is a Good Museum?*, a panel consisting of teachers and museum curators debated this question: Whose responsibility is it to make a museum visit enjoyable: the museum's or the museum visitor's?

Other clusters of students and staff have joined social action projects (assisting crews undertaking rehab work in post-Katrina New Orleans) and participated in intensive language and cultural studies (living with families in a Guatemalan village). Each project is intended to encourage teachers from different disciplines to work together, to orient new students to the school's culture, and to explore issues and ideas that may not lend themselves well to semester-long courses. Graduating seniors often talk about "The Project" as a defining aspect of their Urban Academy experience.

The project concludes as each subgroup presents some aspect of its work to the school as a whole for further discussion and analysis.

The "Project" cultivates equity in numerous ways. First, it makes clear that every place visited, every person spoken with, and every text read has validity insofar as it provides answers to relevant questions. The place can be St. Patrick's Cathedral on Fifth Avenue or a storefront Pentecostal church in the South Bronx. The text can be an excerpt from Summa Theologica, a section of Martin Luther King's last speech in Memphis, or the transcript of a conversation with a subway platform preacher. In conventional school trips, students often visit wealthier parts of town and receive lectures designed to help them process the experience. Students in these project groups, however, have questions *they* have developed, which the visits are expected to help *them* answer. Moreover, students in a diverse group ask different questions, have different reactions to what they see and hear, and hold different opinions that can be shared as they process the visits, the readings, and the interviews.

The project also develops and solidifies the school's sense of community as students and teachers proceed to learn through and with each other. It is a journey that everyone, including the teachers, can take for 2 weeks, and it reinforces the idea that many topics can be interesting and worth exploring

It features different ways of tackling a common problem based on students' strengths and interests. By encouraging students to choose a path they want to follow, perhaps a topic whose details are equally new to everyone, it also levels the playing field, particularly in terms of previously acquired knowledge. Everyone, again including teachers, becomes a novice, and traditional subject area lines are blurred when, for example, an elections project group decides to find out "what makes a swing state swing" and spends 2 weeks in Ohio (hosted by families connected to like-minded schools) following the Obama and McCain campaigns in 2008.

Finally, it allows teachers to work intensively in teams to explore their environment and the resources in it. It promotes their learning from each other and helps them find new ways of engaging kids by interviewing people one might never get into a classroom, making connections beyond the school that can lead to new courses, allowing them to see students in different settings and new ways, or trying out ideas they would be reluctant or unable to embrace in a regular class.

BUILDING COMMUNITY THROUGH DISCUSSION PROTOCOLS

The nature of classroom discussion, instruction, and curriculum; the emphasis on student ownership; and the performance-based assessment system all inform the culture of a school. Students who become familiar with each other's ideas and thinking in the classroom invariably become more comfortable with each other generally.

As a veteran teacher says,

It goes beyond the individual classroom. It transcends that, so that even in a full-group meeting, even if a group of kids is standing around the hallway discussing something, it's the same kind of value system that prevails: people talking from different perspectives, discussing. It's so interesting. When you look at the exit interviews we conduct after graduation, they're not just talking about one particular class, they're talking about an entire school culture.

In this light, it is significant that Urban Academy graduates frequently return to participate in the school's annual pot luck Thanksgiving dinner, bringing dishes and experiences to share as a way of reconnecting with the community. Returning students can include graduates from as far back as 15 years ago. While they always speak with staff members, they come primarily to reconnect with the community and the values it represents.

Rituals lend themselves well to the creation of community. The best of them celebrate both the individual and the community simultaneously. When an Urban Academy student has completed a particular performance assessment, the entire school recognizes the achievement by cheering the student as he or she and his or her bell-ringing mentor walk through the school's hallway. On occasion, when the student completes an assessment after the term has officially ended, many still insist on being "belled" before a much reduced student audience. There is an understanding that whoever is present represents the entire school community.

School communities benefit from meaningful connections to the broader community in which they exist. For 3 hours every week, Urban Academy student volunteers represent the school at an external community service site of their choice. Their community service assessment involves teacher site visits, personal reflections, and the periodic sharing of community service experiences with other students. The community service experience broadens students' perspectives, allowing them to participate in community experiences beyond the school in not-for-profit organizations. For many, it is the first time they have had such a responsibility. The school exposes students to the idea that the larger community is a resource they can learn from, and through community service it is strongly suggested that they have an obligation to reciprocate.

The ideas and practices reflected in these experiences—observations, inquiry discussion, respect for diversity, high expectations of students and teachers, the importance of community—are central to the construction of meaningful alternatives to standardized testing.

BEYOND HIGH SCHOOL: LESSONS LEARNED

Students who graduate from performance assessment schools are products of this equation. As a result, they emerge from high school with the academic skills needed for college-level work as well as with the feeling that they are competent, powerful, equally intelligent, and prepared individuals.

Maria responded to a question about how minority students coming from a diverse Consortium find themselves functioning in colleges that have relatively few minority students. She replied:

> I attend a small rural college with mostly White students, which is a new experience for me. But I came from a high school where I was used to expressing my ideas to students of all different backgrounds and listening to them, too. People at the college could see that, and I was asked to become part of group that deals with race and class differences on college campuses in general. My involvement with this group gave me even more confidence in my classes. It has also taken me to other parts of the country and allowed me to meet civil rights heroes like Joseph Lawson, Marian Wright Edelman, and John Lewis. It gives me another identity to use as a foundation.

Another question asked concerned the adjustment Consortium students coming from a culture of discussion must make when they arrive in college classes that de-emphasize it. Justin explained:

I've been there. I experienced that even when I was at Urban Academy and went to church on Sundays. And because of my mom's wishes, I wound up at a Christian college where most of my classes were lectures. But I always asked questions in those lectures, and I even tried to start discussions in them. I'd stop the professors when I didn't understand their points and ask them to explain more clearly. I would say that I can't really learn fully this way. I have to engage people. And when I couldn't speak up in a lecture, I'd approach the professor after class and ask him for time where we could discuss the topic further. And a lot of them loved this and gave me that time.

Prior to attending Urban Academy, Freddy had never been to school with White students; following graduation he attended a well-known private college on scholarship where the student body is overwhelmingly White. These experiences presented him with unique challenges. As he noted,

I made White friends at Urban Academy, but they were always part of mixed groups. In college, I was sometimes the only minority in a class or a lounge. And most of these kids were really different from the White kids I'd known at Urban. What really helped me, though, was the time in classes. There I always felt like I could participate even when the material was difficult.

When I first got to college, I didn't like it socially. But, I thought, well, you have to take advantage of this as long you have to be here, and so I decided to try to be premed. Ever since high school, I had it in my head that doctors always work and make a good salary. And I liked science at Urban. So I took a class called Evolution of Model Organisms. At first, it was fun, but eventually I started to hate it. It just wasn't that intriguing. Then I thought about majoring in Spanish because some of my friends there were doing that, and I figured I'd grasp it pretty quickly. But then someone suggested a computer science class to me, and I took it. It was really hard, but I wasn't intimidated by the reading and writing because I felt fully capable of doing the work. What I really liked about it was that the class involved problem solving, and I liked asking myself, "How do I figure this out given the problem in front of me?" Of course, I also realized that these were pretty marketable skills to have, so now I am a computer science major.

Freddy's reflection underscores the value of students becoming active learners seeking meaningful knowledge. This is a crucial dimension of equity and the opportunities it presumably makes possible. Freddy's testimony shows that while aspirations of upward mobility can animate students, the motivation that can endure adversity in an unequal world comes best from an ownership of and interest in one's education.

This is where the issue of equity in education meets the problem of equity in society as a whole. Inequality has profound consequences. The failure of standardized testing is that one cannot make young people equal through measures that make them feel inferior and restrict their capacity for analysis and growth. If schools are going to address the issue of equity, they must be more open to new methods of assessing achievement, particularly those that have the potential to allow students to realize that they are capable and smart. Performance assessment creates an environment where a young person's ideas matter and are part of the educational process. This is the foundation for the creation of a more equitable education.

REFERENCES

Brazile, D. (2014, July). Speech presented at the American Federation of Teachers annual convention in Los Angeles, CA.

Dewey, J. (1916). *Democracy and education.* New York, NY: Macmillan.

Foote, M. (2007, January). Keeping accountability systems accountable. *Phi Delta Kappan, 88*(5), 359–363.

Performance Standards Consortium. (2012). *Data report on the New York Performance Standards Consortium.* New York, NY: Author. Retrieved from http://www.nyclu.org/files/releases/testing_consortium_report.pdf

PART III

Making Organizational Meaning

Once leaders have connected with their own personal and then professional core, their next challenge is to connect others—the people within the organization, students, parents, and the larger community—to the larger goal and vision. A critical part of this work is helping others to make meaning of the goal so that "buy-in" and cohesion can be achieved. Victor Frankl (1959/2000), a neurologist and psychiatrist who survived numerous Nazi camps, asserts that people have a fundamental need for meaning in their lives. In the context of equity work in education it is the role of courageous leadership to help others find meaning in their work. Doing so provides coherence instead of mere compliance with administrative directives. When the larger meaning of a goal is valued and firmly understood, all involved can derive a feeling of satisfaction that what they are doing is worth the struggle.

While many education policies use fear as a means to motivate—fear that a school will be closed, that a student won't graduate, that a teacher or principal will be fired if test scores don't improve, and so on—something more than fear and a monitoring of performance indicators on assessments is needed to motivate and inspire stakeholders to work together. The importance of getting all stakeholders to appreciate and embrace a common mission, vision, values, and goals (MVVG) cannot be overstated. It is the deeper meaning of MVVG that moves the hearts of stakeholders and propels their energy toward school improvement. For this to occur, it is critical for leaders to establish a cohesive environment, premised on trust and respect, whether at the classroom, school, or system level. Without a meaningful and concerted focus, a lack of clarity and confusion emerge, making it difficult for forward movement and ultimately improvement.

There are many tools that can assist leadership in making organizational meaning. In the next chapter, for example, Ann Clark describes how she and her team in the Charlotte-Mecklenburg district determined the highest-leverage change they could make in order to affect all parts of the system and then used that as the focus for overall success. This proved to be especially important for schools in high poverty areas where the external constraints (discussed in Chapter 1) had been used as a rationalization for poor performance in the past. To counter this, district leaders reframed the appointment of principals and teachers to under-performing schools from being that of onerous "combat duty" to being a professional honor. The establishment of clarity and meaning resulted in significant gains for all students and prestigious recognition such as the Broad Prize for excellence in urban education.

The importance of meaning and relevance makes it possible for stakeholders to drill deeper than organizational structures; it is a critical component of teaching and learning through curriculum and assessment. Allison Zmuda shares an approach to personalized learning that provides teachers the framework to create instruction that is meaningful and relevant for their students and that builds on the brain research discussed in the introductory chapter. It provides students the opportunity to make meaning, to build from prior connections, and to understand the relevance of their schoolwork to broader world connections. Dennis Littky describes the innovative Big Picture Schools model he established around the idea of providing students with the opportunity to explore their interests and cultivate their passions through real-life learning experiences. He also shows that this model served as a highly effective platform for deep learning. It is the process of learning that is emphasized and transferred to future learning and real work experiences. Finally, Estrella Olivares-Orellana, a bilingual science teacher, uses caring and an understanding of the developmental challenges faced by her students to develop meaningful learning activities for her students. Her approach makes it possible for her "emergent bilinguals" to make connections to the curriculum and to use their culture as a resource in the classroom. She provides concrete examples of lessons that are relevant and meaningful to English Language Learners (ELLs).

In their own way, each of these authors draws upon the new paradigm for excellence through equity that we discussed in the introductory chapter. They have found ways to enable students to establish relevance and personal meaning that sparks the core and gets to their own inner purpose, or core. In each case, the result is that students who have been marginalized are provided the opportunity to experience unprecedented success.

REFERENCE

Frankl, V. (2000). *Man's search for meaning.* Boston, MA: Beacon Press. (Original work published 1959)

Human Capital as a Lever for Districtwide Change

6

Ann Blakeney Clark

THE COURAGE TO CHANGE

Charlotte-Mecklenburg Schools (CMS) is located in a southern banking city. The CEOs of banks do not hesitate to place their top talent in a struggling branch to either turn the branch bank around or close it. In public education, management strategies are not as blunt; however, our district is successfully applying this principle.

Charlotte-Mecklenburg Schools took a courageous step in 2008 by identifying two key reform levers in its strategic plan—an effective principal leading every school and an effective teacher in every classroom. As a first step, the district placed a highly effective principal—one with a proven track record of improving student achievement and narrowing the achievement gap—in 27 of the lowest performing schools in the district. The principal in turn selected a team of highly effective teachers, literacy facilitators, and assistant principals to join the team. The approach was called strategic staffing. The key word is *strategic*. The district was intentional in the selection of leadership and teachers to lead and teach in its lowest performing schools.

While the strategic staffing initiative brought CMS national attention and praise for its courage in placing its best talent where it was needed most, it begs the question: Why is placing your top talent in your struggling schools viewed as a courageous leadership step rather than the standard operating practice in public education?

As the chief academic officer in CMS, with 24 years of experience in the district, I felt a moral imperative to address the chronically low-performing schools in the district. A tough look in the mirror helped me realize that for 24 years I had led and served in a district where top talent was not the obvious choice to take on the challenges in our struggling schools. The opportunity to change that tradition was all the motivation I needed to lead the Strategic Staffing Initiative. Six years later, many of the schools have shown significant academic gains in reading, math, and science, and the district was recognized for its efforts to close the achievement gap with the Broad Prize for Urban Education in 2011. This is the story of this remarkable change and how it provided a foundation for the work we are doing now.

STRATEGIC STAFFING FOR EQUITABLE OUTCOMES

As we began our work on designing the Strategic Staffing Initiative, we met with principal and teacher focus groups to understand what it would take for them to choose to lead an underperforming school. The message was loud and clear from these focus groups and helped shape the five tenets of the district turnaround strategy. Specifically, our teachers told us the following five things:

1. **A great principal with a proven track record is critical to a decision for a highly effective teacher to leave a current teaching assignment and move to a struggling school.** Over and over again, our rock-star teachers told us the leader of the school would be the determining factor in a decision to transfer to a struggling school. Teachers described a principal with the ability to masterfully strike the balance of pressure and support for the academic and cultural changes required to address the lack of student achievement in the school. The teachers were quick to remind us that the principal would need to lead with teachers, not charge up the mountain and leave behind the teachers and staff. While strong instructional leadership was a nonnegotiable for the principal, teachers emphasized the need for strong human relations skills as the game-changer for a principal in leading a turnaround effort.

   Realizing how critical the principal position would be in our turn-around strategy, the district immediately mobilized an effort to develop a principal pipeline program to develop leaders to fill the inevitable vacancies created by the Strategic Staffing Initiative. The district forged formal partnerships with two local universities that included joint design of the program components aligned with the district priorities and initiatives, selection of candidates for the program, and determination of a candidate's successful completion of the program. This unique partnership allowed the district to be in the driver's seat with the higher education programs, ensuring that the principal candidates who completed the program would be ready to lead in Charlotte-Mecklenburg Schools. Today the district has approximately 40 school leaders completing these partner programs each year ready to move into assistant principal and principal leadership roles. The combination of strategic staffing and the principal pipeline program has strengthened the leadership talent bench in the school district and positioned the district to more aggressively place principal and teacher talent in the lowest performing schools.

2. **A principal cannot take on the leadership challenge at a struggling school without a team of talented educators. Teachers want to transfer as a part of a high-functioning teacher team as opposed to transferring solo to a challenging teaching assignment.** Moving to a tough assignment with a group of student-centered and mission-focused teachers is a second critical ingredient in the recruitment of the district's best teachers to a turnaround effort. Teachers were enthusiastic about a leadership role in a like-minded group of colleagues with a genuine belief in every child, a proven track record of moving the achievement dial, and a willingness to do whatever it takes to improve educational outcomes for students.

Based on this feedback from teachers, each principal was able to recruit a team of teachers to join the reform effort at the struggling school. This team was asked to make a 3-year commitment to the school and was recruited based on a proven ability to achieve more than a year's worth of growth in a year's worth of time with students. In addition to signing a contract, teachers were expected to help instill a culture of high expectations for students, collaborate and build the capacity of existing teachers at the school, and be a model of belief in the potential of every student.

3. **Teachers and staff not supportive of the reform strategy were removed from the school in equal numbers to the number of teachers coming into the school.** Teachers were emphatic that toxic teachers at the school needed to be removed in order to allow immediate traction in the entry plan for the strategic staffing team. Teachers who were identified for exit from the school resigned, retired, or, in a few situations, were reassigned to another school.

Teachers identified what they described as a toxic teacher-lounge mentality where a culture of low expectations, complacency, hopelessness, and adult-centered attitudes prevailed. The challenge of entry into a low-performing school needed to be mitigated with an opportunity to balance an infusion of talent with a departure of an equal number of teachers who lacked the will or skill to tackle the academic challenges on the horizon.

4. Principals must be given the freedom and flexibility to reform the school without the constraints of district regulations that limit the ability to use time, people, and money and resources to impact academic progress for students. As part of the contract for strategic staffing, principals were granted freedom and flexibility with accountability to design a tailored turnaround strategy for the school based on an extensive review of a variety of data points. Teachers understood that if their principal earned autonomy, this would trickle down to the classroom and provide them with the necessary flexibility to teach without constraints and unleash their innovation, passion, and creativity to meet the needs of each child.

The autonomy for principals included flexibility with staffing, scheduling, budgeting, training of staff, and selection of instructional strategies. Each strategic staffing school improvement plan was built on the specific strengths of the faculty at the school. At Ashley Park, principal Tonya Kales created a Family Model where a team of teachers owned a grade level of students. Each day, students were grouped based on the previous day's accomplishments. Students, if asked, could not identify a homeroom teacher and instead named all teachers at the grade level as a teacher. The Family Model allowed teachers to teach in areas of their expertise and for the entire grade-level team to touch every student each week. Teachers in turn evaluated their success individually based on the overall grade level performance rather than on the accomplishments of one group of students on the grade level.

Suzanne Gimenez, a strategic staffing principal at Devonshire Elementary, compared her role to the leader of a wagon train in the Old West. She had to line up her experienced drivers every four or five wagons to make sure all wagons stayed on track. As the leader of the wagon train, she would circle back periodically to make sure everyone was still on track. Ms. Gimenez placed a highly effective teacher at each grade to allow that teacher to assist in building the capacity of the entire teaching team. Grade-level meetings occurred on a daily basis, led by a literacy facilitator and a math facilitator. As principal, she realized that a small team of effective teachers could not turn around a large elementary school without a commitment to build the entire school's belief in students and capacity to individualize instruction.

5. **Compensation matters.** When district officials talked to other districts about strategic staffing, educators were frequently shocked that compensation was not the most important decision-making variable for principals and teachers taking on the turnaround assignment. Certainly, our teachers knew that compensation did matter—as one teacher reminded us, the compensation needed to pay for more than a monthly dry cleaning bill.

Financial incentives were structured to recognize that strategic staffing teams were taking on an arduous challenge, and compensation should reflect that. Principals and assistant principals received a 10% pay supplement on top of their base pay. Teachers received a $10,000 recruitment bonus for the first year and $5,000 for years two and three. At the end of 3 years for the first cohort of seven schools, the district realized the need to extend the compensation for years four and five in order to continue to build the teaching capacity of the school staff.

CONTINUOUS IMPROVEMENT

From the beginning, we recognized that this work would be evolutionary. It had to be part of a process of continuous improvement built into the design of the initiative. In addition, we were constantly listening to the principals and their teams and learning about how to improve recruitment, entry and exit, training, turnaround models, and retention processes. Some examples of lessons learned are listed below:

- The first cohort of educators told us that they need to be allowed to enter the school in March, not July, in order to have time to observe teachers, meet the community, analyze the data, assess the culture, and make better staffing decisions. To support this type of strategic preparation, we moved the start dates.
- We learned that allowing principals to select their leadership teams and giving them the freedom to determine how best to meet their training needs was essential for empowering principals and schools.
- We figured out that the central office could best support schools by providing training for school teams in strategic school design to support the effective use of time, people, and money to maximize student achievement results.
- We increased compensation for fourth- and fifth-year teachers to provide a tangible incentive for those willing to take on the extra challenge. This resulted in the teachers selected delivering more than a year's worth of growth in student learning for a year's worth of time.

- The central office provided what we thought of as "911" level-support to these schools. We knew it was important that when a strategic staffing principal called for help, the central office staff had to respond promptly, as they would to a 911 emergency.

As a result of a focus on continuous improvement, the district now finds itself in the enviable position of having principals contact the deputy superintendent to ask how they can be assigned to a Title I school or a low-performing school. The district culture has shifted to one where taking on a tough assignment as a principal or teacher is a badge of honor and thus is highly sought out as a leadership opportunity. Principals and teachers now proudly refer to themselves with the designation "strategic staffing principal" or "strategic staffing teacher." Taking on a low-performing school is comparable to being named principal of the year—that is the culture now in Charlotte-Mecklenburg Schools.

ZERO PUSHBACK FROM PARENTS AND THE COMMUNITY

Uproar would seem a likely outcome if a school community has its star principal and best teachers taken away and placed into a low-performing school in order to achieve equitable outcomes for students. Indeed, we had braced for this potential eventuality. Instead, we had no complaints from our parents or community.

Our amazing principals deserve much of the credit for our school community embracing the strategic staffing initiative. When the superintendent and I invited principals to accept this challenge, we spent as much time talking about their exit from their current assignment as we did on their entry to their new school.

Each of our strategic staffing principals matched their exit strategy to their school community. But a common thread across all exit plans was personal ownership of the decision to take on this new assignment as a moral imperative to ensure that a child's zip code did not determine the quality of education he or she received. One principal brought a cake into her faculty meeting and announced they were having a celebration. She told the staff that the district was celebrating their success as a school team by inviting her to lead a struggling school in the district. She urged them to embrace her new school assignment as a way of honoring the work they had done together.

At another school, the principal displayed the data of the school he was moving to on a projection screen and indicated that it was a moral imperative for him to accept the invitation from the superintendent to lead this school. He made such a compelling case to his school community that his PTA volunteered to adopt his school, provide parent support, and help build parent involvement in his new community.

These two examples of principals making the case for their moves are only two of 27 opportunities where principals exercised their extraordinary leadership skills to make a compelling case to students, staff, and parents that a move to a new school must be supported and embraced rather than challenged and criticized. Just as our culture has shifted among principals to consider a tough assignment a professional privilege, so too have our teachers, parents, and community embraced the need to put talent where it is needed most.

WHAT'S NEXT

Our philosophy was always one of continuous improvement and unwavering commitment to equitable outcomes for students. Many of our gains in the 27 schools were low-hanging fruit—taking single-digit student achievement results to low double-digit successes. Now we want to go to the next level.

With a new superintendent and a new strategic plan, human capital is still a key lever for reform in our district. The urgency to achieve equitable outcomes for every child continues to drive us. Our new strategic plan calls for the development of Strategic Staffing 2.0 that will build on the lessons learned from our first round of strategic staffing and provide more time for root-cause analysis at struggling schools, additional planning time to develop the turnaround strategy, and intentional professional development for the entire school staff.

The district is also exploring new scheduling approaches to maximize opportunities for our neediest students in a given school to be taught by the most effective teachers. Having an effective teacher in every classroom is a long-term strategy. The urgency of the achievement gap in the district requires maximizing the opportunities for our students furthest behind to have increased contact with high-impact teachers each day. New teacher-leadership roles are being created to allow our best teachers to remain in the classroom while teaching more students, building the capacity of their teaching colleagues, and being compensated for their newly expanded roles as teacher leaders.

Charlotte-Mecklenburg Schools has moved from being a courageous district willing to place its best principals and teachers in its neediest schools to a district where talented principals and teachers seek challenging assignments. That culture shift has prepared us to develop our next round of strategies targeting our lowest-performing schools.

Personalized Learning

7

Allison Zmuda

In every school, regardless of its resource, staffing, and leadership challenges, the one constant goal is creating a school and classroom culture that engages students to do their *best* work. What every educator knows, however, is that an appropriate assignment for one student may not be appropriate for the other students. Relevance, prior knowledge, current skill development, mindset, and other factors make it more or less likely that each student will accept the challenge and settle in and do the work. And for our struggling and disenfranchised students, they believe (and perhaps rightly so) their schoolwork is disconnected from the "real work" of supporting a family, pursuing aspirations, tackling complex problems, and navigating the world.

This chapter focuses on shifting toward a personalized learning structure: one where students collaborate with teachers as learning partners to have a mutual stake in performance. The origins of personalized learning can be traced to the Dalton Plan in the 19th century where each student could program his or her curriculum in order to meet his or her needs, interests, and abilities. The goal was to promote both independence and dependability and to enhance the student's social skills and sense of responsibility toward others. In contemporary classrooms, the heart of personalized learning stays much the same; learning is

- owned by the student (student as the heart, teacher as the coach or adviser);
- interdisciplinary in nature; and
- grounded in the exploration of authentic and meaningful problems, challenges, and ideas that have significance to the broader world.

While the original idea has become modernized, especially due to the advent of technology, the challenge of doing this in schools remains quite daunting. This is a fundamental design challenge that requires dedicated, risk-tolerant, intelligent, compassionate educators to reimagine schools in such a way as to deepen who we are as a society. Progressive educator John Dewey (1907) once said,

> What the best and wisest parent wants for his own child, that must the community want for all of its children. Any other ideal for our schools is narrow and unlovely; acted upon, it destroys our democracy. All that society has accomplished for itself is put, through the agency of the school, at the disposal of its future members. (p. 19)

Therefore, as educators we are compelled to figure out how to make what may appear to be competing aims part of school culture:

- Encourage talented learners and struggling learners in the same classroom.
- Manage an increasing educator workload and make time to connect with individual students.
- Routinize classroom procedures and expectations and honor the messiness of learning.
- Provide straightforward assignments that require efficient recall and complex challenges that can be approached numerous ways.

This chapter first responds to the question "why now?" by describing two major tipping points: change in demographics and in economic structure. The discussion then focuses on four major components in the design of personalized learning: clarity, context, culture, and capital. The fundamental shift necessitated for a personalized learning environment to flourish is how we see our students in relation to the work we do— moving from a place where school is something done to our students to a place of collaborative partnerships.

TWO TIPPING POINTS

In a standardized, test-prep, data-driven, risk-averse school world, why change now? There are two tipping points that have also become a reality in the contemporary world that directly impact the education of our students.

Change in Demographics

According to the 2010 census (Center for Public Education, 2012), America's population is growing more racially diverse and, in 30 years, the nation will have a new majority—a majority composed of minorities. These trends reflect who we are seeing in our classrooms across every state in the nation. The Center for Public Education (2012) reported the following to school leaders:

- More than one-third of all Hispanics are younger than 18.
- Using 2005 figures, the Population Reference Bureau estimates that about 45% of children younger than 5 are minorities.
- In 2008, there were 49.3 million elementary and high school age children (5- to 17-year-olds). About 1 in 10 students attended private school in 2008, a ratio that has remained fairly consistent since the 1970s.
- Between 2000 and 2008, 13 states saw increases in enrollment in Grades 1 through 12. During the same period, 37 states experienced decreases, although only 16 saw decreases that were statistically significant.
- In 2010, 21.6% of children under age 18 lived in poverty.
- The percentage of births to unmarried mothers has nearly doubled since 1990, up from 26.6% that year to 40.6% in 2008.
- In 2009, 23% of U.S. students had at least one foreign-born parent; this includes the 5% who were foreign born themselves and the 18% who were born here with at least one foreign-born parent.
- Among the foreign born in 2009, 53% were born in Latin America, 27% in Asia, 13% in Europe, and 7% in other regions of the world.
- Nearly 20% of the nation's population age 5 and older speak a language other than English at home.

According to the editors of this book, "If demography need not determine destiny, and a child's race and class *can* be decoupled from how well they will do in school or college," then we need to embrace the children we have in front of us for their unique gifts, talents, and aspirations. This has been the American challenge since the inception of public schooling: to provide *every child* a quality education where he or she can thrive. As our classrooms continue to become increasingly diverse, moving to a personalized learning framework becomes more essential. In 1999, Ted Sizer contended that personalized learning helps our democratic society tap into the talents of our students and prepare for an increasingly unpredictable world:

The insistent coaxing out of each child on his or her best terms of profoundly important intellectual habits and tools for enriching a democratic society [and] the substance and skills to survive well in a rapidly changing culture and economy. . . . It can be done. It is being done, however against the traditional grain. (p. 11)

It is time to design a pluralistic education that moves beyond skin color, native language, and zip code where everyone is a valued member and has the capacity to learn.

Change in Global Economy

To prepare students to be college- and career-ready and able to compete in a global marketplace, students must be trained to think, problem solve, imagine, and collaborate in the creation and use of new knowledge. Michael Fullan and Maria Langworthy (2014) assert,

For the past century students who graduate have acquired great skills in conforming to the learning expectations defined by others: doing what they have been instructed to do. But today when those students go into the workplace and the wider world, they are suddenly confronted with the expectation that they need to do very complex things without instructions. (p. 35)

A test-prep curriculum with outdated and limited resources, delivered by inexperienced teachers, is prevalent at many urban public schools, which makes it more likely that struggling students will find limited value in their education (Hudley, 2013). An Independent Task Force Report on U.S. Education and National Security (Klein, Rice, & Levy, 2012) reported the following:

- More than 25% of students fail to graduate from high school in 3 years; for African American and Hispanic students, this number is approaching 40%.
- In civics, only one-quarter of U.S. students are proficient or better on the National Assessment of Educational Progress.
- Although the United States is a nation of immigrants, roughly eight in 10 Americans speak only English, and a decreasing number of schools are teaching foreign languages.
- A recent report by ACT, the not-for-profit testing organization, found that only 22% of U.S. high school students met "college ready" standards in all of their core subjects; these figures are even lower for African American and Hispanic students.

- The College Board reported that even among college-bound seniors, only 43% met college-ready standards, meaning that more college students need to take remedial courses.

We are *failing our students* when we believe that the end-all and be-all of a quality education is "passing the test." To become "college and career ready" requires students to see connections—how personal experience, multiple subject areas, and multiple perspectives enrich how we see the world. The content we teach, the problems we assign, and the texts we read are in service to cultivating independent, self-directed learners that are compassionate, productive, creative, and globally minded citizens.

PURSUING PERSONALIZED LEARNING VIA THE FOUR C'S: CLARITY, CONTEXT, CULTURE, AND CAPITAL

For personalized learning to be more than an esoteric ideal, the remainder of the chapter describes each component by offering reflective questions, key ideas, and a deeper dive into what it means for the classroom. Table 7.1 provides a quick synopsis of how personalized learning shifts both classroom pedagogy and leadership structures.

As you read through each component, consider how we are treating our students and ourselves as learners. Do we have clarity on what we are

Table 7.1	How Personalized Learning Shifts Classroom Pedagogy and Leadership Structures

The Four C's	Moving From . . .	Moving to . . .
Clarity	Focus on discrete information and skills	Clarity on the reason for learning, how it is connected to the problem or task at hand, and how it is connected to larger learning goals
Context	Rote, disconnected assignments and assessments that primarily measure retention	Assignments focused on relevance of the topic being studied through authentic, meaningful work
Culture	Culture that sorts students based on test scores and grades	Culture of fairness and equity where students are known, heard, and individually supported
Capital	Culture where teachers are reluctant to take risks and grow practice	Culture that leverages social capital to collectively improve teacher practice

aiming for? Do we believe that what we are aiming for is worthy? Do we have a respected voice in the design, implementation, and evaluation? Do we have opportunities to grow our practice?

Clarity

Student Reflective Question

What am I aiming for?

Key Idea

Articulate learning goals in student-friendly language.

- Long-term goals unify learners in the classroom.
- Short-term goals are within every student's zone of proximal development.

Deeper Dive

There should be consensus around a handful of learning priorities or larger goals to frame assignments and experiences throughout schooling. These larger goals are the knowledge, skills, aptitudes, and dispositions under which specific topics can be explored, problems can be identified and investigated, and performances can be developed and presented. Many of the newer national or state standards have been revised to provide clarity on larger aims of each subject area. Consider the following examples:

- Common Core Anchor Standards in Writing
  - o Write informative/explanatory texts to examine and convey complex ideas and information clearly and accurately through the effective selection, organization, and analysis of content.

- ISTE Standards for Students for Research and Information Fluency
  - o Students apply digital tools to gather, evaluate, and use information. Students (a) plan strategies to guide inquiry; (b) locate, organize, analyze, evaluate, synthesize, and ethically use information from a variety of sources and media; (c) evaluate and select information sources and digital tools; and (d) process data and report results.

- Next Generation Science Standards for Engineering (middle school)
  - o Students define problems more precisely, to conduct a more thorough process of choosing the best solution and to optimize the final design.

By anchoring student learning experiences in these larger learning goals, teachers and students have a wide range of choices of content and methods for personalizing the learning experience. Even when specific topics or content are prescribed, the larger learning goals serve as a North Star for each student's learning path. The contemporary challenge is not the quality of the national, state, or provincial standards we have but rather the way we are leveraging them to create meaningful, personalized experiences for our students.

How do you use existing standards to create goal clarity for students in your classroom, school, or district? Jay McTighe and Grant Wiggins (2012) propose the development of transfer goals to indicate the long-term aims of a discipline, "what we want students to be able to do when they confront new challenges—both in and outside of school" (p. 4). Here are some illustrative examples of long-term transfer goals in connection with short-term outcomes for a given unit.

Mathematics Long-Term Goal. Recognize and solve practical or theoretical problems involving mathematics, including those for which the solution approach is not obvious, using mathematical reasoning, tools, and strategic thinking.

- Short-Term Learning Goals
    - o I can solve problems by writing proportions.
    - o I can find unit rates and prices.

History Long-Term Goal. Apply the lessons of the past (patterns of history) to better understand other historical/current events and issues, and anticipate and prepare for the future. In this unit, students will create and justify a "bill of rights" for Afghanistan or Iraq based on their knowledge of the Declaration of the Rights of Man, the Declaration of Independence, the Bill of Rights, the Universal Declaration of Human Rights, and their own experiences.

- Short-Term Learning Goals
    - o I can use key ideas and phrases of the (listed) documents to defend why this is appropriate regardless of time and location.
    - o I can create a cohesive set of rights that balance the unique cultures, fragile peace, and essential freedoms.
    - o I can articulate why this is a unifying agreement based on my knowledge of the deep-rooted conflict and tradition of this country.

World Languages Transfer Goal. Communicate effectively in the target language, in varied situations, while displaying a sensitivity to culture and context. In this unit, students will get directions (in the target language) for a great restaurant.

- Short-Term Learning Goals
  - o I can explain my food preferences (i.e., level of spiciness, desired cost, type of environment) based on my knowledge of the local area and culture.
  - o I can listen to the directions and summarize back to clarify accuracy.
  - o I can demonstrate good manners throughout the conversation.

To achieve goal clarity, we articulate these goals in direct alignment with the standards, but we move from education jargon to accessible language. Providing clarity for students and teachers does require deep knowledge of grade-level content expectations as well as understanding of the programmatic aims of a discipline. However, this can be drafted and proposed by a smaller group within the school and revised by all staff members as we continue to grow collective expertise.

Context

Student Reflective Question

- Why should I care?

Key Ideas

- Meaningful tasks are born out of authentically messy problems, challenges, and experiences.
- Students have a role to play in shaping the task and evaluating progress.

Deeper Dive

Creating context—*why is this important, and what is its connection to me*—requires transparency about how any assignment is connected to the larger aims. In 2007, Edutopia commissioned a literature review of innovative classroom practices. Below are the key research findings in the review from Linda Darling Hammond and Brigid Barron (as cited in Chen, 2012):

- Students learn more deeply when they can apply classroom-gathered knowledge to real-world problems and when they take part in projects that require sustained engagement and collaboration.

- Active learning practices have a more significant impact on student performance than any other variable, including student background and prior achievement.
- Students are most successful when they are taught how to learn as well as what to learn (p. 37).

In other words, context is essential in how students engage with a problem—their willingness to make sense of ideas, persevere when getting stuck, attending to technical details, and evaluating progress over time. To design real-world problems, as referenced above, necessitates understanding the students we have in front of us and treating them as collaborators in the design and evaluation of their learning.

From a design point of view, our challenge is framing an idea that is connected to both the content area we teach and the students we serve. Let's look at a couple of concrete examples framed by classroom teachers but personalized by the student.

- **An Algebra II example from a school in Philadelphia.** Heat waves are the leading cause of death in the United States compared to all weather events combined. In 1993, there were 118 heat-related deaths in the city of Philadelphia. In 2011, the city of Philadelphia experienced at least 18 heat-related deaths over a span of 5 days. This data concerns you because you worry for the health of your family and community. Based on your knowledge of Algebra II, begin to predict the intensity and frequency of possible future heat waves. Use that analysis to create an explanation of what people can expect during the summer of _____ and where they can seek refuge in their local community through the creation of a map.
- **An interdisciplinary example from Hartford, CT.** Students collaborate to develop and execute an idea that will contribute to the aesthetic beauty and health of a place or community. This development process includes: survey of the area/neighborhood to determine current condition, interview people who use the space to find out their concerns and ideas, propose and get approval for the project, develop a plan of action, and complete the task. Some examples are: cleaning up a common space, creating a community garden, providing trustworthy health information in connection to a community concern.
- **A Grades 3 to 5 language arts task from Carrollton-Farmers Branch, TX.** Think of a disagreement, argument, or fight that you had with someone you care about (a good friend, a sibling, a parent,

or grandparent). Describe what started it, what happened, and how/if it was resolved. Also reflect on whether it changed the relationship or not: the lesson you learned about the other person, yourself, or people in general.

- **A K–1 language arts/geography task from Virginia Beach, VA.** Read *Rosie's Walk* (or play the YouTube version http://www.youtube.com/watch?v=pIQDoOn4mLk). Break students into small groups and have them draw out of a hat a location in the building. Their job is to use positional words to describe how you would get from the classroom to that particular location (can be recorded, written steps, drawing). Have them test out their directions on another student group to see if they arrived at the desired location and make appropriate revisions. Then, have them test on an adult to see if they got to the desired location and make appropriate revisions if needed (adult steps and height are very different from a 5- or 6-year-old).

For each of these examples, there is choice in how to approach the task, creating a plan or an approach, and making ongoing revisions or modifications based on feedback. Each of these examples is also aligned with state or national content standards as well as several 21st century skills. Most important, each one of these examples reflects issues or concerns that are important to our students—considering emergency plans for my family, doing something positive for my community, making sense of a disagreement, or worrying about getting lost.

Now, imagine a recurring task that frames learning over the course of the year or the program that is more student-centered.

- **English/Language Arts.** How do I prove that I'm right? (Or someone else is wrong?) Students apply the construction of an argument to make a case or tear down someone else's case based on logic, bias, cultural influence, experience, or evidence. For example: Should students have some say over the books they read in class? Are the Pittsburgh Steelers the best NFL football franchise? Should euthanasia be legal? Is it possible to end terrorism?
- **Science.** Students pose questions about science topics that they wonder about throughout the year. For example: Why is the sea salty? Why does the moon change shape? Is sugar bad for you? Then, every couple of months, each student selects a question that is still fascinating and investigates the answer.
- **History/Social Studies.** What do people fight over? When is it the right thing to do/justified? How can (or is it possible for) people to

come back together again? Students use these questions as a lens to research different places, times, and experiences where there is substantial conflict. This can be done throughout a course or throughout a K–12 experience.

Students have much more control over the content to be explored, the questions to be pursued, and the ideas to be developed. But, once again, all are aligned with state and national standards.

Another way of collaborating with students is around an investigation, performance, or design that benefits the community.

- Investigate the spread of a particular disease (hereditary or environmental) to determine what can be done to contain it or prevent it from happening.
- Determine the true cost of a particular event, series of events, or life choices. For example, the true cost of the Vietnam War, having a baby as a teenager, a NASA program, or $5,000 of credit card debt.
- Create a tribute to a personal (or fictional) hero through artwork, poetry, a letter, a eulogy, or another form of acknowledgment.
- Design better furniture that can fit in a predetermined space (e.g., dorm room, classroom, living room).
- Investigate conditions in an area devastated by war or a natural disaster to determine the effectiveness of relief efforts. Take action to provide assistance through either communication or fundraising.

Again, these tasks are designed to get insight into how students approach challenges, how willing they are to take risks and make mistakes, and how they can inspire others. They also have the potential to resuscitate the heartbeat of what learning should be—exciting, powerful, and all-encompassing.

We must attend not only to the design of these tasks but also to how teachers and students collectively can evaluate progress. To create such a tool, we identify key criteria of what quality looks like and then discuss how to create accessible descriptions. Here are two concrete examples. The first, in Figure 7.1, comes from a school district in Virginia where math instructional specialists and teachers crafted a mathematics problem-solving rubric for Grades 2 to 5 using the metaphor of a puzzle.

The second example (Figure 7.2) comes from Avon Public Schools in Connecticut, where a group of English Language Arts teachers worked to create a Grades 4 to 8 speaking rubric framed by key criteria, reflective questions, and accessible descriptors.

Figure 7.1   Mathematics Problem-Solving Rubric, Grades 2–5

Key Criteria	Novice—1	Emerging—2	Proficient—3	Exemplary—4
I understand the problem.	I read the problem but did not understand what it was asking.	I read the problem and tried to figure out what was important.	I read the problem and identified what was important.	I read the problem and identified what was important and the idea behind it.
I have a plan to solve this problem.	I selected a strategy to solve the problem, but it didn't work, so I didn't finish.	I selected a strategy to solve the problem, but I needed assistance to get unstuck.	I came up with a strategy, used it on my own, and it worked.	Through lots of revision, I came up with a strategy that worked, or I came up with another way of solving it.
I use mathematical language (numbers, symbols, vocabulary, and representations) to show my thinking.	I used mathematical language, but it didn't help me solve the problem.	I used accurate mathematical language but had minor errors.	I used accurate mathematical language to solve the problem correctly.	I used efficient and/or sophisticated mathematical language to solve the problem correctly.
I explain how my answer makes sense for this problem. I examine someone else's answer to see if it makes sense for this problem.	I explained my answer, but it didn't make sense.	I explained my thinking by restating the steps I took for this problem.	I justified why my answer makes sense for this problem.	I justified why my answer makes sense for this problem and made connections to other types of problems (within and beyond math).

Source: Used with permission of Newport News Public Schools.

Figure 7.2   Speaking Rubric, Grades 6–12

Criteria	1—Beginning	2—Developing	3—Proficient	4—Advanced
Ideas and Content *Did I convey a clear message and stay on topic?*	My topic is not clearly stated. I really don't include details in support of my main ideas.	My topic is stated, and I present main ideas to support the topic. I don't share enough relevant details to support my main ideas.	My topic and main ideas are clearly stated. My main ideas are stated, and the supporting details are relevant to the main ideas.	My topic is presented in a clear, focused manner that demonstrates knowledge and understanding. My main ideas are strongly stated with supporting details that are relevant and appropriate for the target audience and topic.
Claim *Are my claims compelling?*	The claims I present to support my main idea are not convincing or logical.	Some of the claims I have presented are convincing and logical, but they do not fully support the main idea.	All of my claims are convincing and logical.	My claims are so powerful they influence the audience to reconsider or accept the main idea.
Word Choice *Are my words and phrases carefully chosen to express?*	My word choice is unclear or too general.	My word choice is clear but lacks a connection to the topic, purpose, and audience.	My word choice is clear and appropriate for the topic, purpose, and audience.	My word choice is powerful and adds to the audience's understanding of the topic.
Organization *Is my presentation easy to follow?*	My presentation is missing an introduction and/or a conclusion, which makes it difficult for my audience to follow.	My presentation has an introduction and a conclusion, but the lack of transitions makes it difficult for my audience to follow.	My presentation has an introduction, transitions between ideas, and a conclusion so that my message can be followed by my audience.	My presentation's organization adds to my message: an introduction that draws in the audience, smooth transitions, and a conclusion that reemphasizes my message.

(Continued)

Figure 7.2   (Continued)

Criteria	1—Beginning	2—Developing	3—Proficient	4—Advanced
Delivery *Does my presentation support my message?*	I rarely or never look at my audience and/or rely completely on my notes. My gestures, posture, facial expressions, or movement distract from the presentation. How I use my voice keeps the audience from understanding the message.	I look at my notes more than my audience. My gestures, posture, facial expressions, or movements are awkward during the presentation. How I use my voice distracts or occasionally keeps the audience from understanding the message.	I look at my audience more than my notes. My gestures, posture, facial expressions, and movements fit the presentation. My voice is clear and understandable (e.g., volume, rate, articulation, pronunciation).	I look at my audience and use my notes only as a guide. My gestures, posture, facial expressions, and movements add to the presentation. My voice is clear and understandable, and it makes my presentation more interesting.
Presentation Aid(s) *Do my presentation aid(s) support the topic and my message?*	My presentation aids are inappropriate or distract from my message.	My presentation aids support the topic but generally do not add to my message.	My presentation aids support the topic and my message.	My presentation aids support the topic and my message, and they add value through audience engagement (e.g., use of humor, pose thought-provoking questions, surveying, including audio or video clips).

Source: Used with permission of Avon Public Schools.

Culture

Student Reflective Questions

- What is expected from me?
- Are those expectations required from everyone else?
- How do I work to achieve those expectations?
- Who supports me in my pursuit?

Key Idea

Create a culture where students are focused on producing their best work.

Deeper Dive

When a student walks into a classroom, he or she becomes connected to the culture. Seth Godin (2013) demands that we reimagine a compulsory school system where students are motivated by more than obligation.

> We don't ask students to decide to participate. We assume the contract of adhesion, and relentlessly put information in front of them, with homework to do and tests to take. What's entirely missing is commitment. Do you want to learn this? Will you decide to become good at this? . . . We need students who can learn how to learn, who can discover how to push themselves and are generous enough and honest enough to engage with the outside world to make those dreams happen.

To that end, we must create and sustain a daily culture immersed in exploration, problem solving, and failure where students are active, alive, and growing right before our eyes. The following questions and responses can serve as a guide to establishing the kind of learning environment that demands the best from teacher and students:

What is expected from me? Every student is expected to produce his or her *best* work (in light of the long-term goals) inspired by quality examples and common checklists or rubrics. Students are not satisfied with "just getting by" because they see the value and the impact of the work. If there is an authentic audience for the task, there is a different level of energy and urgency to labor over the details, seek feedback from others, and persevere through multiple revisions.

Are those expectations required from everyone else? From a student's point of view, one of the most desired qualities in a teacher is fairness. Students need to see that there are high expectations for everyone (long-term goals as described earlier). However, students also need to see that fair does not mean the same; our individual coaching with students should be tailored based on talents, interests, level of skill development, and need (short-term goals as described earlier). This flexibility allows the students to design work that is more meaningful and appropriate based on their current skill level and area of interest. This flexibility also allows the teacher to provide targeted feedback in light of the student design and to offer tailored suggestions for the student to consider in next steps.

How do I work to achieve those expectations? Students need to see feedback as fundamental to improvement. Jeff Howard (2011), founder of the Efficacy Institute, describes the stakes of not providing actionable feedback for students:

> To make feedback is to prime oneself for effective, improvement focused action; but to fail to do so is equally consequential. Failure to make feedback leaves us with no insight about "what to work on," and therefore no basis for formulating improvement strategies—so learning stops. When normal children are unable to learn consistently in school, it is not because they are stupid; it is because the circumstances of their learning environments render them unable to make and use feedback in this way, so they fall back on the old, destructive stand-by: "I got a D. I guess I just can't do this."

The clichéd phrase "Failure is necessary for growth" has been confirmed by cognitive psychologists and neurologists. When a student arrives at an incorrect answer, presents a flawed statement, or submits an unclear draft, it is how we respond that disarms the "f-word"—providing regular, student-friendly, action-oriented feedback.

- **Regular**. Students need to be updated on the impact of their performance. When students understand that the goal is improved autonomous performance, then the evaluator's job (teacher, peer, expert, self) is to immediately engage the student in describing and analyzing what happened, and the student's job is to focus on what to do next in light of that information. The more time that elapses between the performance and the feedback, the less likely it will have an impact on future performance.
- **Student-friendly.** Feedback should be understood by the student. Many rubrics and criteria fail this test in their obtuseness—some, many, most; inaccessibility for the target age and comprehension level; or the conflation of quality with quantity—counting facts, quotes, or paragraphs rather than controlling focus or a well-justified explanation.
- **Action-oriented.** Students need to focus on one or a handful of improvements rather than be overwhelmed by errors. When students review feedback, they should get good information on how to proceed, places to make adjustments, or how to come up with a new idea.

Who supports me in my pursuit? A culture of excellence requires a range of people to be invested in every student's performance. From a teacher's vantage point, I need to know the student in front of me well enough to know what his or her best work looks like. From a student's vantage point, peer support and feedback can be quite beneficial. This encourages a level of collaboration where students can learn from one another and creates a classroom culture that values feedback and continuous improvement. From a larger community vantage point, offering feedback and guidance shows a level of support for individual student success but also has real benefits in helping students understand the importance of their work in achieving a larger meaningful purpose. Whether it is evaluating water quality in the city, doing the leg work to propose and build a skateboard park for kids to use after school, or bringing in a series of authors to critique student writing, taking the time and interest in student work impacts motivation and development.

To create a culture of excellence, we need to attend to each of the student questions as a design moment as well as a relational moment. For example, the way we provide feedback, both tone and explanation, communicates volumes to students about their capacity to succeed. The power of personalization is grounded in how we treat one another as individuals to gain a better understanding of the material and of one another.

Capital

Educator Reflective Question

How do we collectively improve performance?

Key Idea

Focus on social capital to raise individual teacher performance.

Deeper Dive

Working with students, especially those that are struggling, requires experienced staff with a powerful tool kit to cultivate relationships, content expertise to design authentic tasks, and the ability to provide regular feedback in relation to challenging expectations. But there are two troubling trends that make it problematic for students to receive the assistance they need.

First, there is a lack of employee engagement in school, as reported in an alarming 2012 Gallup poll.

Researchers classified 31 percent of teachers as "engaged" at work under that index, compared with 30 percent of respondents overall. But, among all occupations tracked in the survey, teachers were the least likely to say that their opinions counted at work. (Blad, 2014, p. 15)

Teachers have become disenfranchised themselves: due to the crushing workload, new individual appraisal system, leadership turnover, and initiative fatigue, many are doing the best they can to endure. And many are not long for the profession, which leads to the second point.

Second, teacher experience is at an all-time low, which makes it less likely to have skilled practitioners in every classroom. Michael Fullan and Andy Hargreaves report:

National Schools and Staffing Survey data reveal that the most frequently occurring number of years that American teachers had been in the job was 15 years in 1987–88, between one and five years in 2003–04, and just one year in 2007–08. In other words, there are more teachers in American public schools today with one year's experience or less than any other group. How would you feel if that were the measure of experience, of accumulated human capital, in your local hospital? (2012b, p. 36)

Even the most effective school leaders would have difficulty in building momentum if they had that level of turnover in the building.

The challenge, then, is to build professional capital to ensure stability, effective pedagogy, collaboration, creativity, and energy. Fullan and Hargreaves (2012a) describe the characteristics of "teaching like a pro." Professional capital

- is technically sophisticated and difficult,
- requires high levels of education and long training,
- is perfected through continuous improvement,
- involves wise judgment informed by evidence and experience, and
- is a collective accomplishment and responsibility (p. 14).

Thus, clarity, context, and culture are as important for the students as they are for the entire school community. To reengage staff, to have them commit to the work for the long haul, they have to believe that they have elbow room to create, to take risks, to grow from feedback, and to share practices. While some teachers may be reluctant to collaborate, they need to have confidence that the collective choices they make in meetings are acted upon if they are in the best interest of students.

CONCLUSION

Personalized learning resurrects 19th century ideals through a modern twist by leveraging the global changes in demographics and economics to prepare students for a complex, unpredictable world. From a pedagogical standpoint, we must move beyond the scope of a "test-prep" curriculum to one of teacher-student partnerships in the creation and evaluation of assignments. In *A Rich Seam: How New Pedagogies Find Deeper Learning,* Michael Fullan and Maria Langworthy (2014) assert,

> Effective partnering is built on principles of equity, transparency, reciprocal accountability and mutual benefit. Through such partnering, teachers not only become learners themselves but also begin to see learning though the eyes of their students. This "visibility" is essential if teachers are to continuously challenge students to reach for the next step, and if they are to clearly see whether teaching and learning strategies are achieving their intended goals. (p. 12)

This is as valuable to resurrecting the joy in classrooms as it is in creating an equitable environment.

REFERENCES

Blad, E. (2014, April). More than half of students "engaged" in school, says poll. *Education Week, 33*(28), pp. 1, 14–15. Retrieved from http://www.edweek.org/ew/articles/2014/04/09/28gallup.h33.html?tkn=LONFebxh1gTC9N9vjP%2FZONxxf%2F%2Fa0%2FW7KB46&print=1

Center for Public Education. (2012). *The United States of education: The changing demographics of the United States and their schools.* Retrieved from http://www.centerforpubliceducation.org/You-May-Also-Be-Interested-In-landing-page-level/Organizing-a-School-YMABI/The-United-States-of-education-The-changing-demographics-of-the-United-States-and-their-schools.html

Chen, M. (2012). *Education nation.* San Francisco, CA: Jossey-Bass.

Dewey, J. (1907). The school and social progress. In *The school and society* (pp. 19–44). Chicago, IL: University of Chicago Press.

Fullan, M., & Hargreaves, A. (2012a). *Professional capital: Transforming teaching in every school.* New York, NY: Teachers College Press.

Fullan, M., & Hargreaves, A. (2012b, June 6). Reviving teaching with professional capital. *Education Week, 31*(33), 30, 36.

Fullan, M., & Langworthy, M. (2014). *A rich seam: How new pedagogies find deep learning.* Retrieved from http://www.michaelfullan.ca/a-rich-seam-how-new-pedagogies-find-deep-learning/

Godin, S. (2013). *Stop stealing dreams.* Hubpages. Retrieved from http://www
.squidoo.com/stop-stealing-dreams

Howard, J. (2011). *Feedback is fundamental.* Efficacy Institute. Retrieved from
http://www.efficacy.org/Resources/TheEIPointofView/tabid/233/ctl/
ArticleView/mid/678/articleId/426/Feedback-is-Fundamental.aspx

Hudley, C. (2013). *Education and urban schools.* American Psychological Association.
Retrieved from http://www.apa.org/pi/ses/resources/indicator/2013/05/urban-
schools.aspx

Klein, J. I., Rice, C. (chairs), & Levy, J. (project director). (2012). *US education reform
and national security.* Council on Foreign Relations. Retrieved from http://
www.cfr.org/united-states/us-education-reform-national-security/p27618

McTighe, J., & Wiggins, G. (2012). *From common core standards to curriculum: Five
big ideas.* Retrieved from http://grantwiggins.files.wordpress.com/2012/09/
mctighe_wiggins_final_common_core_standards.pdf

Sizer, T. (1999). No two are quite alike. *Education Leadership, 57,* 1, 6–11.

Who Wants a Standardized Child Anyway?

8

Treat Everyone the Same—Differently

Dennis Littky

Every student comes into school with a different background, personality, skill set, interest, and attitude. As educators, we know this, but somehow dismiss this fact and teach every child the exact same content, in relatively the same way, producing a standardized child. The only times we seem to help kids learn differently and independently are in kindergarten and graduate school. In between, we assume everyone needs to attain the same knowledge base, so we instruct all students in the same way.

At Big Picture Learning (BPL), we have designed a model that teaches every student the same . . . differently. Every student needs his or her own learning plan. We know that every student must maintain and improve studies in reading, writing, and math. We believe that all students must learn how to solve problems and be creative thinkers. For example, they must know how to understand science and history in such ways, in order to think like scientists and historians. Yet, every student needs to do this very differently. The BPL model does not expect a student to adopt knowledge but rather leads students to explore and find their interests and passions to construct their learning platform. We are less concerned with memorizing facts and more focused on inspiring students to want to learn. We want our students to study something deeply, learn how to seek out information, conduct research in depth, and meaningfully apply what they have learned.

The objective is that a student retains what he or she has learned in a comprehensive way and can apply this knowledge to real work.

One of our eleventh-grade students, Joe, came into my office and asked me about the Vietnam War. Having been there after the war, I showed him my slides and shared my stories with him. Consequently, Joe decided that he wanted to study the Vietnam War, which led him to register for a college class on the subject at the community college and obtain an internship with a veteran who was building a war memorial. He read everything he could get his hands on. One day, I asked him where his interest came from. He hesitated; there was a long pause, and he then said, "My dad fought in the Vietnam War, and every year since I was 5 years old, I asked my dad to tell me about the war. Every year, he walked away from me. Now, at 17, I want to learn more."

For Joe's senior project, at 18 years old, he traveled with his father to Vietnam. They had conversations about his war experiences and visited places where Joe Sr. fought when he was just 18. It was an incredible, life-changing experience for both of them. Consequently, they developed a website to assist and support families to talk about the war and process their own hardships. Joe's dad shared his medals and began talking to his family, commemorating his experience rather than hiding it. I loved the fact that Joe learned to study history deeply and meaningfully. Joe profoundly understood war in an amazing way. He went on to college to study history and then returned to The Met (the first BPL school is located in Providence, Rhode Island, and is widely known as The Met) as a teacher. That is what defines learning, one student at a time. Some say knowledge is power. We say the use of knowledge is power.

The structure of Big Picture Schools is designed to allow every student to develop his or her own customized program. There are clear academic goals, yet how each learner achieves them varies tremendously. After an adviser meets with the student and parents, an educational plan is developed. The student begins this process by selecting an interest and then finding a mentor and a workplace, where he or she can learn necessary skills through the chosen interest and passion.

One freshman student, Jose, had decided to work at a hospital to conduct pulmonary research. When presenting his exhibition and work, he confessed that his interest came from his mother's addiction to cigarettes, and that he wanted to better comprehend the dangerous effects of smoking to be able to present them to her. His academic growth was a direct result of using his interest to learn how to become a scientific thinker, an analytical reader, and an in-depth researcher. This is the result of learning The Big Picture way, where every ninth-grade student is encouraged to find an interest, experiment with it, and learn the skills needed to succeed in life. Although their interest may change, this philosophy is reinforced throughout their high school experience. By the time students become juniors or seniors, they are required to take a college course propelling them forward to be advanced thinkers. The studying is done in collaboration with their communities, in a real work environment, where young adolescents are asked to think and act like adults, creating the foundation for life application. A journalist happened to be visiting the hospital where Jose worked while she gathered information for an article she was writing on the effectiveness of student learning in internships versus in schools. The following day, she was on a visit at The Met, and as we were walking down the hall in conversation, she saw a student running full speed, yelling, as many adolescents do. I asked her if she recognized the unleashed teen and told her that it was the same Jose she met a day earlier in his workplace at the hospital. She was shocked at the difference in his demeanor between the two environments, showing that both settings are necessary to cultivate adult thinking.

There was another student, Ramona, who knew she wanted to become a teacher and found an elementary school teacher to be her mentor. Approximately 8 weeks into her internship, she said, "You know what? I don't like working with kids," and had discovered that she loved computers. However, after 6 months of working behind a computer, she became bored with the inactivity of sitting behind a desk. After some additional searching, her love for theater finally led her to an internship with a major theater company, and that is where she has been ever since. At Big Picture Schools, we care about what each student's interest is and the experimentation process in finding that interest. The purpose of the internship is for students to explore and discover personal strengths, learn about their aptitudes and capabilities, and go deep into their learning.

It simply makes sense. This is evidently clear when looking at the data collected by state departments of education on the performance of Big Picture Schools. More kids attend school each day, more kids graduate, and more kids are accepted into college than kids of the same demographic at other comparable schools. BPL hired MPR Associates to conduct a study of graduates from three BPL high schools—MetWest (Oakland), Met Sacramento, and San Diego Met— to determine what life paths graduates pursued after high school and how well their high school experiences prepared them for college and career. Survey data were collected from January through May 2012 from students who had graduated between 2006 and 2010. Data from the National Student Clearing House were used to augment the survey data with additional information about college outcomes. Highlights from the study (MPR Associates, 2012) include the following:

- 74% of BPL graduates enrolled in college within the first year after graduating from high school.
- 44% of graduates enrolled in 4-year colleges within one year of graduating.
- On average, freshmen-to-sophomore persistence was 87%.
- 74% of respondents working and not in school reported securing a job through a high school internship contact.
- The opportunities to work with adults at internship sites and the opportunities to build self-confidence through work-based learning and other activities were cited as the most important aspects of the Big Picture models in terms of contributing to success in life after high school. Other students find work right out of high school connected to their interest. This is not just theory. There are thousands of real examples evidenced throughout our 108 schools established throughout the United States and the world. So we ask, why isn't everyone trying this method? It is a method that takes into consideration where and who the student is. It allows the teacher and the school to educate each student differently, not just with personalized mentorship and tutoring but with an entirely customized curriculum.

Traditional methods have not been consistently working to serve our students. In education, when something isn't working, districts and institutions respond by working harder at it because they are certain that the fundamental system is correct and just needs a boost. The idea that standardized assessments and tests are beneficial has led to a saturation of testing in the classroom. The belief that a standard curriculum is best tightens the controls that govern instruction and learning. Now, it is not just the progressives that are saying the system is not working. Every day, more research and publications are proving that our public schools are not working effectively. Yet, there is still little movement to try to reverse the crisis with significant reform.

A recent article in the April 23rd commentary of Education Week, "Stop Tinkering, We Need a New K–12," written by Paul Reveille, past commissioner of education in Massachusetts, speaks to this very point. Dr. Reveille led a system touted as a model for teaching everyone the same standardized curriculum to pass the Massachusetts Comprehensive Assessment System (MCAS). However, now, after leaving his position, he recognizes that the primary weakness of the current school system is its one-size-fits-all design. He questions how an education system instructing children from such widely diverse backgrounds, assets and deficits, advantages and disadvantages, in the same way, expects universal results. Our belief in the Big Picture model states that one size fits none. It is time to wake up. There is much talk about change in the educational forum, but few are doing it. Dr. Reveille is correct in admitting that the system he ran does not really work. Yes, there are programs that are working to improve education, but none has yet reached the scale necessary to really transform the system. We ask, why not, and what can we do about it?

One problem is that many educational institutions are focused on tweaking around the edges. For example, some educational facilities and programs have progressed to offer online learning, which has some good value today. The flaw is that it is being used to present traditional content in new ways without taking into consideration the students and their specific needs. Many claim to be doing personalized and individualized work: however, they develop programs for students to study a curriculum that does not make any sense because it lacks connection, integration, and application.

The example of putting old wine in new bottles applies here. New programs are implemented every day; and the public is distracted by the next new shiny thing, but in the end, results are not much different. The public seems satisfied by the small modifications introduced in ornate packaging, which prevents many reformists from completely revamping the current system. A significant problem is that our country does not have a common definition of *learning*. Learning is not about memorizing facts. Learning is about being mindful and using imagination and creativity to learn about what works best for each student. Because standardized testing and Common Core State Standards are presently filling the void, they have become the transitional definition of learning in America. We at Big Picture Schools define *learning* differently: Learning is to problem solve and think critically, to analyze and interpret different perspectives, to be creative and use the world as a tool to innovate, to be proficient in reading, writing, and math. Learning is expressing and working with the desire and interest to keep learning. Education is the process by which teachers and learners collaborate in the best possible environment: one where all members feel safe, supported, and respected, and where kids and adults are excited and passionate about learning.

It is time for a major paradigm shift. Anything short of that is unacceptable. This is not to say that there aren't many reputable schools and institutions that serve struggling communities and low-income student demographics. I had the honor to administrate a few myself in New Hampshire and New York. As I witnessed the students grapple with success after high school, I understood with even more purpose that there had to be a greater transformation in learning for students during their formative high school careers to be able to overcome the challenges they faced in the worlds they live in.

If we have any chance of developing a more equitable system, we must place into action something very different. Luckily for Elliot Washor and myself, we had the opportunity to create a school from scratch in Providence, Rhode Island, in 1995, where we were allowed to completely reinvent the paradigm for high school education. We credit the opportunity to a progressive state commissioner of education, Peter McWalters, who was an advocate of educational equity. He saw in our new design a chance for each child to receive the exact resources necessary to succeed. Elliot and I wiped the slate clean of any preconceived notions regarding the constructs of education. We tried to forget what we knew about schools, and instead, we thought about education. Our leading question became "What's best for kids?"

We thought about Margaret Mead's quote, "My grandmother wanted me to have an education, so she kept me out of school." We cared about kids, so we knew we had to change schools drastically so guardians of people like Margaret Mead would not feel compelled to make such choices. We asked that question again: "What's best for kids?" We did not initially ask, "How do we better prepare kids for tests?" or "How do we make the school more efficient?" or "What are the best texts?" The answers didn't look anything like what we were used to. Rather than depending on any set curriculum, we decided to start with a focus on the students to devise an effective program. We thought, if we care about what is best for them and important in their lives, then students and their families would be involved in developing the curriculum. We resolved to construct an educational plan that was student incentive based. It included a split schedule and has evolved into a systemized program that offers resources for successful learning. On Mondays, Wednesdays, and Fridays, each small school is scheduled to follow a structured agenda, while 2 days per week students work on location at their internships or community projects.

Agenda: Mondays, Wednesdays, Fridays

9:00–9:30 **Pick Me Up:** The entire school gathers to commence the day in a positive, uplifting way as students present their projects, research, and studies and discuss ideas and share stories about their internships, projects, and community involvement.

9:30–10:15 **Advisory:** Students work on planning their daily and weekly calendar books, discuss their project developments, share ideas, communicate any current event issues affecting their lives, and receive feedback.

10:15–12:00 **Curriculum and Project-Based Learning:** Students work independently with their advisers to study academic content, review their customized curriculums, assess progress, discuss their projects and personal learning plans, consult with core academic specialists and tutors, and receive instruction.

12:00–12:30 **Lunch**

12:30–2:30 **Independent Work, Small Group Work, Seminars:** Students work independently to study, research, or complete instruction-based assignments, work in small groups, or attend seminars and workshops.

2:30–3:00 **Advisory:** Students return to advisory groups that are led by teachers to review the day's tasks and determine what needs to be completed for homework in order to prepare for the next day or meet their educational objectives.

Agenda: Internship Work Days

Plan of Study: The adviser, student, and internship mentor devise a plan of study that must be completed at the student's internship. The plan of study is based on student interest, particular work objectives, and integrated studies.

Advisers: Advisers visit student internship locations to observe the student's work ethic, placement, and adaptability. The adviser conferences with the mentor to discuss the student's aptitude, capabilities, placement, and progress.

Student Work: Curriculum studies and research conducted at school are specifically designed to support the projects students are working on at their internships.

Assessments: Students are formally assessed by their mentors and their advisers on their daily performance at their internships.

Three times per year, students deliver an hour-long presentation to their parents, staff, fellow students, and internship mentor, demonstrating their completion of integrated study. The exhibition consists of the student's portfolio, prospectus paper, daily journal, internship project, visuals, and media presentations. Because formal assessment is so comprehensive, it is written in narrative form.

Our learning model allows for every student to make the work his or her own with the support of the advisers, core teachers, specialists, staff, parents, fellow students, and community. This is due to the fact that the adviser/teacher role is very different from that of a traditional teacher. Teachers are often generalists that support their students on all their varied projects. They use community experts and other specialized teachers to lead students to go deeper into certain content. This method supports teachers to work with the whole child and makes it possible for students to integrate their program. What makes the job challenging is they themselves did not attend schools that function in this way, so they were not subject to this type of instructional model. Simply, they were not trained to be teachers like this in college. This is why we have placed significant emphasis on staff development and training.

As seasoned, experienced educators, we know that when students are motivated, they are engaged. Yet, to establish a rapport with each student to identify those points of connection takes more than a 45-minute-period class each day. Therefore, it makes logical sense to start the year by guiding the students to explore their interests. Most have never before been asked what they were interested in learning. We developed a scaffolded process for the teacher to lead the students to thinking about their interests in a reflective way and then begin to synthesize that interest with academics, internships, and community partnerships. In our model, learning is about personally experiencing an interest in a profound way that leads to growth. We believe school should be life to text, with real work application in the world in order to inspire each student to study and learn deeper. All the pieces are in place, but the dots have not been connected. It is necessary that all of the innovative schools and programs written about in this book and beyond come together for the greater good and not just to serve our own programs.

We are entrusted with the next generation's education. The paradigm shift will only work effectively if we redefine learning. It is time.

REFERENCES

MPR Associates. (2012). Big Picture Learning: High school alumni report. Berkeley, CA: Author. Retrieved from http://www.bigpicture.org/wp-content/uploads/2013/05/BPL-Report-Final-Jan-2013_2.28.13.pdf

Reville, P. (2014, April 23). Stop the tinkering: We need a new K–12 engine. *Education Week*. Retrieved from: http://www.edweek.org/ew/articles/2014/04/23/29reville_ep.h33.html

Equitable Ways to Teach Science to Emergent Bilinguals and Immigrant Youth

9

Estrella Olivares-Orellana

The population of immigrant youth in U.S. secondary schools has increased steadily in the last few decades. The total number of immigrants in the United States hit a record 40 million in 2010, a 28% increase from 2000. Of these immigrants, 10.4 million are students in U.S. public schools (Camarota, 2012). The last report by the National Clearinghouse for English Language Acquisition (NCELA, 2013) indicates that more than 4.65 million students have been identified as Limited English Proficient (LEP) in K–12 schools. Most policy makers and educators refer to this subpopulation of students as English language learners (ELLs). I refer to them as "emergent bilinguals," drawing upon a term developed by García, Kleifgen, and Falchi (2008), who argued that by referring to students as ELLs or LEPs, we discount their potential to become fully bilingual. Such terms and the practices that frequently accompany them also perpetuate the inequities and disadvantages that emergent bilinguals frequently encounter in their education because their home languages and cultural understandings are ignored when it is assumed that their educational needs are the same as those of a monolingual child.

Emergent bilinguals comprise the fastest growing group of students in U.S. secondary schools (Menken, Kleyn, & Chae, 2012). Teaching subject matter content in topics such as math and science to emergent bilingual adolescents can be especially challenging. Teachers must find equitable strategies to make the content accessible to students who often have considerable variation in their language abilities, background knowledge, and learning styles. Drawing upon my experience in the classroom as a bilingual science teacher and a teacher educator, I use this chapter to analyze instructional strategies that have proven successful in making science content accessible to emergent bilinguals. In many of the examples presented, I draw upon what education anthropologist Luis Moll describes as "funds of knowledge" (González, Moll, & Amanti, 2005) so that my students can use their cultural and linguistic resources to acquire new knowledge and language skills. I also employ culturally relevant pedagogical techniques in ways that are additive, equitable, democratic, and empowering.

Low-income immigrant youth typically must overcome many challenges to be successful in school. In addition to the psychological and emotional toll many endure as they adjust to a new country and culture, it can be said that newcomer immigrant youth must also undergo a double transition. One transition is related to the emotional, mental, and physical changes that occur among all young adults at this stage of human development. The second transition is related to the social adjustment of moving and finding a place in a new country. For many immigrant youth, the two processes are occurring simultaneously and can produce a sense of uncertainty and vulnerability. They live in what Prieto and Villenas (2012) call *nepantla*, "a space of in-between-ness, transformation, frustration, discomfort, and spontaneous ways of adjusting and learning." *Nepantla* is a "Nahuatl word for the space between two bodies of water, the space between two worlds" (Ikas, 2002, p. 13). It is a place where significant transformations can take place because of malleability provided by adolescence. Prieto and Villenas describe this space as providing potential for "magic" because anything can happen in *nepantla*. For recent immigrant youth in U.S. schools, the *nepantla* provides the space where navigation between different worlds is possible. It is also where new identities can be discovered, and agency can flourish. This space may also be a period of life fraught with stress and frustration, and for that reason it is essential that educators pay particular attention to the developmental needs of their students during this stage.

Studies have shown that most immigrant students in the United States attend schools that offer fields of endangerment rather than fields of opportunity (Suárez-Orosco, Suárez-Orosco, & Todorova, 2008), imperiling possibilities for immigrant youth to be successful during this state of transition and transformation. Endangerment occurs when the educators who serve emergent bilinguals lack the skills to meet their needs and display a lack of awareness toward the complex transition they are undergoing. In the sections that follow, I draw on my experience as a teacher in bilingual classrooms to propose ways in which we can provide opportunities for academic success to recent immigrant students, who also happen to be emergent bilinguals. I focus on the implementation of what I call a "pedagogy of care and trust," which uses strategies that build upon students' experiences, background knowledge, and interests in order to achieve excellence.

A BILINGUAL HIGH SCHOOL SCIENCE CLASSROOM FOR NEWCOMERS

As about 32 ESL (English as a second language) students walk into their Bilingual Living Environment classroom, a girl asks: "¿Compartiremos nuestros artículos hoy? Tengo uno bueno." The girl wants to share an article about a Salvadoran scientist who discovered a new method to treat Leukemia. Her teacher responds, "Si, hoy si. We will share our science articles right after we tackle a few Regents questions. Tienen que estar listos para el regents." This is a living environment and the students will be required to take the state's Regents exam at the end of the semester. The school calls the course Bilingual Living Environment because only Spanish-speaking newcomer students are placed in it. It is also designated as an ESL class, which means that the science teacher, who also happens to be bilingual, can use the students' language to provide instruction as she prepares them for the New York State Living Environment Regents exam. Students can take this exam in Spanish or English, whichever language they prefer. The class is comprised of students who arrived in the United States 1 or 2 years ago, who therefore have acquired some fluency in English, along with students who arrived in the United States only a few days ago. Given the diversity in their backgrounds and in their command of English, the teacher must find ways to use bilingualism as a bridge to learning science, and she must do so with minimal support from the administration.

As part of her effort to prepare students for the state exam, students are given a sheet with five living environment Regents questions. They have to answer them in 10 minutes. They start working right away, because by now, this is a familiar practice in their science classroom. When the timer goes off, students are instructed

(Continued)

(Continued)

to exchange their papers with their closest partners. Students' hands start going up. The teacher takes turns calling on students, and they share their answers. As they do, the teacher either confirms the response or gently lets it be known that the answer offered is incorrect. Students correct the papers of their partners, and as they do, the teacher stresses the importance of reading carefully when answering Regents questions. "Every day un quiz?" complains a male student in the back of the room. "Tenemos que practicar," the teacher reassures him.

Despite the diversity in their backgrounds, approximately 80% of the students placed in this bilingual science class will obtain a passing score on the Living Environment Regents exam. Their passing rate is equal to or sometimes higher than the school's overall approximate passing rate, which ranges between 70% and 80% for mainstream students. The high rate of success is the result of a teaching strategy that allows students to use their native language as a resource. These ESL students must meet the same standards as the mainstream students, but the teacher understands that in order for them to be motivated and engaged, they have to see the applicability of science to their daily lives. She does this by embedding a variety of language arts skills and culturally relevant themes that help to make science meaningful. She also uses examples of appropriate role models that she hopes they will be able to identify with, while maintaining high standards and expectations.

PEDAGOGY OF CARE

As the vignette above illustrates, creating a caring learning environment is essential for teaching new immigrants and emergent bilinguals. Several researchers have found that care is the essence of human life, and that a caring relationship is essential to the growth and development of human beings (Noddings, 1992).

John Dewey (1938/1963) argued that teachers must start with students' experiences and interests to create connections to the content of the material being taught. Drawing upon these two important principles, care and relevance, I suggest that a pedagogy of care must begin with the assumption that all students are capable of learning when their relationships with their teachers are strong and nurturing and when the teacher understands how to capitalize on the students' experiences and interests. In my opinion, the most difficult aspect of relationship building is the simple recognition of the need for its existence. Once that desire is there on the part of the teacher, the relationship develops naturally. Forming a relationship with a student could be as easy as inquiring about the activities they enjoy and making personal connections regarding these activities. For immigrant youth, who are defining their identity in a new environment, these connections could have a profound impact on their academic success.

In my experience, meaningful connections with students can take a variety of forms, from briefly discussing a sporting event, new song, or TV show, to showing an interest in some of the activities students enjoy by attending or participating in it. Most students respond positively and become more engaged and motivated to learn when the educator displays a strong interest in them. When a meaningful connection is built, a sense of reciprocal respect and responsibility not to let the other one down is born. Over time, a degree of trust and understanding begins to develop between teacher and student as the relationship becomes rooted in confidence and a belief that the teacher has the best interest of the student in mind. Based on my classroom experiences, I have found that most students are open to building strong, positive relationships with their teacher when the teacher shows an active interest in them. I have also found that this is especially true for immigrant emergent bilinguals. Once a connection has been made, the possibilities for learning are endless. As the adult, the teacher must enter into this relationship with an understanding that respect and responsibility must be mutual. Therefore, if I, as the teacher, expect students to work hard, then I must also work hard. If I expect students to put forth their best effort, then I must do the same. It should be evident to students that their teacher works just as hard as they are expected to work in order to provide opportunities for academic achievement.

Connections with students' families are of equal importance. Whenever possible, an effort should be made to include the families and the community in the education of their children. Immigrant parents are often reluctant to become involved in school activities, especially when they have limited ability to speak English. However, parents or guardians can be encouraged to assist with school or classroom events, and they can be invited to be present for student demonstrations or presentations. They can also be included on fieldtrips by asking to serve as chaperones. For some, such forms of involvement may be difficult due to work responsibilities, but parents or guardians should still be encouraged to participate to whatever degree is possible. By treating parents as partners, we send a message to our students about the importance of their parents and reinforce a bond that is invaluable to their success.

In addition to care, it is important for teachers to build upon students' experiences and interests. This can be done as easily as asking students if they have prior experiences with a certain topic before introducing it. Before starting a unit on rocks, a teacher may ask students what types of rocks they are familiar with, or if there were rocks were they lived before or where they live now. Such questions allow students to become part of the dialogue and contribute to the lesson. New knowledge about rock properties and categories can be built on the information students have provided.

At the introduction of a unit on homeostasis, a teacher may ask students if they have a thermostat at home and if they know how it makes the heating system go on and off to maintain a stable temperature. After taking a few responses to the question, the teacher can point out that our bodies work in a similar manner, making us sweat or shiver to maintain a stable body temperature. Similarly, a teacher can ask if the students know anyone who lives with diabetes and has to check blood sugar levels constantly. She can then explain that this occurs as a consequence of their bodies not responding to or not producing sufficient insulin, which is the hormone that maintains our blood sugar levels stable. If students get the sense that what they know is considered valuable knowledge onto which new information can be built, they take ownership of their understandings and expertise and become more invested in furthering what they already know. They are also more likely to continue making fruitful contributions to classroom discussions. They may even go home and find out more about what they know because they understand that the information they bring with them to class matters and makes it possible for them to make valuable contributions.

The Next Generation Science Standards (NGSS) were released in 2014 and have currently been adopted by 26 states. The standards are founded on a view of science as a body of knowledge that is evidence based, that uses models and theory building to advance. Three dimensions inform each standard: Practices, crosscutting concepts, and disciplinary core ideas. The practices define behaviors that scientists employ as they explore and build models and theories about the natural world. Crosscutting concepts are used as a way of linking the different domains of science. Disciplinary core ideas focus the K–12 science curriculum, instruction, and assessments on the most important aspects of science (Next Generation Science Standards, 2014). The NGSS foster the idea that content and practice are intertwined, and students should be presented a practical view of science rather than a static list of scope and sequence items to be learned. To that end, whether the audience is mainstream students or emergent bilingual immigrant students, science should be taught in a way that is pragmatic and connected to students' lives.

Similarly, it is important to demystify science and the work scientists do. Many students have long held a rigid perspective of what is considered science and of the work scientists engage in. Students tend to have a vision of science as something that happens only in a laboratory setting, directed largely by males in white coats. In an effort to unsettle this notion, clarify misconceptions, and promote science learning as something anyone can engage in, teachers are encouraged to introduce science through everyday practices.

For this reason, I often ask students to describe a scientist. This elicits a variety of responses, which may fuel a conversation on the different types of sciences and different members of a community who practice science. It also provides an opportunity to debunk stereotypes that may make science seem inaccessible to my students. Since science can explain events that are happening around us, it is vital for educators to assist students in coming to the realization that science is not as hard as they may think. Teachers can ask students to consider some of the common practices they participate in, such as cooking, growing plants, measuring, riding in a vehicle, eating, or inflating a balloon, among many others.

Through my involvement in classrooms with emergent bilinguals, I have experienced firsthand the importance of trust between teacher and student. Trust is important for all students but even more for immigrant youth populations who are navigating a new educational space and constructing and negotiating new relationships. A strong relationship with an educator can be key in students' academic success. In an ethnographic study of a large inner-city Texas high school, Valenzuela (1999) found that for many immigrant Mexican and Mexican American students, schooling is a subtractive practice. Rather than it adding to their prior knowledge, these youth experienced school as an ongoing exercise in feeling deficient and inadequate. As opposed to this type of schooling that strips diverse youth of significant cultural resources, it is possible to create a classroom that employs additive pedagogical methods founded on caring and trusting relationships.

DYNAMIC BILINGUALISM

In addition to teaching subject matter content, it is crucial to promote the value of bilingualism and biculturalism to emergent bilinguals. In a $4\frac{1}{2}$-year qualitative research study of a New York City high school, Bartlett and García (2011) found that the success of the school to serve newcomer emergent bilinguals was related to the fact that it did not categorize students based on their deficiencies as "limited English proficient" or "English language learners." Instead, educators within this school viewed the adolescents they served as students for whom bilingualism will undoubtedly emerge. They found that the success of this school was a result of extending students' home language practices and developing their academic use by integrating them effectively to teach them new content knowledge. This school resourcefully opened up bilingual spaces within content classes, such as math, science, and social studies, where both the home language and English are used to make academic content accessible to all students. As explained by García (2009), this hybrid use of language in learning and teaching is referred to as "translanguaging," which has the potential to develop into the kind of language, whether in English or the home language, needed for academic success.

In many cases, immigrant youth have a relatively short amount of time to develop the complex literacy practices required for academic success and, ultimately, high school graduation. For this reason, it is particularly important and beneficial for educators of newcomer youth to make use of students' languaging practices. García (2009) has proposed a model of dynamic bilingualism in which the languaging practices of emergent bilinguals are considered in interrelationship. I have used this approach in my science classrooms. I consciously create spaces that allow students to engage in complex multiple language practices to construct new knowledge. This does not mean that teachers of emergent bilinguals must translate every lesson and offer every concept in both English and the home language. Rather, it means that there must be a flexible understanding of language practices so that students' language abilities can serve as a resource rather than a hindrance to learning.

For example, in a high school Regents-level science classroom, lessons are planned with the content in mind; however, language is always the medium of instruction. The focus of a science lesson on human impact on the environment should be the ways in which humans impact the environment. Students were asked to research how their particular communities affect the environment. They were told to interview relatives or members of their community in their native language or in English about waste disposal, energy use, recycling, purchasing locally grown goods, and other practices. Later, they were asked to organize their data so that they could share it with their classmates, teachers, and administrators in a presentation. Their presentation could be done in English, Spanish, or both. As long as they had learned the ways in which humans impact the environment they could demonstrate their knowledge in any manner that seemed most comfortable, and the lesson could be regarded as successful. In this case, the emphasis was on the content, but it also provided numerous opportunities for them to use English, or any other language. In this way, they have the opportunity to transfer the knowledge they acquire to the language they are learning, while still using the language they know as a resource. Dynamic bilingualism expands opportunities for teachers to provide students with authentic learning experiences and helps to facilitate students becoming fully bilingual.

The Common Core State Standards require every teacher to focus on the development of reading and writing skills. For most students, context is crucial for the development of literacy. Whether in the home language or in English, science classrooms can provide the perfect environment for the development of all language arts skills. This is particularly the case for classrooms that provide experiences with inquiry-based science methods. Scientific inquiry requires planning investigations, identifying assumptions, using critical and logical thinking, and considering alternative explanations for observed phenomena (National Research Council, 2000). Communication skills are essential for participating in these scientific processes and for sharing scientific discoveries. It is important to emphasize, however, process over results, because it is through explaining scientific processes that new knowledge is constructed. It is equally important to highlight that scientific processes should not be followed like cookbook recipes. They should be adapted to the matter being explored. By stressing the importance of engaging in scientific inquiry, teachers empower students to take more responsibility for their own learning. Some ways in which educators of emergent bilinguals can promote language arts development through science are by implementing science journals, weekly science news sharing, debates, and student science demonstrations.

Science Journals

Included in the inquiry-based science methods are skills such as researching, formulating hypotheses, making detailed observations, analyzing observations, drawing conclusions, and considering alternate hypotheses. Whether in a physical notebook or digitally, science journals can serve as instruments for students of science to document and communicate their detailed work. Scientists are constantly making observations and considering explanations. The maintenance of detailed science journals is another way to support the development of students' language arts skills. For emergent bilinguals, these journals should allow for dynamic bilingualism, and the language of choice may change as the student progresses in acquiring English language skills. Bilingual teachers can evaluate journals based on students' ability to record information that leads them to discover scientific knowledge. The emphasis should be placed on content, such as scientific observations and descriptions, rather than language.

Teachers who do not speak the students' first language, or teachers in ESL settings, in which a variety of languages may be spoken by students, may encourage students to support their English language skills with pictures, diagrams, charts, or tables to communicate their scientific observations and explanations. Furthermore, a variety of scaffolding strategies can be implemented to assist emergent bilingual students with their English language skills.

1. Teachers can provide sample questions in science journals to help students who are developing their English language skills. Here are some sample questions:

   What is the main question you are trying to answer with this experiment?

   How will you answer that question?

   What material do you need?

   What do you predict?

   What do you expect?

2. Teachers can provide sentence starters for students to use when hypothesizing and making scientific observations on their science journals, such as the following:

   I am investigating the effect of . . .

   I already know that . . .

   I wonder . . .

   I predict that . . .

   I expect to see . . .

   I observed . . .

   I found that . . .

   I was amazed when . . .

   I identify patterns in . . .

   The data reveals that . . .

   My results demonstrate that . . .

   This reminds me of . . .

   I made connections with . . .

   I conclude that . . .

3. Teachers can provide word boxes with the terminology pertinent to science experiments in general and with words specific to a given scientific investigation. For an experiment regarding "Diffusion Through the Cell Membrane," for example, students may be provided with the following word boxes:

General Terms
Hypothesis Independent Variable Dependent Variable Observations Data   Control   Experimental   Results
Specific Terms
Cell Membrane   Diffusion   Osmosis   Transport   Concentration Concentration Gradient   Balance   Homeostasis   Water

4. An additional scaffold for students to organize scientific information in their science journals is the use of graphic organizers, since they provide an excellent venue for students to demonstrate understanding. These could be concept maps, word webs, Know-Wonder-Learned (KWL) charts, time lines, flow charts, planning charts, or T-charts, among many other types. Graphically organizing information requires independent reflection and comprehension. For emergent bilingual students in nonbilingual settings, graphic organizers provide an excellent tool for students who may be in the beginning stages of second language development to express mastery of scientific concepts. Teachers can provide partially completed graphic organizers for students to incorporate into their journals in order to systematize information and demonstrate understanding.

The assessment of these journals can take many forms, but it should mainly focus on whether or not students are able to exhibit understanding of scientific concepts. I suggest setting time aside to meet individually with each student, at least once per academic quarter, to review, assess, and discuss their journal entries. This could be done during extra help sessions, class time while students work independently, or any other time available during the school year. For emergent bilingual immigrant youth, who may be unfamiliar with the education and evaluation system in U.S. schools, it is crucial not to make assessments a mystery. Students should know exactly what is expected of them in order to succeed. An effective way to do this is by always providing multiple exemplars of the work expected of them. Teachers can keep exemplar journals from previous years to demonstrate expected outcomes.

Weekly Science News

A practice that I engage both my high school and college students in is to look out for current science events news articles and select one that they can share with the class each week. It seems tedious to students at first, but as they become comfortable with the notion that they are considered knowledge providers in my classroom, they take ownership of this role and take it very seriously. This assignment has become very useful for developing language arts skills, as students are required to read the article, answer a few simple questions about it (such as where the article was found, its significance, its implications, etc.), and be prepared to briefly share its contents with their classmates. Considering the linguistic abilities of my emergent bilingual students, I do not restrict the language in which students perform this assignment. Since it requires the sharing of information in the form of an informal presentation in front of the class, this assignment has also proven to be helpful in developing students' confidence and self-esteem. This is vital for immigrant youth who are negotiating their place in a new environment where they are often seen as unsuccessful. Furthermore, as high school students prepare for science Regents exams, which are filled with difficult scientific text, this assignment gives students much-needed practice with reading about science and discussing what they understood from the reading. To our delight and surprise, on a few occasions, science Regents examinations have presented reading passages that discuss scientific discoveries we have already analyzed in the classroom. These weekly science news articles have sparked great conversations, and to my enjoyment, students continue to communicate with me about science news they find long after they are out of my classes.

Classroom Debates

Scientists often have to discuss and justify their discoveries and points of view. Classroom debates about scientific topics provide excellent platforms for science learning and the further development of language arts skills. Students have an opportunity to collaborate as they research and present information on a given topic in order to express their support or opposition to it. In science, the topics that can be examined in the form of debates are countless. Some of the topics I have used include evolution, the use of vaccines, vegetarianism, human cloning, government subsidy of renewable forms of energy, the use of genetically modified foods, stem cell research, global warming, and school lunch nutrition, among many others. Debates provide students with the opportunity to develop their language skills while simultaneously showing them the value of using evidence to support well-developed arguments.

Student Science Demonstrations

The work of a scientist includes communicating discoveries and sharing information often. Students should see themselves as scientists, and as such, they should be encouraged to disseminate information about topics they learn in class. Science fairs provide great platforms for such propagation of information and collaboration. However, more intimate events can be just as beneficial, if not more fruitful because they encourage dialogue in a smaller setting. Classroom group presentations can be great tools for cooperative learning and for solidifying material covered in class.

For example, after finishing a unit on gas laws in a chemistry class, I arranged my students in groups of four and randomly assigned a gas law to each group. Their task was to explain their assigned gas law to their peers with a demonstration. Group members were asked to take on different roles, such as leader, timekeeper, or spokesperson, and to be accountable for those roles. Time was allotted for students to interact with each other to research the topic and to prepare their presentation. Emergent bilinguals were given the flexibility to select the language in which they wished to present. As the teacher, I took a backseat during the presentations, allowing students to take charge of their learning. In this way, I became just a resource rather than controlling the direction of the discussion. On the day of the presentations, other teachers, parents, and administrators were invited to listen as guests. This positioned my students as experts who were educating others about what they had learned, providing yet another opportunity to practice their language skills while demonstrating scientific knowledge. Their classmates were encouraged to prepare questions for each presenter to address after their demonstrations were completed. In this way, students engaged in collaborative discourse about the topics covered in class while also learning from each other.

MAKING SCIENCE CULTURALLY RELEVANT

As classrooms become more diverse, it becomes vital for information to be disseminated in ways that are equitable and meaningful to all students.

Culturally relevant pedagogy can significantly enhance the academic success of ethnically diverse students. It provides a way for students to thrive in school while maintaining their cultural integrity, and it allows them to draw upon their cultural resources as they learn. Successful educators must know their students and content area. I argue, as many supporters of culturally relevant pedagogy do, that a successful educator's ability to engage and motivate students can be enhanced considerably by getting to know his or her students and using that knowledge to facilitate learning. Among the many aspects encompassed by one's culture, those more germane to education are cultural values, traditions, communication styles, learning modalities, relational patterns, lifestyle priorities, and acceptable practices, among others (Gay, 2002; Boykin & Noguera, 2011). By getting to know our students, we become better equipped to design lessons that promote student investment in the content being taught. Culturally relevant science teaching is a way for science educators to make science accessible to all students by making meaningful connections between the content being covered and students' lives.

A common misconception among certain members of minority groups is that in order to succeed academically, conformity to mainstream society is a necessity, and academic attainment will come at the expense of their cultural identity. This need not be the case. Students, especially emergent bilingual immigrant youth, need to get a clear message that their ways of knowing and learning are not only acceptable but also legitimate. Equally important is for teachers to help students acknowledge when this is not the case and engage in fruitful dialogue to propose ways in which these situations can be remediated. In order to implement this type of pedagogy, I propose the use of culturally relevant science demonstrations and the infusion of relevant role models within the curriculum.

There are different ways in which teachers of emergent bilinguals can provide learning environments that are culturally relevant. The science classroom offers many opportunities. An activity that I enjoy doing with my students is the *"Culturally Relevant Science Demo."* I ask students to share a cultural or traditional practice they engage in that relates to science or can be explained using science. I describe some home remedies commonly used in my country, such as eating a spoonful of sugar to cure hiccups, and how I did not accept it as real science until I later learned that sugar has been proven to modify nervous impulses, preventing the diaphragm from contracting spastically. I ask students to recall home remedies or cultural practices that they have grown up with and to research the science behind them. Through this project, I have learned of numerous traditional practices, some of which are supported by scientific facts while others remain unfounded but provide for excellent learning moments. Students are then encouraged to demonstrate and explain the science behind their cultural scientific practice to their peers in a presentation to which family members and administrators are invited. It is a very enjoyable and motivational activity that promotes learning and empowers students as experts and knowledge providers.

RELEVANT ROLE MODELS

Inspiration and motivation are important ingredients to promote academic success, particularly for emergent bilingual students or members of minority groups that may not be equally represented in positions of power and knowledge. Illuminating appropriate role models becomes instrumental for students to envision themselves succeeding academically and becoming knowledge holders. Science teachers of immigrant populations have to work hard to move students away from the assumption that most scientists or people who make scientific discoveries do not look like them. It is important to take the time to look for literature that highlights the work of scientists that resemble the student population. Since I teach Spanish-speaking immigrant youth exclusively, I include in my lessons the work of science contributors such as Mexican engineer Guillermo González Camarena, inventor of the color television; Dominican marine biologist Idelisa Bonelli, considered the mother of marine conservation in the Caribbean; Argentinian officer Juan Vucetih, who created the first fingerprint system of identification; Mexican researcher Luis Miramonte, who synthesized the key chemical compound in the contraceptive pill; Argentinian biologist Raquel Chan, who led the team of scientists who created a more drought-resistant seed; Chilean engineer Arturo Arias, who first envisioned instrumental seismic intensity; Salvadoran inventor René Nuñez, who developed a new method of combustion to make fire and produce heat; Chilean astronomer María Teresa Ruiz, who discovered, among various cosmic objects, the first brown dwarf ever observed; Honduran-British pharmacologist Salvador Moncada, whose work contributed to the understanding of how low doses of aspirin prevent cardiovascular episodes and stroke; or the first Latin American astronaut, Costa Rican physicist Franklin Chang-Díaz, who is working on building a plasma engine that allows the realization of faster and cheaper space travel. These are only a few that pertain to the student population I teach; many more can be found to be presented as relevant role models in the science classroom.

THE POWER OF EXPECTATIONS

Children have a natural drive for learning and an innate curiosity that needs to be fed and challenged. Everyone loses when expectations are lowered in order for students to easily meet them. Throughout my years as an educator, I have experienced firsthand the power of expectations. If students perceive that minimal work is acceptable, it would make sense that unless they possess an inherent drive toward hard work, they will produce only what is expected of them. Suárez-Orosco, Suárez-Orosco, & Todorova's (2008) study, focused exclusively on the experiences of recently arrived foreign-born youth, revealed that most newcomer immigrant students attend less than optimal schools, which, in many cases, obstruct learning and engagement. Possibly, if the conditions are less than optimal for students, the case might be the same for teachers. This may cause frustration and unease as a result of having to deal with issues of regulatory curricular and instructional mandates in addition to crowded classrooms; lack of resources; lack of planning time; and students requiring differentiated instruction, scaffolding, and other teaching strategies due to their diverse backgrounds and educational experiences. This frustration and anxiety can in turn translate into hostility toward students and low expectations. However, as hard as it may seem, we have to remember why we became teachers, and if the answer is to help children learn and achieve success, we must deeply consider the impact of our assumptions. Rather than lowering expectations based on the assumption that children from diverse backgrounds cannot achieve under the circumstances in which many of them are schooled in the United States, we must raise our expectations and work hard to create environments that demonstrate to students they can achieve with our help.

The conditions under which many newcomer immigrant youth are schooled in the United States often exacerbate the stress they experience related to their transition to a new country and culture. Educators who believe students can achieve and who work hard to set up environments that are conducive to learning are vital for the academic success of emergent bilinguals. If we really want students to excel, it is important to continuously set high expectations for all types of learners, regardless of their circumstances. Teachers can maintain high expectations by implementing a rigorous curriculum with the necessary scaffolds to make it accessible to students. Scaffolding and differentiating instruction should not equal weakening or diluting the curriculum. Students are capable of achieving success when instruction is provided in ways that are meaningful and equitable. If students are preparing for a state exam, they should know exactly what the exam and its acceptable responses look like.

If students will be assessed on their ability to prepare a project or presentation on a given topic, they should be provided with exemplars and rubrics in order to effectively prepare. Expected outcomes should be clear to students to allow them to take responsibility for their path toward academic success.

CONCLUSION

I recall reading somewhere that students learn best when instructed by educators with the passion of an apprentice and the aptitude of a professional. From my personal experiences with teachers and prospective teachers, I would say that most teachers have a desire to make a difference with the students they serve. However, for this to happen with emergent bilinguals and new immigrants, we have to find ways to support them so that they can be effective regardless of the situation they find themselves in. There is nothing more beautiful and inspiring than observing a veteran teacher who is on the verge of retirement and still maintains that passion for teaching. Whether we are in classrooms with mainstream students, emergent bilinguals, or special education students, it is important to have high expectations and set up learning environments for all types of learners. Students will rise to the occasion when they know their teachers care about them and expect nothing less than greatness from them.

For emergent bilinguals in particular, it is imperative that teachers employ pedagogical methods that are additive rather than subtractive and value students' knowledge and ways of learning. Some of the basic elements for effective additive education in bilingual settings include setting up classrooms that scaffold rigorous content matter so that all students can access it; providing role models in whom students can see themselves represented; having teachers that include students' family and community members; setting high expectations for all students; creating connections to students' lives; having faculty who demonstrate high content-area and pedagogical capabilities; allowing for dynamic bilingualism and translanguaging; and offering high-stakes content exams in the students' language of choice.

I have tried to provide concrete instructional strategies in this chapter that I have had success with, to make science content accessible to all students, including emergent bilinguals. Teachers of immigrant youth must be attentive to the many challenges faced by this population of students, and with that in mind, set up classrooms that employ a pedagogy of care and trust, using additive strategies, which build upon students' experiences and interests in order to achieve excellence. Critical for the success of emergent bilinguals is the recognition that students' language ability and potential bilingualism is an advantage rather than a hindrance for academic success. Therefore, successful bilingual classrooms extend students' home language practices and develop their academic use by incorporating them effectively to teach new content knowledge, allowing for dynamic bilingualism and trans-languaging. As with any subject matter, it is important to make the content material accessible by emphasizing its practicability and relating it to students' daily lives. In my science classrooms, I stress the fact that students are already practicing scientists and use common culturally relevant daily activities they engage in to explain scientific concepts. Additionally, I believe that inspiration and motivation are key ingredients for academic success; consequently, I include appropriate role models to demystify students' assumption that most scientists or people who make scientific discoveries do not look like them. Last, I strongly believe that students will rise to the occasion when instructed by teachers who build caring connections with them and have the ability to see their potential rather than focus on their shortcomings. When teachers build caring and trusting relationships with students, set high expectations for all learners, and build on students' experiences and interests, the possibilities for academic success are limitless.

REFERENCES

Bartlett, L., & García, O. (2011). *Additive schooling in subtractive times: Bilingual education and Dominican immigrant youth in the Heights.* Nashville, TN: Vanderbilt University Press.

Boykin, W., & Noguera, P. (2011). *Creating the opportunity to learn: Moving from research to practice to close the achievement gap.* Washington, DC: ASCD.

Camarota, S. A. (2012). Immigrants in the United States, 2010: A profile of America's foreign-born population. *Center for Immigration Studies.* Retrieved from http://www.cis.org/articles/2012/immigrants-in-the-united-states-2012.pdf

Dewey, J. (1963). *Experience and education.* New York, NY: Touchstone. (Original work published 1938)

García, O. (2009). *Bilingual education in the twenty-first century: A global perspective.* Malden, MA: Wiley/Blackwell.

García, O., Kleifgen, J. A., & Falchi, L. (2008). From English language learners to emergent bilinguals. *Equity Matters: Research Review No. 1. A Research Initiative of the Campaign for Educational Equity,* 1–59.

Gay, G. (2002). Preparing for culturally responsive teaching. *Journal of Teacher Education, 53*(2), 106–116.

González, N., Moll, L., & Amanti, C. (2005). *Funds of knowledge: Theorizing practices in households, communities, and classrooms.* Mahwah, NJ: Lawrence Erlbaum.

Ikas, K. R. (2002). *Chicana ways: Conversations with ten Chicana writers.* Reno, NV: University of Nevada Press.

Menken, K., Kleyn, T., & Chae, N. (2012). Spotlight on "long-term English language learners": Characteristics and prior schooling experiences of an invisible population. *International Multilingual Research Journal, 6,* 121–142.

National Clearinghouse for English Language Acquisition (NCELA). (2013). *The biennial report to congress on the implementation of the Title III state formula grant program.* U.S. Department of Education. Office of English Language Acquisition, Language Enhancement, and Academic Achievement for Limited English Proficient Students.

National Research Council. 2000. *Inquiry and the national science education standards.* Washington, DC: National Academy Press.

Next Generation Science Standards. (2014). Retrieved May 18, 2014, from http://www.nextgenscience.org

Noddings, N. (1992). *The challenge to care in schools: An alternative approach to education.* New York, NY: Teachers College Press.

Prieto, L., & Villenas, S. A. (2012). Pedagogies from Nepantla: Testimonio, Chicana/Latina feminism and teacher education classrooms. *Equity & Excellence in Education, 45*(3), 411–429.

Suárez-Orosco, C., Suárez-Orosco, M. M., & Todorova, I. (2008). *Learning in a new land: Immigrant students in American society.* Cambridge, MA: The Belknap Press of Harvard University Press.

Valenzuela, A. (1999). *Subtractive schooling: US Mexican youth and the politics of caring.* Albany: State University of New York Press.

PART IV

Ensuring Constancy and Consistency of Purpose

Pursuing excellence through equity requires an ability to avoid distractions that may come from political opposition or competing priorities. In our current climate, when budget shortfalls and a relentless wave of reform initiatives compete for our attention, courageous leadership is necessary to keep us focused on our goals. Those in leadership must protect educators from the ever-changing initiatives and directives that push their way into districts and schools through the guise of policy and reform. The business of education is bigger business than ever before in America (Ash, 2012), and along with it comes a continuous pull on school leaders to buy more and adopt the "solution du jour." New standards, curriculum, programs, technologies, and professional texts are created, and schools purchase, implement, and abandon these products just as rapidly. Staying focused on equity requires constancy and consistency of purpose so that educators are able and willing to support the vision of their organization. Such an approach is necessary because it accomplishes two major goals. First, it reduces stress that arises from multiple priorities and a lack of time to complete them. This allows staff to focus on the purpose without losing time changing directions. Second, it provides clarity. Leaders who provide clarity contribute to the success of high-performing systems (Evans, 1996).

Paul Reville, former Education Commissioner of Massachusetts, exemplifies this principle in the next chapter. Reville shares six contributors to the "uncommon success" of his state. The first two reasons are leadership and clear rationale. The concluding reason is "long-term commitment by various partners." Reville highlights the various initiatives and responsibilities put forth to schools over time with an emphasis on the fact that structure (the amount of time) doesn't change; however, the list of responsibilities grows. He describes an effort that began 21 years ago and resulted in powerful results (as measured by the National Assessment of Educational Progress [NAEP] and the Program in International Student Assessment [PISA] scores). Constancy and consistency of focus at the state level fostered these results. However, Reville emphasizes that the goal of eliminating gaps has still not been fully met, and in so doing, he again exemplifies the continuous commitment to the stated purpose while offering eight suggestions for advancing it.

REFERENCES

Ash, K. (2012, February). K–12 marketplace sees major flow of venture capital. *Education Week, 31*(19), 1, 10–11.

Evans, R. (1996). *The human side of school change.* San Francisco, CA: Jossey-Bass.

The Journey Toward Equity and Excellence

10

The Massachusetts Experience

Paul Reville

Massachusetts is the nation's leading student achievement state. The Commonwealth is at or near the top of numerous national achievement scales and even some world rankings. More than 2 decades ago, prompted by a group of business leaders who became education advocates, the state decided to embark on a set of ambitious reforms driven by an urgent interest in excellence and equity. The concepts of excellence and equity were seen as mutually reinforcing rather than competing interests. Taken together, the reforms were designed to address the need to ensure a prosperous future for Massachusetts by preparing all children, not just some, for success in work, citizenship, and life. By many indicators, the Massachusetts excellence and equity strategies have been highly successful, however much more remains to be done.

How did it start?

In the late 1980s, some Massachusetts business leaders became convinced that the state's education system needed an overhaul. These leaders, many of whom had been inspired by the clarion reform call of the Nation at Risk report, had learned about public education's strengths and weaknesses by engaging in school-business partnerships (National Commission on Excellence in Education, 1983). These partnerships, often more "feel good" than strategic activities, nonetheless served to educate businesspeople as to the operations and limitations of the state's K–12 school system.

Among the most salient features of the schools that made an impression on business leaders were

- the system's lack of clear goals, performance targets, and metric systems for measuring progress;
- the lack of any accountability system;
- the schools' lack of any clear talent development or human resource development systems;
- the uneven performance of schools and high failure rates in some areas and for some children;
- the inadequacy and irrationality of the state school finance system;
- the lack of completion and choice in the education system; and
- the hard work and good intentions of educators who often lacked professional supports and sometimes worked in substandard conditions.

These observations led to deep concern about whether Massachusetts had the human capital system needed to ensure a prosperous future. Business leaders asked: Where would they find workers with the skills and knowledge necessary to compete in a 21st century, postindustrial/information economy? These business leaders in Massachusetts, like many of their counterparts across the country, determined that school-business partnerships alone were insufficient to the scope and scale of change necessary to turn public education into a driver of 21st century prosperity. They wanted to transform a system they saw as outdated and outmoded. They wanted a high performance system that succeeded for each and every student.

Not only did the business community worry about having the skilled, knowledgeable workers they needed for successful high-skill, high-knowledge 21st century enterprises, but they were concerned about the quality of the citizenry and the quality of our communities. They worried, too, about increasing poverty, the inability of people lacking a quality education to support themselves, and the prospect of a growing underclass that would become financially dependent on government and, effectively, a drag on economic growth.

A group of prominent business leaders decided to spearhead this work. The group, led by highly regarded businessman Jack Rennie, was called the Massachusetts Business Alliance for Education (MBAE). (*Disclosure: I served as MBAE's founding executive director.*) MBAE's pathbreaking report and reform manifesto, issued in 1991, laid out a set of policy reforms and strategies designed to remedy the shortcomings of the public education system while building its capacity to achieve excellence.

Significantly, the report's title, "Every Child a Winner!" trumpeted the equity concerns business was bringing to the table (MBAE, 1991).

Prominent in MBAE's call for transformative change in the state's education system were the following appeals to both equity and excellence:

> The strength of the Commonwealth will be a direct function of the capability of public schools to provide an adequate education to all children, regardless of race, ethnic background, social or economic status or location.

> The challenge is to improve the Commonwealth's system of public education so that each child will have the opportunity to achieve his/her maximum potential to go on to a productive life as a participant and a contributor to American society and the American economy. This challenge embraces all children . . .

That the business community put forth such a clear and powerful call was a catalyst to a policy process ultimately embraced by the governor and the legislature. MBAE was reflecting a growing national leadership consensus on the need to reform education so that it prepared all students for success in the modern economy. Government and business leaders could see clearly that the jobs of the future would require improved knowledge, skills, and disposition if America was to remain competitive, the economy prosperous, and the democracy vibrant. Leaders also saw that the status quo school system wasn't up to the task of educating the vast majority of students to unprecedented levels of mastery. Typical of the discourse of the time are the following quotes from major national reports:

> If our standard of living is to be maintained, if the growth of a permanent underclass is to be averted, if democracy is to function effectively into the next century, our schools must graduate the vast majority of students with achievement levels long thought possible for only the privileged few. The American mass education system, designed in the early part of the century for a mass-production economy, will not succeed unless it not only raises, but redefines the essential standards of excellence and strives to make quality and equality of opportunity compatible with each other. (Carnegie Forum on Education and the Economy & Task Force on Teaching as a Profession, 1986)

> It is not enough to establish a high performance standard. It is essential that everyone meets it. Above all, we must avoid creating

a system of educational "haves" and "have nots" in which some students attain the Certificate of Initial Mastery while others are permanently relegated to the backwaters of our society. The purpose of the Certificate is to improve the lifetime education and employment opportunities of all students. (National Center of Education and the Economy & Commission on the Skills of the American Workforce, 1990)

MBAE's "Every Child a Winner!" called for transforming Massachusetts's schools, and its strategic outline became the background of historic legislation that reshaped the Commonwealth's public education system with a combination of standards and accountability measures, systems improvements ranging from new executive authority for superintendents to the establishment of charter schools, and a finance system overhaul resulting in a more progressive distribution of school finance and a doubling of the state's financial commitment (in real dollars) over a 7-year period.

"Every Child a Winner!" set the stage and served as a foundation for a vigorous and successful march to education reform in Massachusetts. Driven by the business community, largely supported by the education field, and ably shaped and led by the governor and the legislature, education reform became a reality with the passage of the sweeping Education Reform Act of 1993, the most significant set of school reforms in a century.

Massachusetts was by no means the first state to enact standards-based reform, but having learned some lessons from other states, Massachusetts's leaders were able to be particularly effective in implementing the new strategies which, within a matter of years, catapulted the Commonwealth's student achievement performance from the middle of the pack to first in the nation.

How did this happen?

This uncommon success was accomplished for a number of reasons, including these:

1. **Leadership.** The leadership for the reform campaign and implementation was deep, diverse, nonpartisan, consistent, and unusually persistent.

2. **Clear rationale featuring economic, excellence, and equity arguments.** Leadership, especially the business community, which was viewed as disinterested, made a compelling case that the reforms were essential to future economic success, job growth, and general prosperity. The reform agenda was systemic and promoted as a way not only to improve overall education performance but also to improve every school

and the education of each and every child. Reformers believed that the education of all children was a matter not only of fairness but of economic self-interest. Consequently, the reforms were simultaneously promoted as both excellence and equity strategies.

3. **High expectations: high standards and high stakes.** The reforms demanded high levels of performance from all the key constituents in education. The state not only set high goals (by many accounts the highest in the nation) but made the goals count by attaching real consequences, high-stakes accountability, to the achievement of those goals. In furtherance of these strategies, the state developed a high-quality and much admired assessment system, the Massachusetts Comprehensive Assessment System (MCAS).

4. **Significant investment in building capacity and achieving financial equity.** The state not only set high standards but significantly invested (doubling the state's financial commitment to education) in building the capacity of educators to achieve those new goals. The legislature revised the funding formula in ways that rectified historical inequities that had short-changed communities with high proportions of low-income students. In fact, the new funding formula included provisions for providing extra funding to communities in direct proportion to the number of low-income children being served. Massachusetts's investment in education reform stood in sharp contrast to many states that established historically high, unprecedented goals for schools but provided no strategies or resources for achieving such revolutionary goals.

5. **Inclusive approach to policy and implementation.** Reform was done with the field, not to the field. Policy proposals were drawn up after exhaustive consultation. Implementation plans were influenced and shaped by those responsible for the work. It wasn't reform by consensus, but consultation and conversation were deeply embedded features of the change process. Thus, Massachusetts was able to achieve great success in education by "doing reform with the field, not to the field." In this regard, unions were seen as partners rather than adversaries in the reform process, and Massachusetts achieved exceptional results while being a strong union state.

6. **Long-term commitment by various partners.** Governors, the legislature, business groups, education advocacy groups, the media, urban superintendents, and many others maintained long-term commitments to implementing the work of education reform. Legal pressure also came from the state's highest court, the Supreme Judicial Court, which accepted the reforms as a remedy to a long-running equity finance case while demanding consistent, long-term commitment by the state to the reforms.

Now, 21 years after the 1993 education reform policy victory and deep into successful implementation, it is all too readily apparent that although Massachusetts has done very well, comparatively speaking, we are a long way from achieving our original goal of closing pernicious, persistent achievement gaps.

For example, on the NAEP, the nation's school report card, Massachusetts has been first or tied for first in English and math at both measured grade levels, fourth and eighth grades, for the last five, biannual administrations of the test. For a decade, Massachusetts has been first in the nation. We've seen steady improvement on our own MCAS scores and some significant gap closing at lower levels of performance. We do extraordinarily well on SAT scores and participation rates, on drop-out rates, and in international tests of student performance when Massachusetts is measured as a separate jurisdiction.

However, our MCAS tests regularly show significant, persistent gaps in the attainment of proficiency by various subgroups. For example, on the 2013 MCAS third-grade test of English, 65% of White students were proficient or higher, but only 34% of low-income students or 19% of English language learners were. In fifth-grade math, 67% of Whites scored at the top levels while only 41% of low-income students did. In eighth-grade science, 46% of White students achieved proficiency or above, but only 19% of low-income students did. White males drop out at the rate of 1.8%, while Black males drop out at the rate of 5.4% and Hispanic males at 6.8% (Massachusetts Department of Elementary & Secondary Education, 2014).

When we set out on the education reform journey in the early 1990s, we aimed to eliminate achievement gaps, to get all students to proficiency, and to once and for all eliminate the correlation between various factors like socioeconomic status and educational achievement and attainment. Echoing our early reform friends from Kentucky (Shriner, Ysseldyke, Thurlow, & Honetschlager, 1994), we said, "Massachusetts will educate all students to high levels, and all means all." However, that has yet to happen. As well as we have done, judged by the standard of "all means all," we have failed. As long as we still have an iron-law correlation between poverty and lower levels of achievement and attainment, between socioeconomic status and educational achievement and attainment generally, our work is not done. We can and must do better.

THE LIMITS OF STANDARDS-BASED REFORM

It is now obvious from our current vantage point, more than 2 decades after the original reforms, that, as a strategy, standards-based reform, while necessary to drive the improvement of education in Massachusetts, was insufficient to achieving the equity-driven goal of "all means all."

Why was this the case? Was standards-based reform the wrong strategy? Some argued, for example, that the standards strategy was too narrow, too prescriptive, and overall inimical to the development of the whole child. Others hated the emphasis on testing and felt that testing corrupted good classroom teaching.

The state's improved performance and prominent national rankings refute the argument that standards-based reform was an ineffective strategy. Nonetheless, an unfortunate and overheated debate developed between standards advocates and those arguing for the whole-child approach. This kind of either/or, simplistic, dichotomous warfare sometimes divided the field and, in my view, missed the point.

The school system's limitations were the point. An alternative explanation for the insufficient performance results was that perhaps schools, as currently conceived, are simply too limited, too weak an intervention to achieve the education reform goal of "all means all." The idea that as a result of well-intentioned school reform strategies, systems like the one in Massachusetts could transform themselves from organizations that produced high achievement for some students into engines driving high performance for all students turned out to be naive.

Standards were necessary but not sufficient for establishing the kind of high performance, continuously improving education and human capital development system that business leaders had envisioned. You had to have ambitious goals, measure progress, and use the data on performance to improve in order to achieve success. This just seems like common sense and a theory of action used in most other human endeavors. But standards alone, grafted onto to an inadequate school system, would not suffice to eliminate historical inequities in student outcomes. In fact, it became apparent that standards-based reform could have a perverse effect if schools didn't change to accommodate the new strategy.

For example, the theory behind the standards paradigm dictated a mastery system where advancement should no longer be determined by "seat time" or courses completed but by demonstrated proficiency in mastering the desired standard of achievement. Such a model necessitates a flexible time system that would provide each student the time and attention needed to achieve the standard. Such a differentiated approach to learning is in sharp contrast to the one-size-fits-all time model that is pervasive in American schools. As the National Commission on Time and Learning observed in 1994, the "design flaw" in schooling needs to be fixed: "Above all, fixing the flaw means that time should be adjusted to meet the individual needs of learners, rather than the administrative convenience of adults" (p. 12).

To do standards-based reform right, we would have had to modify the schedule and calendar of schools to meet the needs of each and every learner. Furthermore, we would have had to expand the amount of time in which schooling occurred in order to meet the need to get *all* students to proficiency in core subjects while simultaneously accommodating other increased demands on schools.

Asking schools to get all students to high standards, even in a couple of tested subjects like English and math, turns out to take much more time than the old system of educating only a few students to a high standard. Schools were expected to get all their students to high standards in core subjects while continuing to provide students with a well-rounded education. There wasn't enough time to do all of this, so the curriculum narrowed in order to make more time for improving student learning in the core subjects which were the tested subjects at the center of the accountability system. What was measured became what was taught. This wasn't necessarily a bad thing, because the measured topics were important, but the overall education was inadequate to what was needed to prepare students for success. The school system was indeed a "prisoner of time" (National Education Commission on Time and Learning, 1994).

The narrowing of the curriculum became a perverse effect of implementing standards-based reform without allowing adequate time for the achievement of the standards. Students everywhere were short-changed by this narrowing effect.

The push for achievement in core subjects came at just the time when, in the 21st century, we are asking schools to do more than ever before: not only to attain unprecedented, high standards in English, math, and, now, science for all students but also to provide students with an education that would not only prepare them to get and hold high-skill, high-knowledge jobs but also ready them to be active citizens, heads of families, and lifelong learners; impart to them the 21st century skills of creativity, communication, and collaboration so important to success in the world of work; and inspire and engage them in science, technology, engineering, and math (STEM) topics, including the mastering of new forms of technology while at the same time addressing the need for the development of character and grit. At the same time, schools could not afford to neglect, though they often were forced to give minimal attention to, important core subjects like history, art, music, and foreign languages. On top of all this, schools continued to be expected to perform various practical and social functions ranging from driver education to providing nutritional meals to solving various social problems from violence to teen pregnancy. Schools were and continue to be overloaded because the time devoted to education has not been expanded to meet the rapidly increasing demands made on schools.

Massachusetts, like virtually all of the other states, didn't make the major changes necessary to add more time (there is a limited but successful experiment with expanded school time, but it has not been scaled up [National Center on Time and Learning, 2011]) or to introduce a more flexible school time system. It would have been costly and too inconvenient for adults. So, Massachusetts's educators tried to make standards-based reform work within the old one-size-fits-all fixed-time model, but that strategy was doomed to limited success.

Despite our good intentions and strong school reform strategies, we have clearly failed to get all students to proficiency, in spite of 2 decades of investment and hard work. In Massachusetts, 20 plus years of reform have proved that high standards, rigorously implemented, can make a significant difference in improving student performance in core subjects, but it has also demonstrated that if the standards-based reform strategy is not fully and appropriately implemented, if it is modified to fit into an inadequate system of schooling, then this strategy cannot and will not yield its promised results.

A WORD ON SCHOOL CHOICE

There have been other reforms operating parallel to, in concert with, or subordinate to standards-based school reform. For example, school choice has been a prominent reform strategy for the last quarter century in Massachusetts. More controversial than standards-based reform, choice initiatives like "interdistrict choice" and charter schools have been viewed variously by business and government leaders as either competitive with (or, in some cases, destructive of) standards-based reform or as complementary strategies driving market incentives for change, new options, especially for disadvantaged parents, and the development of new models of schooling. Choice has many strong proponents in Massachusetts and across the nation. Massachusetts takes justifiable pride in its choice programs.

However, notwithstanding the vigorous advocacy for choice and the fact that Massachusetts has produced some of the nation's most successful charter schools, growth in school choice has been highly constrained due to the realities of education politics, competition over scarce financial resources, the resistance of the status quo, and fierce debates about the success or lack thereof of charter schools. In 21 years since the creation of charter schools in the Education Reform Act of 1993, less than 4% of the state's students are enrolled in charter schools, while roughly 1% of children participate in the state's school choice program that was established in 1989.

The failure of these choice reforms to catch fire and spread suggests their limitations. It is irrefutable that for the foreseeable future, the overwhelming majority of our students will be served by mainstream public schools where choice and innovation are urgently needed. The choice movement has put constructive, competitive pressure on mainstream schools to embrace a wide range of reforms and compete for students. In addition, the charter movement, at least here in Massachusetts, has produced some exemplary, innovative, and highly successful school models that hold promise even if they are only starting to be scaled.

Choice will continue to be an essential companion strategy for the reform of public education. Choice options will likely grow incrementally, and experimentation with new hybrid forms of school governance and service delivery can and should continue. Experiments like the recent state receivership of the Lawrence Public Schools show great promise. Efforts to scale choice successes will be watched closely, and positive results should be embraced. However, choice is not a silver bullet; it is a mechanism for distributing services rather than a prescription for providing students what they need to achieve proficiency.

Choice provides autonomy, but autonomy does not automatically confer superiority on its possessor. As in the case of additional money or time, it's not having these elements that improves performance but rather what you do with the opportunities presented by money, time, or opportunity. These factors, well used, can make an important difference. Poorly used, they are simply wasted.

SCHOOLS ALONE ARE NOT ENOUGH

As the Commonwealth's secretary of education from 2008 to 2013, I often articulated, startling many education audiences, that I believed, along with Richard Rothstein (2004) and other observers, that schools, as currently conceived in America, based as they are on a model that consumes only 20% of a child's total waking hours between the time of kindergarten and high school graduation, provided much too weak an intervention to overcome substantial disadvantages, especially those associated with poverty.

What's the evidence to support the proposition that our current model of schooling is failing? After more than 20 years of implementing standards-based reform in Massachusetts and across the country, there is still an iron law correlation between a child's socioeconomic status and his or her educational achievement and attainment. In other words, standards-based reform has, thus far, not succeeded in its equity mission. Schools were failing prior to this set of reforms, and equity gaps have, indeed, narrowed in some places, notably here in Massachusetts, where implementation has been robust and effective. However, it is also the case that when we set out to reform education in Massachusetts, we wanted to eliminate the correlation between zip code and educational achievement; we wanted to establish that ideal meritocracy Horace Mann had envisioned "common schools" bringing to this Commonwealth (Danns & Span, 2004). While we have promisingly narrowed some of the gaps, we still have a long way to go to achieve our ambitious objectives.

The evidence suggests that to achieve equity and excellence, we will need a set of policies and practices designed to transform public education into a system that can educate all of our students, and all means all, to a high standard while giving them the necessary skills, knowledge, and dispositions to succeed in 21st century work, citizenship, and life. We have done as much as we can with the old engine, the early 20th century model of schooling. We now need a new engine strong enough and complex enough to do the job of educating all students to high standards for 21st century success.

A NEW ENGINE

While Massachusetts and the nation can be proud of the education reform policy changes and investments we have made, as well as individual schools and programs that are beating the odds, we now face a moment in education reform history when we must take stock once again, consider our successes and failures, and plot a course of action, based on what we have learned through experience, and more likely to help us achieve our aspirational goals.

I begin this critical self-examination with reconsidering the paradigm of schooling in which we operate. School reforms have been just that—*school* reforms. They have focused almost exclusively on modifying our current K–12 system, what I call "the old engine," which was designed and built in the early 20th century to do a very different job than the one we are asking schools to do today. At the dawn of the 20th century, America wanted a school system that would rapidly educate and socialize large numbers of young people, many of them immigrants, so that they could fill low-skill, low-knowledge jobs in a burgeoning industrial economy. Schools were designed to batch-process, mass-produce education and to deliver a bell curve distribution of student achievement over a low center. We needed only a few highly educated people (graduation rates then were barely 10%), lots of people in the middle well enough educated to do routine work, and a group of others, barely educated, to fill society's menial jobs. The old engine successfully delivered what the nation needed, and while it was significantly improved over the course of the 20th century, the basic engine remained intact.

Policy makers have modified the old engine in various ways by introducing accountability mechanisms and supports that make the existing structures as efficient and effective as possible. The core remains the same. The vast majority of American children still attend schools that look much like the institutions of the early 1900s; they spend a relatively limited amount of time each day on less than half the days of the year sitting in classrooms with peers of roughly the same age, guided by individual teachers whose preparation, methods, and curricula adhere to basic pedagogic principles not unlike those that prevailed in the industrial era. While virtually all other aspects of society have changed over the past century, schools have not.

The old industrial-era engine of schooling is simply too weak for the job we are asking it to do; it is too limited in capacity to educate all students to the level the economy and world demand. Education reformers were ambitious—perhaps naive—to think we could close such enormous gaps by focusing on schools alone. School-based learning is a critical *piece* of the solution and must remain a priority, but closing achievement gaps requires more. This job calls for a whole new engine.

The new engine must incorporate a comprehensive redesign of existing schools, the capacity of the system to differentiate its approach to meet the needs of each learner, the integration of health and well-being supports, and easy accessibility for all to out-of-school learning opportunities. This new engine should be designed to ensure that all of our students will be challenged to realize their full potential while economically disadvantaged students will always have a fair chance of mastering the skills and knowledge necessary for success.

Features of the New Engine

America is not about to abandon schooling even if its educational performance is subpar. Schools, like it or not, perform an important child custodial function in our society, and the need for that function, the need for child care, so adults can go to work, will continue. Schools also have social and practical advantages for educating children. Consequently, we need to deepen and extend all of our reform efforts to optimize the current system of schooling. For example, efforts designed to build a genuine teaching profession, deepen student learning, deliver more effective instruction, accelerate early literacy, and ready students for careers—all these and many other school reforms must continue.

However, building a new engine will require a dramatically broader conception of schooling—a reimagined system that will attend to child and youth development as well as education. It must be a braided set of education and support systems that is explicitly designed *to meet all children where they are in early childhood and give them what they need—the quantity and quality of instruction, the level of support and opportunity, in and out of school, to enable them to enter young adulthood ready for success in work, citizenship, and lifelong learning.*

The design, building, and implementation of this new engine will require a national dialogue, an open design process, model building, implementation, testing, evaluation, and an iterative cycle of redesign and improvement. Such a plan will need to be accompanied by education and advocacy efforts aimed at engaging key constituency groups, policy development initiatives targeted at enabling the new designs, comprehensive research and evaluation of new models, and communication efforts built to create a sense of urgency and a clear value proposition for major changes to the status quo.

An open design process for this new engine will need, at a minimum, to address the following three challenges:

1. School Redesign

In a 21st century system, schools must be

- *Extended* to provide guaranteed education and support services for children and youth from birth to young adulthood. The education system will need to begin in early childhood and extend to providing all youth some measure of postsecondary education. The new system will have a particular focus on ensuring that truly disadvantaged children, at each stage of their lives, will have access to the services and supports needed to ready them for success.
- *Expanded* in its daily schedule and annual calendar to offer the time, services, and enrichment opportunities needed to level the playing field for all students by tailoring the quantity and quality of instruction to meet the needs of each child. The new design must solve the 20% problem: it is impossible to achieve a 100% meritocracy on a school intervention that now involves only 20% of a child's waking hours, especially in a society with pervasive inequality in resources and learning opportunities available to children.
- *Differentiated* to meet all students where they are and provide them with the educational services they need to achieve mastery. The last frontier of school reform may well be breaking down the rigid,

one-size-fits-all model and allowing for the kind of differentiated treatment that characterizes other customer-driven systems like health care.

2. Health and Well-Being Supports

No matter how much schools improve, children need more than academic supports to thrive; they must also be physically and emotionally healthy to be ready to learn each and every day. If we are to close achievement gaps, we must eliminate the impediments that prevent children from coming to school or distract them from providing their best, motivated effort when they are in school. Untreated dental, vision, and asthma problems, to name just a few such barriers, will often present insurmountable obstacles for students even when attending ideally optimized schools. We need a braided system of health, mental health, and human services to ensure children are genuinely ready to learn.

In this expanded model, health and mental health services must be comprehensive, integrated with educational services, and designed to support students in dealing with myriad problems that threaten to obstruct their education. Such a system might be modeled on standard, corporate human resource practices that provide employees the support they need to cope with problems that threaten job performance. At the same time, schools must work on helping children to build the noncognitive skills that make such important contributions to life success, skills like self-mastery, resilience, interpersonal facility, and grit.

3. Out-of-School Learning Opportunities

Children live 80% of their waking hours outside of school. Affluent children have virtually unlimited access to learning opportunities in this nonschool time. The privileged learn and grow through opportunities in camp, sports, travel, tutoring, music lessons, access to learning technology, and countless other opportunities. Children of poverty generally have little or no access to such opportunities as their parents struggle to make ends meet and survive. It turns out that the learning that occurs, or fails to occur, outside of school has every bit as much to do with achievement gaps that show up in school as anything that happens within the four walls of school.

To address these out-of-school learning gaps, a richer, more coordinated, educationally aligned system of programs and services needs to be developed so that all students have access to a full complement of extended-learning, after school, summer, and work-based opportunities that enrich them as learners and help them build the important skills and networks that will serve them in the future.

POLICY IMPLICATIONS

Obviously, there are no silver bullet policies that will automatically lead to both excellence and equity in American education. Based on the Massachusetts experience, I'd recommend the following policy starting points:

1. Change the policy framework. Future policies must link education tightly to child and youth development. Education policy, narrowly defined as "school policy," will not be enough to build a platform for achieving equitable outcomes. Schools alone cannot do it.

2. Policy and incentives must encourage differentiation, meeting students where they are and giving them what they need to be successful. As in the case of special education, so now, all students need individualized attention and learning plans. The one-size-fits-all model will not work. We need a flexible, adaptive system, like a health care system that individualizes diagnosis and treatment. Students should get the quantity and quality of learning experience that they need to be prepared for success.

3. Policy and incentives should aim to braid health and human services so as to mitigate the problems that get in the way of children coming to school ready to learn. Interventions should be designed to assist children and families in mitigating sources of toxic stress in their lives (Center on the Developing Child, 2010). While the system should have the capacity to address acute problems, it should be coupled with affirmative, in-school programs and standards designed to help students develop the nonacademic characteristics, like resilience and self-management, that are necessary for success.

4. Policy and incentives must be developed so as to create a system that provides a rich variety of out-of-school learning opportunities for disadvantaged students. Options like out-of-school vouchers for economically disadvantaged children should be tried.

5. An early education entitlement must be created from birth for all low-income children.

6. Policy must seek to build healthy, income-integrated communities with education service organizations that engage parents and community members in supporting children's learning.

7. Policies should expand and extend schooling while embracing evidence-based school reforms dealing with key current reform issues like the provision of high-quality teaching; deep, student-centered learning;

career readiness; effective use of data to guide educational strategy; and application of technology to accelerate and expand student learning.

8. Policy should aim to open the sector and encourage new providers and entrepreneurs, operating in a public environment of transparency and accountability, to provide the necessary services and supports for children. The public sector needs help in building its capacity to deliver high-quality, effective services. Education should not be a monopoly system.

These will not be easy policies to promote either politically or financially. Leaders will need to make the space, politically and culturally, to discuss these policies and the problems they are designed to address. As always, complacency, that inherent American conservatism about educational change, will be one of the biggest obstacles. Presidents, governors, and business leaders can catch the nation's attention with an urgent call to reinvent human resource systems designed for a rapidly changing economy and world. Without this sense of urgency, change is unlikely to happen.

In this time of growing inequality and diminished social mobility, America desperately needs powerful, effective, and equitable education and child development systems. The education work of the 21st century requires transformational new approaches to how we educate our children. There is no work more important to the future of this nation and its people. If we fail at this work, not only will we have failed morally, but our economy will suffer, our democracy will be at risk, and millions of families and children will suffer the consequences. Under these circumstances, we will surely fail to thrive as a nation. The alternative, expressed in the title of MBAE's historic report, is to design a new education system that makes "every child a winner" and in so doing, the nation wins, we all win.

REFERENCES

Carnegie Forum on Education and the Economy & Task Force on Teaching as a Profession. (1986). *A nation prepared: Teachers for the 21st century.* Washington, DC: The Forum.

Center on the Developing Child at Harvard University. (2010). *Key concepts: Toxic stress.* Cambridge, MA: Author.

Danns, D., & Span, C. M. (2004). History of schooling. In T. L. Good (Ed.), *21st century education: A reference handbook* (p. 267). Thousand Oaks, CA: Sage.

Massachusetts Business Alliance for Education. (1991). *Every child a winner!* Billerica, MA: Author.

Massachusetts Department of Elementary & Secondary Education. (2014). *High school dropouts 2012–13: Massachusetts public schools*. Malden, MA: Author.

National Center on Education and the Economy (U.S.) & Commission on the Skills of the American Workforce. (1990). *America's choice: High skills or low wages!* Rochester, NY: Author.

National Center on Time and Learning. (2011). *Time well spent: Eight powerful practices of successful, expanded-time schools*. Boston, MA: Author.

National Commission on Excellence in Education. (1983). *A nation at risk: The imperative for educational reform*. Washington, DC: Author.

National Education Commission on Time and Learning. (1994). *Prisoners of time: Report of the national education commission on time and learning*. Washington, DC: Author.

Rothstein, R. (2004). *Class and schools: Using social, economic, and educational reform to close the black-white achievement gap*. Washington, DC: Economic Policy Institute.

Shriner, J. G., Ysseldyke, J. E., Thurlow, M. L., & Honetschlager, D. (1994). "All" means "all": Including students with disabilities. *Educational Leadership, 51*(6), 38–42.

PART V

Facing the Facts and Your Fears

At the heart of courageous leadership is the ability and willingness to face the facts and one's fears around ensuring equity for all students. Data analysis by educators forces a critical eye on performance for all subgroups, which often reveals disparities. While it is easier to stick to the status quo, courageous leaders face the data and use them as a catalyst for improvement. Superintendent Amy Sichel, with co-author Ann Bacon, shares her experience as the leader of one of the few school districts in the nation that has made steady and consistent progress in closing the achievement gap. On the surface, the district was performing well and meeting adequate yearly progress (AYP) in most disaggregated groups. However, through a deeper analysis of the data, Sichel and her colleagues identified significant concerns related to the performance of African American students and students receiving special education. Overall, the district data showed positive performance, but she knew that further progress was possible for these groups as well. Sichel and her colleagues chose to face the facts, using the data and support to help people overcome their fears so that they could take the courageous road to excellence.

Similarly, Darlene Berg describes how she and other teachers critically analyzed the math performance in her district. This analysis brought to light a disparity between high and low socioeconomic status (SES) students. Berg made the choice to face this challenge by raising the bar for all students. Her approach focused on a process for strategically infusing instructional materials in all classrooms, which resulted in improvement for all students. In both cases, these leaders leveraged the facts the data provided to courageously engage school boards, administrators, teachers, parents, and other stakeholders to collectively overcome fears and the challenges inherent in assuring success for every student. Leaders like these establish organizational norms and moral imperatives to accurately and regularly examine progress in fostering improvement, optimism, and action.

Focusing on Equity Propelled Us From Good to Great

11

Abington School District's
Opportunity to Learn Initiative

Amy F. Sichel and Ann H. Bacon

In 2004, Abington School District experienced a rude awakening. Analyzing data and achievement results has always been at the core of our work, and our results have been a source of justifiable pride. An analysis of the Pennsylvania System of School Assessment (PSSA) results showed that each of our schools and each of our disaggregated groups achieved adequate yearly progress (AYP). This result had reaffirmed and reinforced our continuing practice and commitment to planning. However, the authorization of No Child Left Behind and the requirement to disaggregate data challenged our success. A deeper analysis of the disaggregated results identified that the achievement profiles for special education and African American students presented significant areas of concern. This information changed our course. We not only acknowledged our reality; we made a commitment to change these outcomes.

What began as the journey of our district's efforts to narrow achievement gaps turned out to be a model of how equity can be the route to excellence for all, including wealthy, White students who are in the majority and already succeeding! During the initial stages of this journey, our plans were shared at a board meeting in which outraged parents were vociferous about how our plan would "dumb down" the curriculum for their high-achieving students. Interestingly, within 2 months of implementation, the same parents reported the rigor had increased, and at present, we've been the recipients of several prestigious awards. This is what happened.

The story begins with our reform efforts to narrow and hopefully close academic achievement gaps between the White population and children with economic needs as well as African American children and students who have a disability with an individualized education plan (IEP). Our reform efforts focused on planning, communication, and implementation that have now been memorialized as "The Abington Way." With ongoing leadership and, most important, a cooperative board of school directors, our strategies resulted in very positive academic gains for students as well as some unanticipated wins.

In 2001 I (Amy Sichel) was a new superintendent but had worked for 25 years in the district in a variety of roles. This experience was extremely helpful as it gave me a great deal of institutional knowledge and ability to deal with the challenges of implementing change. Fortunately, I had a seasoned superintendent's cabinet that included the building principals and central administrative staff. In addition, I had a committed board of school directors and teachers, parents, and community members who were focused on quality education for all. Some decisions we made were possibly considered risky or politically incorrect. As some saw it, we were "putting the have-nots before the haves." The challenge noted by the authors of this book regarding zero-sum thinking was definitely a factor we had to address. However, we were committed as a district to serve all children as if they were our own children and prove that equity can be a course to excellence for all!

RECOGNIZING AN ISSUE

Located in suburban Philadelphia, a first ring community outside of the city, our district serves approximately 7,640 students of which 19% are on free/reduced lunch, 23% are identified as African American, 6% Asian, 5% Hispanic, and 66% White. The district has been diverse for many years with relatively stable demographic data. The district's demographic data 30 years ago showed 13% African American and 3% Asian with about the same rate of economically needy children. By intent and through much effort, the district has one of the lowest placement rates in the county of children placed in special education at 12%. Abington School District has seven neighborhood elementary schools serving Grades kindergarten to 6, one large junior high school housing Grades 7 to 9, and a senior high school with Grades 10 to 12.

A plan for continuous improvement is not new in Abington School District. In the mid-1990s, the school district examined data from standardized assessments and adopted goals through which each of the nine schools had to improve its average score in each tested area by 5%. Our problem was not embracing our diversity; rather, we were concerned with ensuring all students were served equally with the same standards regardless of wealth and affluence. We thought we were innovative and ahead of the curve because we asked our building administrators to raise the level of expected achievement for the overall average of all students regardless of their socioeconomic background.

However, the analysis of the 2004 PSSA data was a turning point; the Grade 8 mathematics and reading results clearly illustrated "the brutal facts" (Collins, 2001), showing the significant achievement gaps illustrated in Figure 11.1. It became evident that we were resting on the high achievement of the majority without adequate attention to the minority. Consequently, we began to take a close look at the achievement results for our disaggregated groups at all grade levels with a focus on our African American and IEP students.

This data review prompted us to ask, "Why is there a dichotomy—where some students achieve and some students do not?" We believed that all students should receive what they need and deserve. It was clearly stated in the district's strategic plan that all Abington students should receive a first-class public education. We realized our beliefs were in alignment with the definition of equity asserted by the authors in the

Figure 11.1   Grade 8 Achievement Gap in Mathematics and Reading, 2004

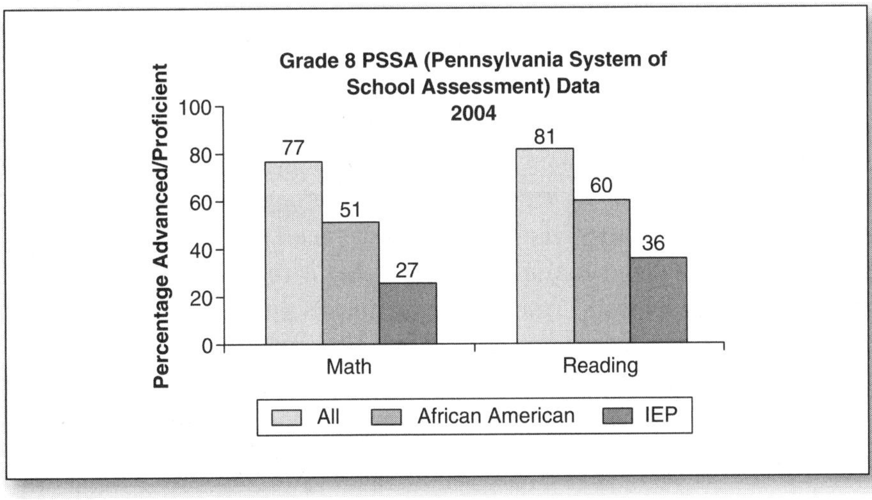

introductory chapter; however, our results were not in alignment. This forced the district to reexamine our situation.

Since results clearly indicated that all students were not achieving to potential and not advancing our mission, we began the difficult work of critically analyzing our context. We followed the process outlined in *Good to Great* (Collins, 2001); we explored our "Hedgehog Concept," determined our focus by establishing our "big, hairy audacious goal," and initiated our "flywheel" (p. 65). We needed to redefine our course of action because more-of-the-same would not create the change necessary to serve the underserved. As Alan Blankstein reiterates in *Failure Is Not an Option*,

> One aspect of building internal capacity relates to developing one's ability to reframe or redefine the problem in order to solve it. This generally takes a deeper analysis on the part of the learning community and highly skilled guidance from the leader or leadership team. (2013, p. 167)

As we were grappling with this process, the Delaware Valley Consortium for Excellence and Equality (DVCEE) was established as a collaborative network committed to work together to support, encourage, and acknowledge the success of their students. This network served as a resource for taking systemic, districtwide, and proactive leadership responsibility for significantly improving the academic performance of all students and at the same time eliminating the observed achievement disparities among racial/ethnic subgroups. As a result of our participation in this program, we were challenged to develop a plan that would result in all of our students having the "opportunity to learn" (OTL). This became the driving force of our reform effort (Schott Foundation, 2009).

DRAFTING THE COURSE TO "GREAT"

It has been the custom in the district to approach many of our problem-solving tasks by creating a Superintendent's Taskforce that includes district and building administrators, teachers, parents, community members, representatives from the Board of School Directors, and students. Each taskforce is guided by a committee charge that details the background of the problem, the objectives, the timeline, and a list of the committee members. In the spring of 2005, at a public meeting of the Board of School Directors, we restated our commitment to continuous improvement by citing strategies and programs that were in place, and we proposed to create a Superintendent's Taskforce entitled Opportunities to Learn (OTL) whose charge would be *"to identify, collect, and analyze appropriate data and to formulate cost effective strategies, programs, activities, and other initiatives, which encourage and support broader numbers of students to achieve proficiency and success in rigorous academic courses."* The key outcome of this committee was to transform Abington's K–12 educational program to ensure that all students would be served. The committee had a set of objectives to accomplish the charge:

- Collect and analyze data
- Review the research and literature to identify best practices
- Develop strategies to place students in challenging classes with the goal of broadening participation of underrepresented populations in academically demanding courses, including honors and advanced placement courses
- Identify support programs for students who require additional assistance to achieve academic success
- Identify professional development needs required to implement this new model
- Propose programs to increase parental involvement
- Evaluate effectiveness of recommendations and initiatives and propose action plans for the 2008 Abington School District Strategic Plan

The larger committee was broken down by instructional levels (elementary Grades K to 6, junior high Grades 7 to 9, and senior high school Grades 10 to 12. Each level had the same subcommittees with areas of focus as indicated in Table 11.1.

We believed that "making the statement that all children will succeed (or learn to high levels) can be energizing. Trying to operationalize it as the sole leader of the school can be depleting" (Blankstein, 2013, pp. 208–209). So, during the next few months, we recruited volunteers for the taskforce.

Table 11.1 OTL Committee's Focus Areas

Elementary Team	Junior High School Team	Senior High School Team
Topics for Study for Each Team		
• Data (achievement, course enrollment, graduation) • Student support • Parental involvement • Placement procedures • Professional development		

With a lot of support, we had no trouble forming a committee of 119 individuals that included one school board director, 36 administrators, 64 teachers, nine parents, six students, and three community members. It was decided that I, as the superintendent of schools, would be the chair, and three principals would chair the senior high school team, the junior high school team, and the elementary team. The three taskforce teams were divided into subcommittees to study each of the topics: data, placement procedures, support programs, professional development, and parental involvement. Prior to preparing the taskforce report, these subcommittees met across all three grade spans. This structure allowed the participants to share ideas and concerns across the elementary, junior high, and senior high school levels.

The final report of the taskforce focused on areas of commonality as well as on areas that were specific to a grade span. There were seven overarching recommendations in the taskforce's final report:

- Provide more classes that are grouped heterogeneously
- Increase participation of minority students in the gifted program and honors/advanced placement (AP) courses
- Increase inclusion of special education students in the regular education program
- Provide student support and mentoring programs
- Stress the importance of differentiated instruction
- Make data more accessible, and increase the use of data to drive instruction
- Work with parents and staff to develop strategies to engage more parents in the students' learning processes

TESTING THE OPPORTUNITY TO LEARN PROTOCOL

Armed with direction and support from the stakeholders, we developed and implemented a plan to address each of the recommendations. This effort began at the high school in the spring of that year when the staff members were beginning to plan for the incoming Grade 10 students. At that time, it was decided to create a pilot program for Grade 10 that would address issues of *equity*, *access*, and *time*. The pilot program consisted of the following:

- **Detracking** to offer only two levels of each major subject course—honors and college preparatory (this was determined to be the vehicle for designing a program focused on equity for all students by offering only rigorous courses focused upon college admission)

- **Designing** a school-day schedule to include time for academic support for students for whom additional time for instruction and skill practice was considered essential to address the fact that some students require more time to achieve mastery
- **Providing access for all students to all courses** by opening courses to students with IEPs and by offering open enrollment for honors and AP courses
- **Providing professional development for staff members** to help them prepare and plan for the new instructional model as well as address any resistance

Detracking eliminated basic skill-level courses that did not adequately prepare students for college and careers and created classes where students were working toward achieving high academic goals. The work of Jeanne Oakes in *Keeping Track* (1985) and *Making the Best of School* (with Martin Lipton, 1990) drove our thinking, and the results from Dr. Carol Burris's (2003) research conducted in Rockville Centre Union Free School District, Rockville Centre, NY, helped us to set the course.

Our initiative created a during-the-day support program for both the general education students who aspired to be successful in college prep classes and special education students who were moving into an inclusion setting. For general education students requiring academic support, we created a similar program where teachers instructed beyond the traditional five periods per week to reteach and review important material with students. In many instances, this required creativity in the students' schedules and permitting students to flex the number of periods required in some classes. In the big picture, a lot of this was about personalizing the instruction to meet the needs of the students.

For special education students requiring support in mathematics, science, English, and social studies, their schedules were structured and focused on academic success. As shown in Table 11.2, this special education student was enrolled in a full complement of college preparatory courses, 10 periods of Itinerant Support, and an elective, Chef's Workshop. The Itinerant Support classes were taught by certified special education teachers who were knowledgeable in mathematics, science, social studies, and English as well as study skills.

The critical cement for solidifying this plan was the support of the staff members and professional development to prepare them for new challenges in the classroom. Areas of focus for the initial year were *Failure Is Not an Option* (2004) by Alan Blankstein and *Differentiation in Practice* (2005) by Tomlinson and Strickland. Strategies for professional development included book discussions led by the principal and staff

Table 11.2   Grade 10 Sample Schedule for an IEP Student

M	T	W	TH	F
Geom	Geom	Geom	Geom	Geom
Itin. Math/Sc.	Chef's Wkshp	Itin. Math/Sc.	Chef's Wkshp	Itin. Math/Sc.
Chem	Chem	Chem	Chem	Chem
PE	Itin. Math/Sc.	PE	Itin. Math/Sc.	Chem
W Civ II	W Civ II	W Civ II	W Civ II	W Civ II
Eng	Eng	Eng	Eng	Eng
Lunch	Lunch	Lunch	Lunch	Lunch
Itin. Hum.	Itin. Hum.	Itin. Hum.	Itin. Hum.	Itin. Hum.

participation in training sessions focused on *Reading Apprenticeship*, a practitioner-tested and research-validated approach that promotes students' engagement and achievement in subject area literacy (http://read ingapprenticeship.org/about-us/).

ANALYZING THE PROTOCOL

It was important to establish criteria for determining the success of the program. As the pilot program began, we decided to monitor course grades both for college preparatory courses and for honors courses that now offered open enrollment, since there were no state assessments administered in Grade 10. At the end of the first year, in June 2006, the results, listed in Table 11.3, revealed that grades were no different than the previous year. However, when special education students are included in college preparatory courses with regular education students and have the appropriate support system, they are able to achieve at a level that is quite comparable to that achieved by the regular education students. The largest discrepancy was noted in Biology and became a goal for improvement.

With the introduction of open enrollment to give more students the opportunity to opt for honors and AP courses, it was important to review the percentage of students passing these courses and the percentage of students earning As and Bs. As shown in Table 11.4, results were positive. In general, students found the high-level science courses to be the most challenging.

Table 11.3   Percentage of Students Passing Courses

Subject	All Students	IEP Students
English II	89%	89%
World Civ II	90%	85%
Algebra I, Part 2	88%	87%
Biology	80%	71%

Table 11.4   End-of-Year Results: Honors Programs—Percentage of Students Passing the Course and Percentage of Students Earning As and Bs

Subject	Passing	As and Bs
H—English II	98%	81%
H—English III	97%	84%
H—English IV	100%	93%
H—World Civ II	99%	84%
AP American Studies	99%	75%
AP American Studies II	100%	95%
H—Algebra 2	98%	74%
H—Intro to Calculus	99%	86%
AP Calculus/AB	100%	69%
AP Biology	96%	76%
H—Chemistry	100%	68%
H—Physics	93%	62%
AP Chemistry	90%	66%
AP Physics	91%	85%
AP Environmental Science	97%	89%

The overall conclusions drawn from the data included the following:

- Students were finding success in the program.
- There was a need to focus additional support for students who were not successful at this point.

Although the data indicated that there was still a lot of work to be done (particularly in the high-level science courses), it also pointed to a high level of success for students. Consequently, the recommendation was made to the Board of School Directors to continue the model in Grade 10, to extend it to Grade 11 and to Grades 7 through 9 at the junior high school. Over the next 2 years, we worked to complete a full implementation of our OTL model across the secondary Grades 7 through 11.

THE RUBBER HITS THE ROAD: FULL PROGRAM IMPLEMENTATION

As a result of the efforts of the high school team, the following goals were established for the 2006 to 2007 school year:

- To keep the high school program academically sound
- To focus on the needs of *all* students
- To provide instructional opportunities to prepare students for college admission or for entry into the highly competitive job market

To address these goals, the changes that were tested in the 2005 to 2006 Grade 10 pilot program were extended to include Grades 7 through 12. These included

- Open enrollment in honors courses
- The elimination of second and third tracks with the result that students choose either an honors or a college preparatory level course
- The inclusion of as many special education students as possible into the regular education program for all major subjects.

To continue the efforts to reach higher levels of achievement, professional development remains a critical piece, fostering the understanding of the importance of providing all students with opportunities to learn and developing the skills and strategies needed to plan and deliver effective instruction. Table 11.5 reflects this focus.

At the conclusion of the 2006 to 2007 school year, when we had implemented our OTL program in Grades 10 and 11 at the senior high school, we again reviewed final grades of the students in the college preparatory classes and of the students in the honors and AP classes. In this data review, we looked at the students in Grade 11 who were completing their second year in the program and at the Grade 10 students who were introduced to OTL for the first time. The data are shown in Tables 11.6, 11.7, and 11.8.

Table 11.5 Professional Development

Topic	Resources
Rationale for the Opportunities to Learn Initiative	• *"You Don't Know Me Until You Know Me"*—Presentation by M. Fowlin • *"The Greatest Educational Challenge"*—Presentation by P. Noguera • *"Opportunity to Learn: Pursuing Equity and Excellence to Close the Achievement Gap"*—Presentation by P. Noguera • *Class Struggle* (1998)—J. Mathews • *Responding to Class Struggle*—Presentation by J. Mathews • *Failure Is Not an Option* (2004 & 2013)—A. Blankstein • *Good to Great* (2001)—J. Collins
Differentiated Instruction	• *Differentiation in Practice* (2005)—C. A. Tomlinson & C. A. Strickland
Using Data to Design Instruction	• *Results Now* (2006)—M. Schmoker • *THE OPPORTUNITY: From "Brutal Facts" to the Best Schools We've Ever Had*—Presentation by M. Schmoker • *Data Analysis for Continuous School Improvement* (2004)—V. Bernhardt

Table 11.6 Cohort 1: 2005–2006 and 2006–2007—Percentage of Students Passing the Course

	English 10	English 11	Soc. St. 10	Soc. St. 11
All Students	83%	85%	88%	91%
IEP Students	74%	74%	78%	73%

Table 11.7 Cohort 2: Grade 10—Percentage of Students Passing the Course

	English 10	Soc. St. 10	Math.	Science
All Students	83%	89%	86%	85%
IEP Students	81%	81%	78%	80%

For the second year, the staff felt that the data, while pointing to areas needing additional attention, also reflected highly positive outcomes for the OTL initiative.

Continuing to monitor progress of the project, in 2008 we turned to the brutal facts that we noticed in 2004. Again, we looked at the results

Table 11.8	2006 and 2007 End-of-Year Results: Honors Program—Percentage of Students Passing the Course

Subject	Passing 2006/2007	As and Bs 2006/2007
H—English II	98%/99%	81%/80%
H—English III	97%/99%	84%/91%
H—English IV	100%/100%	93%/91%
H—World Civ II	99%/99%	84%/81%
AP American Studies	99%/99%	75%/74%
AP American Studies II	100%/100%	95%/90%
H—Algebra 2	98%/99%	74%/65%
H—Intro to Calculus	99%/97%	86%/61%
AP Calculus/AB	100%/100%	69%/94%

for the students who were in Grade 8 in 2008. These students were in their second year of OTL in the junior high school. Figure 11.2 shows that not only did each group—all students, African American students, and IEP students—achieve higher scores than the students in 2004, but the gap between the African American students and all students and the gap between the IEP students and all students had narrowed. We concluded that our efforts were taking us in the right direction and that our goal had to be to continue on this path.

GETTING FROM GOOD TO GREAT LEADS TO ACCEPTANCE

The results of this extensive planning and our reform initiative identified instructional strategies that are now ingrained in our culture. Essentially, we are committed to *Excellence Through Equity,* as seen through our OTL outcomes:

- Make data accessible, and increase the use of data to drive instruction
- Ensure that all courses are college preparatory, which are high level and rigorous to prepare students for college or the world of work
- Increase participation of our diverse population in the gifted program and honors/AP courses

Figure 11.2 Grade 8 Achievement Gap in Mathematics and Reading, 2004 and 2008

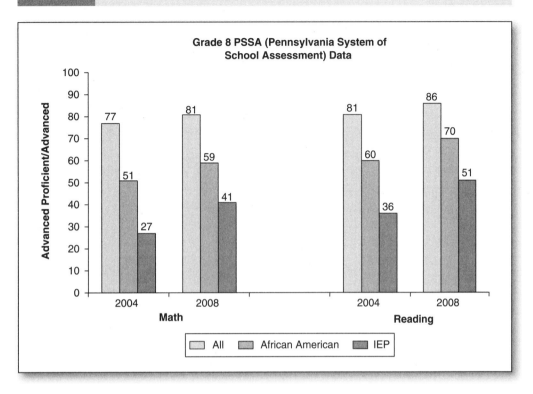

- Increase inclusion of special education students in the regular education program with needed supports
- Provide student support and mentoring programs
- Stress the importance of differentiated instruction and flexible grouping
- Work with parents/guardians and staff to develop strategies to engage more parents/guardians in students' learning processes

The change in culture from good to great is illustrated by this example of two ninth-grade academically talented African American twin girls, from a family of supporters of the district, who asked their principal to create what they termed an "honors tour." They wanted to engage a few other students in the junior high school and organize a PowerPoint presentation for orientation sessions for incoming sixth-grade students to be delivered at each elementary school. The primary purpose of the presentation was to encourage more students to register for the honors classes beginning in Grade 7, a step even beyond college preparatory courses for all. They felt that by diving into at least one honors class beginning in Grade 7 they would experience the high-level rigor and become accustomed to the required preparation, homework, and needed study with the goal of aspiring to AP courses in the high school. What better way to market your successes than through the students themselves!

So here we are 5 years since the full implementation of OTL and concomitant changes to our academic program. Our results from hard data of grades, test scores, and attendance show that our quest to provide a rigorous college preparatory program for all students was and continues to be worth the effort. In the beginning, it was difficult to ask teachers and administrators to think outside the box and move away from past practices, but our results speak the truth—we have narrowed the achievement disparities. The concern many addressed as we embarked on our journey regarding "putting the have-nots before the haves" has not been supported. Making equity the focus of our reform effort produced positive results for all. These examples have helped to support our philosophy that equity fosters excellence for all. What are even more compelling are the unanticipated outcomes, positive "wins" that were not expected.

UNANTICIPATED "WINS"

Matriculation to College/Universities

Traditionally, we experienced a consistent rate where 80% of our graduates entered postsecondary education, including 2- and 4-year colleges and universities. In the 2-year period since detracking, we achieved a 90% matriculation rate to college/universities. When we talked to students, the response was obvious: they were all placed in a college preparatory program and a self-fulfilling prophesy had occurred: 90% of the students now believed they were college ready and worthy! Additionally, as students came back to visit the high school, they continued to state that they were well prepared. We have found that we are producing graduates who are prepared to be collaborative learners in rigorous courses to be well prepared for the future!

Advanced Placement Course Enrollment

Another interesting outcome was an increase in participation in AP courses. Due to our OTL initiative, the number of students enrolling for AP exams increased from 168 to 252 from 2009 to 2013, and the number of AP exams taken increased from 321 in 2009 to 620 in 2013. Students were accepting the premise put forth more than 20 years ago by Jay Mathews that to be ready for college a student had to experience at least one AP class (Mathews, 1998). Not only did they enroll in the AP courses; our outcome rate of a score of 3 and higher on the AP tests also increased. For this achievement, Abington Senior High School was recognized by *U.S. News & World Report* as one of the best high schools for increasing students' participation in AP classes with a 3 or better. In 2013, 80.2% of the students in Abington who took an AP exam earned a 3 or higher as compared with Pennsylvania's average of 68.3%, and the national average of 60.9% earning a score of 3 or higher.

Inclusion of Special Needs Students in General Education

Our special needs students experienced a win. A goal of OTL was to educate more students by including them in the college preparatory classes with supports. Some skeptics believed that not only would students fail but also our parent community would be averse to this change and possibly initiate more due process hearings. In the summer prior to the full-blown implementation, all parents/guardians of an IEP student had a meeting with the supervisor of special education to augment the IEP if it was appropriate to have their child included in the college preparatory program. No parent objected, and every parent was ready and open to embrace our initiative. In fact, in some instances students with prior behavioral issues were better behaved and responsible when attending classes with their classmates. Parents/guardians believed we were prepared to serve their child with equity.

Increased Rigor of the Elementary Curriculum

The initiative has had positive effects on our elementary program. Since all students from Grade 7 on are to be included in college preparatory programs, our K–6 elementary schools had to ensure that students were well prepared. We looked closely at and increased the rigor of our elementary school curriculum and have achieved excellent results. One case in particular involves an elementary school that served the majority of our economically disadvantaged students as well as children of color. It previously showed the lowest school performance, below our other elementary schools. With increased efforts and reforms in that building, we achieved good results. Students' scores have steadily risen. Their efforts were rewarded in 2012 to 2013 when, based on their academic growth in science as measured by the PSSA, the school was designated as a Title I Distinguished School, and in the fall of 2013 it was recognized with a Title 1 Federal Accountability Designation as a Title 1 Reward, High Progress School!

Rising Student Population and Increasing Market Share

School district enrollment has slowly increased for the past 5 years. We have had about 7,400 students enrolled in the district for many years with slight increases and decreases. However, beginning around 2011, enrollment was increasing and by 2012 was 7,640, reaching an all-time high for the last 30 years. This increase became very concerning since space could become an issue; clearly we needed to plan.

This increased enrollment was quite perplexing because the communities of Abington and Rockledge, of which the school district is comprised, are well-established older communities that are built out with little to no land for development. To plan for the future, the Board of School Directors accepted our recommendation, and we engaged the Pennsylvania Economy League (PEL, 2013) to help us with future enrollment projections. The results were fascinating. Overall, the PEL study anticipated that by 2022 the district will have 1,200 more students, around 8,834. They indicated that there were no more live births than previously in the community and confirmed that housing development was not an issue; however, they were clear in stating that as a district we were capturing a larger share of school-age children. Clearly parents are considering the merit of the public schools in Abington prior to considering nonpublic or charter school options as a new sample of this shift in thought. One new parent of a kindergarten youngster shared that her daughter had received a scholarship to a prestigious independent school but, after examining our district results, she turned down the offer.

National Recognition Through Awards and Presentations

Abington School District has also been the recipient of several prestigious national awards including a six-time winner in General Colin Powell's *America's Promise Best Communities for Young People* competition and recognition by *Money Magazine* as a best community in *America's Best Places to Live!* Also the district has been a two time winner in 2014 and 2011 in the College Board AP Annual Honor Roll for increasing participation and outcomes for all students as well as minority children in rigorous AP classes. These prestigious honors are results of the efforts of Abington School District and the Abington and Rockledge communities to ensure that our schools deliver the very best to serve all children—no easy feat.

Our continued participation in the DVCEE offered us the opportunity to share our OTL initiative and its results. Following this, we were accepted to present sessions at the PA/Title I Improving School Performance

Conference (Opportunities to Learn Yield Results—January 2007), at the Pennsylvania Association of School Administrators/Pennsylvania School Boards Association School Leadership Conference (*Opportunities to Learn: Equity, Access and Success for All!*—October 2009), and at the Pennsylvania Association for Supervision and Curriculum Development Annual Conference (*Success for All: Equity, Access, Time*, November 2011). Responses to these presentations were extremely positive and resulted in frequent requests from schools for more information and to visit Abington School District.

EPILOGUE

Clearly there is no silver bullet to our success in meeting our students' needs. It is not technology, nor a magic or hidden curriculum, but rather a will to strive for *Excellence Through Equity.* Our unwavering commitment to keeping equity at the heart of our reform efforts has taken the hard work, research, and creative thinking of many people and the dedication to never lose sight of our focus: to provide a college preparatory program for all (or at least as many as possible)! We removed low-level classes, focused on our outcomes, dug deeper with data, and continually examined what was and was not working and tweaked our schools' continuous improvement plans.

Now it is time to step back and identify other underlying factors that intertwined themselves into our work toward closing the achievement gaps. Recently, I met with a focus group of new administrators (in the position less than 3 years) who had not worked in Abington School District prior to their administrative appointments. The established purpose was to uncover the "special sauce" that contributes to the district's success in efforts such as the OTL initiative. It was noted that planning is always rooted in the district's mission, vision, values, and goals; communication involves not only administrators, but also the Board of School Directors, the community, parents, students, and the entire district staff; and implementation is tightly organized with ongoing communication and participation that includes representation of all constituents and with a strong focus on student achievement. There is no doubt in my mind that these descriptors of the district's culture provided a sound foundation on which we were able to construct our OTL Initiative and to support our *Constancy of Purpose* which guides us in creating such initiatives and supports the continuation of successful programs.

While it has certainly been an honor to be recognized, this work highlights the desperate need for a call to action. In the text by A. Wade

Boykin and Pedro Noguera (2011) entitled *Creating the Opportunity to Learn: Moving From Research to Practice to Close the Achievement Gap*, the authors' state:

> Sadly, the number of suburban districts that are also achieving progress is smaller. Montgomery County, Maryland; Abington, Pennsylvania; and Brockton, Massachusetts, stand out because they have made steady progress in reducing academic disparities between affluent White students and more disadvantaged children of color. However, these districts are the exceptions. (p. 146)

We needed to provide equity to achieve, including anything and everything a student needs to be successful. We continue to examine and ask ourselves what does that look like? What adjustments need to be tailored? We continue to lead with vision and professional purpose and stay the course with focus on student achievement! In the Abington School District we continue to repeat and reaffirm that *Excellence is our standard, and achievement is the result!*

REFERENCES

Bernhardt, V. (2004). *Data analysis for continuous school improvement.* Larchmont, NY: Eye on Education.

Blankstein, A. (2004). *Failure is not an option: Six principles that guide student achievement in high-performing schools* (1st ed.). Thousand Oaks, CA: Corwin.

Blankstein, A. (2013). *Failure is not an option: Six principles that guide student achievement in high-performing schools* (3rd ed.). Thousand Oaks, CA: Corwin.

Boykin, A. W., & Noguera, P. (2011). *Opportunities to learn: Moving from research to practice to close the achievement gap.* Alexandria, VA: Association for Supervision and Curriculum Development.

Burris, C. C. (2003). Providing accelerated mathematics to heterogeneously grouped middle-school students: The longitudinal effects on students of differing initial achievement levels. *Dissertations Abstracts International, 64*(5), 1570.

Collins, J. (2001). *Good to great: Why some companies make the leap.* New York, NY: Harper Business.

Fowlin, M. (2005). *You don't know me until you know me.* Presentation to the Abington School District.

Mathews, J. (1998). *What's wrong (and right) with America's best public high schools: Class struggle.* New York, NY: Random House.

Mathews, J. (2003). *Responding to class struggle.* Presentation to the Abington School District.

No Child Left Behind Act of 2001 (Public Law 107-110).

Noguera, P. (2008). *The greatest educational challenge.* Presentation to the Abington School District.

Noguera, P. (2013). *Opportunities to learn: Pursuing equity and excellence to close the achievement gap.* Presentation to the Abington School District.

Oakes, J. (1985). *Keeping track: How schools structure inequality.* New Haven, CT: Yale University Press.

Oakes, J., & Lipton, M. (1990). *Making the best of schools.* New Haven, CT: Yale University Press.

Pennsylvania Economy League. (2013). *Analysis of demographics and housing and related activity and projections of public school enrollments in the Abington School District, 2012–2013.* Author.

Schmoker, M. (2006). *Results now: How we can achieve unprecedented improvements in teaching and learning.* Alexandria, VA: Association for Supervision and Curriculum Development.

Schott Foundation. (2009). *The opportunity to learn.* Cambridge, MA: Author.

Tomlinson, C. A., & Strickland, C. A. (2005). *Differentiation in practice: A resource guide for differentiating curriculum.* Alexandria, VA: Association for Supervision and Curriculum Development.

Equity and Achievement in the Elementary School

12

*How We Redesigned Our
Math Instruction to Increase
Achievement for Every Child*

Darlene Berg

I recently attended a meeting of elementary school math educators, who came together to discuss classroom instruction. The morning's speaker was hoping for a responsive and engaged audience. For an ice-breaker, letter-size paper and markers were placed on the tabletops. Each audience member was asked to use a sheet of paper to construct a simple tent and to write their name in the center of one side. Additionally, we were asked to think of numbers or symbols that would in some way identify our own district's experiences relative to the teaching of math in our elementary schools. We had to place one symbol or number in each of the four corners of the paper name tent, and as we took turns to introduce ourselves, we were asked to explain our choices.

Without hesitation, I wrote one of each number in a corner around my name: 3,400, 7, 4, 87%. When it was my turn to share, I explained, "Each day the teachers and administrators that I work with are responsible for changing the lives of 3,400 children. We are a culturally and economically diverse district with seven elementary schools. We are approaching our fourth year of the full implementation of the revision of our math program in Grades K through 5, and on the recent Common Core State Standards testing, our students in Grades 3 through 5 demonstrated, on average, 87% math proficiency, up from 74% in 2009." I could have continued, but they said to be brief!

Some of the more interesting data about our district's math instruction is in the details that I didn't have the opportunity to share that day. I work as the elementary-math supervisor in the West Orange, New Jersey, school district. In this focused area of the curriculum, we have begun to significantly close our economic and cultural achievement gaps, and we have done so not at the expense of the economically advantaged. We did not lower our standards, and as a result, even our previously successful students are demonstrating greater success. Not only have we reduced the percentage of children who are nonproficient in math, but we have also shifted large numbers of children up the continuum into the area of advanced proficiency performance. Some of our individual schools' scores rival those of the less economically disparate communities close to us, which have elementary schools with nearly 0% economically disadvantaged student populations. We also know that we are at the beginning of this process, and while the data does show significant and good things are happening here, we still have a way to go, and more improvement is needed.

West Orange is located about 15 miles from New York City as the crow flies, in the most densely populated state in the United States. Our town has been described as a miniature version of Manhattan because of the economic and cultural diversity of the community. Physically and symbolically, our town lies between two mountains. Our residents include the rich and famous as well as recently arrived immigrants of modest means. Our district has identified more than 50 unique languages being spoken in the homes of our students, in addition to English. It is a vibrant town, and as a school community it presents challenges and opportunities.

As a school district, one way that we are able to analyze our elementary students' math proficiency is through reports that are generated from the administration of the annual state exams: the New Jersey Assessment of Skills and Knowledge (NJASK) in Grades 3 through 5. These data help us to see how we are doing academically for math, language arts literacy, and Grade 4 science. This information also describes who we are, demographically speaking.

Using the defined subgroups taken from the No Child Left Behind Act of 2001 according to the most recent data, our district's Grades 3 through 5 population is 33% economically disadvantaged. Culturally, we are 39% African American/Black, 26% Hispanic, and 25% White. About 7% of our student population is Asian, and 3% of our students combined are identified in the subgroups of American Indian, Pacific Islander, or two or more races. While testing data don't tell us everything we need to know about student success or the lack of success, this information provides a basis for conversations and opportunities to identify trends and to inform decision making. All of these data are publicly available through the New Jersey Department of Education website (New Jersey Department of Education, 2013). As you can see in Table 12.1 and Figure 12.1, within these data we have begun to see the academic improvements for all of our students by grade level, comparing cohorts from 4 years ago to cohorts in the latest testing cycle. To demonstrate the progress we've made as a district, I've chosen to compare our levels of proficiency for our three largest identifiable subgroups and the economically disadvantaged. I've included the noneconomically disadvantaged to show that they too have demonstrated significant improvement.

The school year 2008 to 2009 was the year before we began piloting new curriculum resources embedded with the identifiable instructional practices that have been at the core of our success. The school year 2013 provides our most current data (see Table 12.1 and Figure 12.1).

As a math supervisor, I work with and support an instructional team of seven elementary school principals and more than 150 teachers who interact daily with our 3,400 elementary school students. Together with our district administrators, our job is to improve the academic performance of each child as we prepare our students for 21st century citizenship. More than 5 years ago, we embarked on a rigorous course to improve how we were teaching mathematics in our seven elementary schools, because having one out of every four students fail math on the state exams was not a result we were willing to live with. The process was challenging and involved a lot of information, cooperation, energy, and hard work. It seems to be working. We see our success in a number of ways. We analyze the student performance data for the testing of Grades 3, 4, and 5 through the annual School Performance Reports (New Jersey Department of Education, 2013) issued by our State Department of Education. The columns of disaggregated data show significant increases in proficiency by cultural and economic subgroups. The data are useful, and standardized testing provides some insight as to what is occurring, but we also know that we are successful by the level of academic conversations we hear our students having in their math classes. We know that things are moving in the right direction because, when asked, many of our students identify math as their favorite subject. Our hard working teachers discuss the significant shifts in student learning as a result of the instructional strategies that they use in teaching math, and they are happier with the math instruction that they are delivering because of the success that their

Table 12.1	Comparison of Percentage of Proficiency by Demographic Group in 2009 and 2013*				

	Total All Groups	Whites	Blacks	Hispanics	Economically Disadvantaged	Noneconomically Disadvantaged
Grade 3						
2009 District	74.0%	90.0%	68.0%	62.4%	58.8%	80.8%
2013 District**	84.0%	93.4%	81.0%	74.5%	75.1%	88.5%
Grade 4						
2009 District	67.8%	83.3%	60.6%	58.5%	57.1%	73.5%
2013 District**	87.1%	93.0%	83.2%	83.1%	80.4%	90.4%
Grade 5						
2009 District	79.2%	93.9%	74.5%	70.4%	65.4%	85.2%
2013 District**	88.7%	94.3%	84.3%	86.8%	82.2%	91.9%

* Data included on the NJ DOE School Report Card 2009, NJ DOE School Performance Report 2013, New Jersey Department of Education.

** First year of implementation of the new Common Core State Standards for Mathematics.

students are demonstrating. Parents share insights about their children who are finding success in math. I began to realize that something really significant was happening, too, when I no longer heard conversations that began with "My students can't because . . . "

In our elementary-math classrooms, we are closing the achievement gap that has existed for some of our students. We did this by recognizing that the most important resource that we had to guarantee student outcomes was the teacher in the room. We had to look at what was not working for the teachers, what challenges the teachers were facing, and then support the teachers to overcome those challenges. We all had a common vision: we all wanted all of our students to be successful learners. Making that happen equitably in all of our classrooms was the mission.

Early in my career in West Orange as the district math coach, my responsibilities included providing teachers with support to improve student learning through increased use of research-based instructional

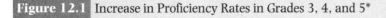

Figure 12.1   Increase in Proficiency Rates in Grades 3, 4, and 5*

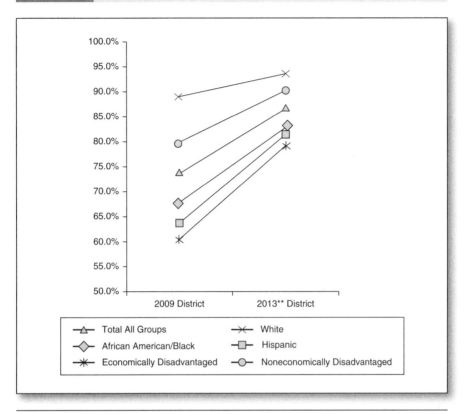

---

* Data included on the NJ DOE School Report Card 2009, NJ DOE School Performance Report 2013, New Jersey Department of Education.

** First year of implementation of the new Common Core State Standards for Mathematics.

strategies. I visited classrooms and worked with the teachers by modeling math lessons using a variety of resources and differentiation strategies to connect with the varied learning styles and needs of the students. Most of the teachers were very receptive to the teacher/coaching model, and they saw that the students' level of engagement was high. During these lessons, one of the most significant ways to reach students who had difficulties grasping math concepts was to introduce the use of manipulatives to support the progression of understanding by helping them to make concrete-iconic-symbolic connections (Bruner, 1976). Examples of the types of resources that incorporated multiple representations of math concepts were the lessons from the *Illuminations* series provided by the National Council of Teachers of Mathematics (NCTM, 2014) and also the lessons found at Marilyn Burns's Math Solutions (Mathsolutions .com). These resources were effective in demonstrating to teachers how to support students' explorations of math concepts such as what pi represents by measuring around soda cans with pieces of string (Burns, 2014) or comparing and contrasting properties of shapes and angles by using origami or drinking straws to create geometric models (NCTM, 2014). These websites also provided ideas to incorporate math games to help students to develop procedural fluency by practicing operations with whole numbers, fractions, and decimals.

We helped students to build on their conceptual knowledge, too, by developing their skills with reasoning and communicating. We had them write out their work onto transparencies that were then placed on overhead projectors. With their work displayed for the class, students would demonstrate and discuss how they solved a problem while their classmates asked questions or critiqued their work. To further our own understanding on how to close some of the experiential gaps that prevented students from seeing math connections in real life, the teachers and I would use in-district workshops to investigate the use of children's literature during the math lesson (Burns, 2014).

Through these classroom visits and workshops, I got to know most of the teachers, and I recognized that we did have a very caring, hardworking staff, but progress was slow. Many of the ideas and lessons that were presented worked their way into lesson plans throughout the district, but it was neither consistent nor systemic. Many teachers were still uncomfortable with making dramatic adjustments to their own familiar instructional practices. This was understandable and especially true in the testing grades, where for some teachers, the fear of potentially lowering test scores by making dramatic shifts in instruction was a paralyzing impediment to change. Through several years of coteaching experiences, it became clear that while teachers saw the value of the instructional strategies that were demonstrated and discussed, they did not see how these fit into their math lessons on a daily basis for the entire school year. Additionally, many conversations focused on the concern that some students faced challenges outside of the classroom that some teachers felt we could not overcome in the classroom, and the thinking was that somehow, by deviating from traditional teacher-centered instruction, we might make it harder for struggling students to learn. During these discussions with my teachers, I agreed that inequitable life experiences did impact how some students processed learning, but I also believed that the experiences we presented in the learning process should be varied enough to overcome the disparities and bring all students to the table. One way to do this was to learn how to incorporate effective instructional strategies equitably for all of our math lessons in all of our classrooms.

What was needed to make this the new norm was a yearlong curriculum of research-based materials that consistently guided the teachers at the point of instruction in math content and rigor and also gave them options for scaffolding or extending the learning based on what the students needed, when the students needed it. And it was not going to be enough to just hand over resources to the teachers; we had to have a clear plan for the sustained professional development needs from the start. This placed a greater responsibility on finding the right resources to support the district's guidelines for instructional strategies and then implementing those resources correctly. As one teacher told me, "We will do what is best for our students, but please make certain that they (central office) know we need time to make this work and we need training."

Eventually, we looked to a revision of our math teaching resources as a means to support a foundation upon which to make the instructional shifts in math education to promote success for all of our students. Our approach to equity was to provide a solid framework so that every teacher could implement the instructional strategies that would support the diversity of learning among our students. Over the next paragraphs, I will recount the process as it evolved for us.

When the district had to consider purchasing new math resources for the elementary schools, we were fortunate to have a committee of teachers who brought a tremendous level of professionalism and insight to the process. Collaboratively, they reviewed resources and analyzed sample lessons. They identified what support was embedded in the materials that would help teachers to make decisions to use research-based instructional practices in the daily math lessons. A group of teachers wanted to find a successful school district similar to ours in demographics and see what its teachers were doing in their classrooms. That was a great idea! We set about looking for a district as large as we were, with similar social and economic demographics and whose students were successful. We looked up scores. How were the neighbors doing? When we located a district that agreed to host us, we took a group of teachers out to see them, to sit in their classrooms and watch them teach. Our teachers talked to their teachers about what was working and to their students about what they liked about learning math. They asked what challenges the faculty faced as they made the shift in instructional practices. The group brought that information back to the district, and it became part of the conversation about change.

I remember thinking that throughout the entire process of redefining our classroom instruction and choosing the support materials that were going to help us do it, as a teaching community, we were working toward developing a common understanding of what equitable instruction looked like, and we were identifying opportunities to support and maintain what the professionals in the room had to do. The process sometimes included debates and sometimes heated discussions, but ultimately the teachers saw for themselves how they could effect positive change for all of our students.

Eventually, two series were chosen and piloted in several of the schools, in the testing grades. Surveys were conducted among the teachers asking what worked and what didn't work, and then ultimately a final choice was made. Then the real work began.

We understood that the process we had undertaken was not so much about which resources we were purchasing as it was about creating a consistent, systemic application of instructional strategies that would increase opportunities for all of our students to be successful in learning math. The materials had to support this goal. Professional development had to support the teachers in the application of the process.

The first year, we delivered the resources to the teachers during the summer months prior to the start of the new school year. Just before classes began in September, full day workshops were held by grade level, to talk about lesson structure and share tips on "how to." We made certain that the workshop presenters were teachers or former teachers who had used the resources and understood the instructional practices that we were asking our teachers to use. They could relate anecdotally about what worked in classrooms with diverse student needs. We had teachers critique the presenters so that we understood who had been most helpful to them and why. We paid attention to what the teachers told us, and we used their feedback to design each next level of training. Principals attended the trainings with their teachers so that they could understand the overarching ideas, the instructional strategies, and provide the moral support. They became an additional resource to the teachers to solve problems and answer questions and concerns.

During this time, anxiety was high. We listened to the teachers' concerns. They were worried that they would not have everything that they needed. The district made certain that they had the classroom resources that they needed to achieve the practices that they were being asked to do; manipulatives, charts, graphic organizers, classroom sets of slates and markers, materials for academic games, and student practice books.

Teachers were asked to walk a narrow corridor and to implement the design and structure of the lessons with fidelity. Some teachers felt that this approach curbed their creativity. The district offered a solution. If teachers could maintain fidelity to the lesson structure we presented, we would build in a "Flexible Friday" that each individual teacher could use in any number of ways based on the instructional needs of their students. Friday's math lesson could be devoted to centers, to extension activities, to projects. This became a popular component of instruction and is still used in all of our schools. Teachers were worried that the training was not going to be enough. The professional development continued that first year and each year since. The most useful workshop presenters were brought back. Teachers were guided in the use of effective grouping techniques for students: heterogeneous pairs, homogeneous pairs, small-group activities, and whole-class instruction. Teachers were shown how to implement formative assessment in the daily lesson to help them to make adjustments to their teaching based on realizing where their students were in their learning. Teachers were shown how the structure of the lessons encouraged learning dynamics in children who previously had been totally passive in the math classroom. Teachers became proficient in using a gradual release of responsibility model of instruction (Pearson & Gallagher, 1983), rather than a traditional teacher-centered approach. Once these instructional strategies were happening consistently and systemically in every building, positive results started to show.

One of the best comments that we received from the teacher feedback following our first workshops was a request to provide differentiated workshops to the teachers. Among the teaching staff were varied levels of expertise and confidence, and the suggestion that our training for the faculty should reflect our understanding of differentiated instruction was right on the money. That first year, as we approached our 100th day of school, we sent out an electronic teacher needs survey. We asked teachers to identify the areas they most wanted additional help with, choosing from five categories: demonstrating an upcoming lesson, demonstrating technology support, pacing the lessons, incorporating differentiation, and other. The responses were collected and organized by building and then by grade level within the building. Specific trends in the needs analysis started to appear. It was decided that in order to make the professional development as supportive as possible, we would send a workshop presenter to each building for the day. We gave each presenter, in advance, the results by grade level of what the teachers felt they needed the most help with. The principals supported this by arranging for a workspace and organizing the schedules so that each grade-level team of teachers could meet with the trainers as a small group. I attended many of the training sessions, and each one started with these questions: "What three things are working? What three things are not working?" The groups celebrated the things that were working, and interestingly, most of the responses to this question started with "The students are really enjoying math!" The items that were not working were discussed, and suggested solutions were shared.

Building-based professional development has been one of the best received ideas. In their small groups, teachers focus on the math instructional needs specific to their population of students. The atmosphere is relaxed, professional, supportive, and productive. Students don't have to lose a full day of instruction so that their teachers can attend the workshop; the workshop comes to the teachers. Principals have been very receptive, and only a few substitutes need to be brought into the building for the day, as we rotate them through the grade levels so that small groups of teachers can move through the training throughout the day.

Each successive year has included training opportunities for teachers new to the district's elementary-math classrooms, as well as opportunities to continue the training for teachers experienced in the math program. Special education and basic skills teachers are included in trainings with the general education teachers so that a consistency of expectations is achieved. The instructional route map has been established, and all of our teachers are better able to make informed decisions about the learning needs of each student.

One of the obstacles we had faced for years was how some classrooms seemed to be individual silos of learning. As we began to develop a common language of instruction, opportunities for teachers to meet as a grade level to work together increased. Where we see some of the largest percentages of student success are in those grade levels in which the teachers meet regularly, plan together, help each other to solve instructional problems, and share ideas. One of my teachers described how she uses her experiences as a member of a professional collaborative group as an example for her students in how to work together collaboratively to problem solve.

Meeting the needs of our diverse student population by providing diverse instruction has helped us to increase the levels of math proficiency for our students. Traditional modes of instruction are not equitable. Only a segment of the learners demonstrate proficiency. As we have evolved as a teaching community through equitable use of instructional strategies through the orchestration and refinement of our math program, greater numbers of our students have begun to demonstrate proficiency, and the achievement gap has narrowed significantly. The effort has involved leadership among the administrators but to a greater degree leadership among the teaching staff. Teachers understand that their students are learning more efficiently because the teachers are using their instructional toolboxes more effectively. The change is consistent and systemic. Through hundreds of observations and walk-through visits, it is evident throughout our elementary classrooms that high expectations for math learning are the same no matter where between the two mountains your school building lies.

Now that we have a level of consistency with the math instruction in the classrooms, we are better able to look at areas where the success rate for our students in math may still not be as strong and determine what other factors or challenges may be impeding student success. We can devise additional methods to support the students to be successful learners. One of our schools was able to boost proficiency rates from 75% math proficiency for Grades 3 through 5 up to 90% in one year by implementing a Saturday Academy for identified children at risk. The population of students is 57% economically disadvantaged, which is considerably higher than our district average. The teachers for the Saturday Academy were provided materials that were aligned with the daily classroom instruction. Teachers were able to target areas where students had gaps in their understanding and then scaffold the learning. By maintaining the common math language, continuity of the expectations, and the use of instructional strategies that the students were familiar with, the program was successful in supporting student achievement.

Not long ago, I stopped by one of my buildings to see a teacher. While I waited for her preparation to begin, so that we could discuss a lesson I had observed earlier in the week, another of my teachers approached me. She was telling me about how she had recently hosted a visit from a teacher from another school district who came to see what we were doing in math instruction. Her guest wanted to watch her teach and ask questions about what worked and what advice she would share. The neighbors wanted to see what we were doing! How awesome!

Hopefully, sharing the story of the work of the teachers and students in West Orange's elementary schools will contribute positively to the conversation that equity in instruction can support accomplishment for all students. In the classroom, focusing on students' need for some does not prevent good teaching for others, and the data prove this. In our district, the average mean scale scores in the elementary-math program have risen, in concert with the number of students leaving partial proficiency behind. If there is reservation on the part of parents of noneconomically disadvantaged students that is based on a concern that when teachers focus on students with needs, their own children will receive less opportunity to grow academically, I can only point to the data that we are generating in our district to show that a diverse learning environment benefits all students. For our students who are economically advantaged and are classmates in diverse classrooms, the data show that this subgroup of students has experienced growth, too! In our district, the achievement of these students has risen to more than 91% proficiency in mathematics, and within that group, nearly 60% are advanced proficient. Even with increasing diversity in the classrooms, our most advantaged students have excelled. All students have needs, even the academically and economically advantaged. A teacher who promotes a student-centered environment and understands how to scaffold instruction to support gaps for one student will use that same set of skills to extend the progression of learning for the child who is ready for more.

A parent recently approached me to ask how to help her child during the summer months to prepare for the challenges of the next school year's math. As we reviewed materials and discussed the progression of skills, she shared with me an earlier discussion she had with her husband about possibly moving to another school district. They were concerned that being in such a diverse district might be an educational disadvantage, and they wondered if they would better serve their child by moving to a nearby district that had a reputation for being successful, and which I knew to be more economically homogeneous. She told me that a friend, who was also an attorney, questioned why she would do that, when the West Orange school that her child was already in was more successful than the school she was thinking of moving to. He was able to show her information on the computer that confirmed his statements.

I appreciated her candor, as well as her desire to advocate for her child, but it made me uncomfortable to know that this parent did not know about our success, and that this lack of information might have contributed to a decision to leave our school community. We have the responsibility to communicate this success to our parents, and perhaps this is the next step in the process for us.

REFERENCES

Bruner, J. (1976). *The process of education*. Cambridge, MA: Harvard University Press.

Burns, M. (2014). *Math reads*. New York, NY: Scholastic. Retrieved from http://mathsolutions.com/about-us/marilyn-burns/

National Council of Teachers of Mathematics (NCTM). (2014). *Illuminations for teaching math*. Verizon Foundation. Retrieved from http://illuminations.nctm.org/Lesson.aspx?id=1992

New Jersey Department of Education. (2013). *NJ DOE school performance report*. Retrieved from http://education.state.nj.us/pr/

Pearson, P. D., & Gallagher, M. (1983). The instruction of reading comprehension. *Contemporary Educational Psychology, 8*, 317–344.

PART VI

Building Sustainable Relationships

Effective leaders understand that relationships premised upon trust and respect are key to learning and essential to success. Without an atmosphere of trust among the *adults* in school, students' success rates drop significantly (Bryke & Schneider, 2004; Bryke, Bender Sebring, Allensworth, Luppescu, & Easton, 2010). Relationships occur through and within each principle of courageous leadership, starting from the beginning—getting to your core. A meaningful relationship has to be present between you and your mission. This is at the heart of getting to your core. This becomes an attractor to like-minded colleagues who then comprise the leadership team. The team, in turn, builds sustainable relationships with the staff members who ultimately reach all children.

These relationships are formalized organizationally through common mission, vision, values, and goals (MVVGs) of the organization (Blankstein, 2013). In short, "Quality relationships, are even more powerful than moral purpose" (Fullan, 2003, p. 35), and the development and sustainment of them is critical for success. In the following pages, Marcus Newsome shares his strategic approach to building relational trust when he became the superintendent of Chesterfield County Public Schools. He provides a unique view on what it takes to navigate the waters of opposing viewpoints among various stakeholders. Newsome used a deliberate approach to build and sustain relationships as he built support for an agenda of excellence through equity.

Lucy Friedman and Saskia Traill provide an example of building and sustaining relationships on an organizational level to establish and grow successful after-school programs. They highlight the relationships among schools and community partners that are necessary for success. In their chapter, Friedman and Traill share early lessons learned, beginning with #1: Change occurs only at "the speed of trust." These authors understand the power and importance of relationships, without which success will be limited, short-lived, or both.

REFERENCES

Blankstein, A. (2013). *Failure is not an option: Six principles that guide student achievement in high-performing schools* (3rd ed.). Thousand Oaks, CA: Corwin.

Bryke, A., Bender Sebring, P., Allensworth, E., Luppescu, S., & Easton, J. Q. (2010). *Organizing schools for improvement.* Chicago, IL: University of Chicago Press.

Bryke, A., & Schneider, B. (2004). *Trust in schools.* New York, NY: Russel Sage Foundation.

Fullan, M. G. (2003). *The moral imperative of school leadership.* Thousand Oaks, CA: Corwin.

A Journey Toward Equity and Excellence for All Students in Chesterfield

13

Marcus J. Newsome

A journey of a thousand miles begins with a single step.

—Chinese philosopher Laozi (604 BCE–531 BCE)

When I began my journey as an educator in the District of Columbia, I did not foresee myself accepting the position of superintendence of Chesterfield County Public Schools (CCPS).

I began my career in South East Washington where I taught for more than a decade in some of the poorest neighborhoods in Southeast Washington, DC. Educators in these schools (primarily racially segregated) faced difficult challenges working through issues often associated with poverty: crime and violence, drugs, physical and mental abuse, neglect, teen pregnancy, and disengaged communities. I loved my students, and they loved me back. I had come to the conclusion that I had to be the difference in their lives, and if I did not pour my heart and soul into them, they would have limited opportunities to break the cycle of poverty that had been so prevalent in their families. For more than 25 years, I had served as a principal, central office administrator, and superintendent, primarily in urban, high poverty, majority minority populated school districts.

Now in Chesterfield, after a thorough examination of student achievement results, I realized that in this community, *respectable was the enemy of excellence.* Moving to the next level with 21st century ideas in a community content with their results and so resistant to change would be one of the most daunting challenges of my career; even more so than moving schools from failing to average.

EQUITY AND EXCELLENCE
IN CHESTERFIELD COUNTY PUBLIC SCHOOLS

When I first arrived in CCPS, the district was basking in the glow of an exemplary reputation, which continues on today. The district had a history of stable leadership. My predecessor had just been appointed by the governor to serve as state superintendent for public instruction in Virginia after 6 successful years leading CCPS. His predecessor had held the same position with the State Department of Education. The shoes I had to fill were enormous. This was a dramatic change from anywhere I had ever worked. Overall student achievement was not a real concern in the district. The most prominent challenge at the time was overcrowding. For several years the student population was growing by almost 1,000 students a year, and a large segment of the students were educated in classroom trailers. The district was in the midst of building new schools as mandated by a 2004 bond referendum. In my first 3 years in the district, we built and successfully opened two new high schools, two new middle schools, and two new elementary schools and made major renovations to 10 others.

But with little public discussion, the demographics were changing faster than many citizens realized. In 2006, student enrollment was 62% White; 27% Black; 6% Latino; 4% Islander, American Indian, Asian/Pacific, and unspecified; and 22% of the students were on the federal meals program. Since then, the percentage of White students enrolled in CCPS has declined to 54%, African American student enrollment has increased slightly, and Hispanic student enrollment has grown to 12%.

One prevalent narrative in the United States is that schools and districts where children of color form the majority student population tend not to perform as well academically as those in which the majority of students are White. Schools that are majority Black and Hispanic are commonly located in areas that are relatively more impoverished and have higher crime. Those schools also tend to have less qualified teachers, lower expectations for student achievement, and more student discipline issues. Interestingly, these conditions and outcomes are often true for children of color even in districts where the majority of students are White. Chesterfield County faces numerous challenges in reversing these trends.

In 2014, over 35% of the student enrollment in CCPS is identified as economically disadvantaged. That translates to more than 20,000 of our children living in poverty as defined by the federal government. There are segments of the community who believe it is the parents' fault, and *we should not be "wasting tax dollars on the children of lazy parents."* This mindset has contributed to Chesterfield County's ranking as having the lowest per pupil funding allocation of any large locality in Virginia. Additionally, segments of the teaching population have struggled with rapidly changing demographics. The teaching workforce is dedicated and as talented as any in which I have ever worked. Yet some teachers acknowledged that they did not have the skill sets to effectively address the struggles associated with the many changing social forces affecting families. This played out when I attended a school board public engagement session with approximately 125 of our teachers in the spring of 2007.

During that session, teachers in attendance lamented the fact that they had to teach students who had discipline problems and did not want to learn. Their suggestion to the school board was for the administration to create more alternative schools. The sentiment was, " . . . *those kids* are a distraction for the students who want to learn." I distinctly remember one courageous first-year teacher in the room who tried to turn the conversation to teacher accountability and their responsibility for educating all children. She was met with a resounding rebuke from her more senior peers. The stark reality of this disturbing culture was like a slap in the face for me. Bill Daggett from the International Center for Leadership in Education has frequently stated that *"culture trumps strategy."* I realized changing the culture and steering this ship on a course that embraces equity and diversity while maintaining excellence was going to agitate some already rough waters. And any public discussion about race was going to be very risky.

In the United States, political correctness often causes people to shy away from open and honest conversations regarding diversity, that is, disabilities, age, gender, ethnicity, geographic origin, or even politics among other topics. As a result of our nation's history, perhaps there is no topic of discussion more sensitive or polarizing than race. This was certainly the environment in Chesterfield County.

Our work ahead would require some strategic and courageous conversations. So rather than focus on any single group of students, I framed the discussion around *No Child Left Behind* (NCLB) and the subgroups identified by the U.S. Department of Education: race, students with disabilities, ESOL (English for speakers of other languages), and economically disadvantaged students. When I discussed achievement gaps, I did not compare the performance of one subgroup with another. I compared each subgroup with a standard of 100%. For example, if the state reading assessment pass rate for our White students was 90%, and the pass rate for Hispanic students was 80%, I presented the achievement gap for White students as 10% and the achievement gap for Latino students as 20%. Thus, we needed to close gaps within every group in the district. The community seemed to buy in to this approach.

I had transitioned into the district in October 2006, almost 6 weeks after the school year had begun, so the summer of 2007 was my first opportunity to speak directly to our teachers. The event was an annual curriculum academy where we typically established the instructional priorities for the upcoming school year. In my opening remarks to the group, I discussed our commitment to raising the bar for all students; closing achievement gaps; treating everyone with respect and dignity (adults and students); and taking responsibility for the success of all students, not just those in our classroom or our school. These four commitments are explained in greater detail in Michael Fullan's (2003) book entitled *The Moral Imperative of School Leadership*.

I also talked to the group about my experience at the school board's public engagement session earlier in the school year, and my disappointment in hearing some students being referred to as "those kids." I explained that I was once one of "those kids." My brothers and sister and my parents were "those kids." Additionally, I pointed out the fact that some of the teachers in the audience were also "those kids" at some time in their lives. "Those kids" was the term used to describe students who did not conveniently fit into our comfort box. It would be our job as educators to adjust and adapt our instructional strategies and practices to meet the individual needs of every student. My focus was on the needs of every student and appealing to the core beliefs of our teachers, who genuinely wanted to do their best to help students. Some of them just lacked the cultural understanding and tools to overcome the challenges. My job was to support them and help provide them with the resources and training necessary to master the changing dynamics of our community. I was pleased to see that most of our teachers accepted the challenge and did whatever it took to help students succeed. During the 7 years since this session, I have never heard anyone in our district use the term "those kids" again . . . not once.

THE FIRST 100 DAYS

> With a clever strategy, each action is self-reinforcing. Each action creates more options that are mutually beneficial. Each victory is not just for today but for tomorrow.
>
> —Max McKeown

Throughout my career, I have been fortunate to experience significant increases in student performance taking place over a short period of time. As a school administrator and superintendent, I have learned that every new leader has to adjust and adapt to a new culture.

Frequently, when new superintendents accept their positions, they begin to change things around based on their previous experiences or preconceived notions of the school district. Some often bring a cookie-cutter approach design to replicate their work done in a previous position, school, or district. These changes frequently include bringing friends and former colleagues to serve on their new leadership team. Perhaps this process may work in some cases, especially where the district is in crisis. In each of my two superintendencies, I purposefully did not bring a new team with me. The districts were not in crisis, so I had the opportunity to listen and learn about the culture and assess the skill sets of the leadership team already in place. Only then did I feel comfortable making changes, and always with the participation of stakeholders. This process fostered early credibility and trust with employees and the community.

As a superintendent in Chesterfield County Public Schools and Newport News Public Schools, I created a *100-Day Entry Plan* to clearly articulate my transition into the school districts. The purpose of the plan was to

1. establish strong team-oriented working relationships with each individual school board member and key personnel;

2. establish strong and collaborative relationships with the district's professional associations and groups of employees;

3. establish strong partnerships with local, state, and federal officials;

4. understand and develop an appreciation for the district, communities, demographics, and cultural norms; and

5. clearly articulate goals and expectations with print and electronic media.

The plan included three phases:

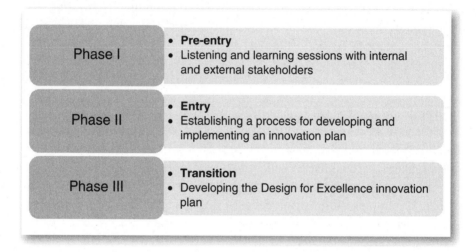

Phase I	• **Pre-entry** • Listening and learning sessions with internal and external stakeholders
Phase II	• **Entry** • Establishing a process for developing and implementing an innovation plan
Phase III	• **Transition** • Developing the Design for Excellence innovation plan

Phase I of the plan was dominated by listening and learning sessions consisting of numerous meetings with constituent groups: internal leadership groups, central office administrators, principals, teachers, and staff, as well as external leaders to include parent groups; business and civic organizations; and federal, state, and local elected officials. Weekly updates were provided to the school board and school administrators along with a process for their feedback. A formal report was given at the conclusion of the initial phase.

I recall a conversation with one of our school board members during my first month on the job. He said he wanted me to be more vocal and forthcoming with my ideas. I was appreciative of his confidence in me and his respect for my opinions—I certainly had plenty of ideas and opinions. However, the dynamics of the school district and culture of the community was somewhat foreign to me. I had no intentions of vocalizing many of my thoughts until I had a better understanding of the lay of the land. I needed to conduct my own historical research, learn who the movers and shakers were, and better comprehend the pain points. When I spoke, I wanted to speak with wisdom and authority.

It is worth noting here that one of my most important conversations with the leadership of the school board came prior to my acceptance of the job. When the board offered me the job in August 2006, I did not immediately accept their offer. Two major issues needed to be addressed. First, I said to the school board chair at the time, "Your interview questions were centered on adult issues. I want assurances from you that the board is committed to focusing on students as their top priority." Second,

I said, "Many of the interview questions from the school board were micromanagement in nature. I want assurances from the school board that it will not try to micromanage the superintendent." After the chair discussed these issues with his colleagues, he assured me the board would focus on students as their top priority along with governance, and they would leave the day-to-day operations of the school system to me and the staff. In fairness to the board, they felt like the administration and staff members were doing a good job of educating students, and they wanted to make sure the adults were being held accountable. These were critical and nonnegotiable issues for me. It helped establish the atmosphere for an honest, open, trusting, and productive relationship going forward.

Phase II was dominated by leading. After listening, observing, and learning more about the district and community, my confidence and comfort level to exert a more aggressive leadership style grew. During my first several weeks in the district I read and studied every document about the school system I could find. I committed information and statistics to memory on everything from soups to nuts: student test scores, graduation rates, discipline, attendance, curriculum design, programs, survey and audit, professional development, budget, capital projects, facilities, local business, economics, political influences, and much more. I was able to set the directions for how the superintendent and school board would communicate and hold ourselves accountable to the governance and operations of the school system. This led to the initial stages for the development of our new strategic plan that we later called our innovation plan.

Phase III—Strategic planning: The Virginia Department of Education requires each local school district to develop a strategic plan that is to be updated every 2 years. However, there are no parameters regarding the content of the plan. The plan I inherited was in the form of a short PowerPoint presentation. I was very experienced in developing strategic plans, so this was an exciting opportunity to powerfully shape the work and future of the school system.

I began by summarizing everything I had learned about the district into a simple mission, a vision, and four priority goals. I remember sharing these in a one-on-one meeting with the special assistant to the superintendent. She was a brilliant lady who had previous experiences leading policy development at the Virginia Department of Education. She liked what I had put together, and asked me, "What are you going to call the plan?" I responded with "the Design for Excellence, because my expectation for the district is excellence, and every action of our work should be by strategic design." She reinforced my ideas, and the rest is history. I presented the foundation of the plan to the school board and public. But the actual objectives, driver actions, and key measurements for accountability took almost a year to complete.

ENGAGING THE COMMUNITY
IN THE DESIGN FOR EXCELLENCE 2020

> In a fast-changing world, looking at tomorrow and seeing it only
> as a little bit more or a little bit less of today won't cut it as we
> move into the future. As educators and community leaders, we
> need to use powerful trends data, coupled with imagination, as we
> plan ahead. A challenge will be to not only develop a plan but to
> turn it into a living strategy—a strategic vision that will help us
> lead our students, schools and communities into an even more
> successful future.
>
> —Gary Marx

The original Design for Excellence was adopted in December 2007 and
modified in June 2008 and again in June 2009. The plan contained five
goals addressing student goals and employee goals.

1. Academic excellence for all students (while narrowing achievement
   gaps)

2. Safe, supportive, and nurturing learning environment

3. Knowledgeable and competent workforce

4. Community investment

5. Effective and efficient operations and management

In 2010, we made significant changes to the plan and updated the
name to the Design for Excellence 2020. This plan continued to address
expectations for students and employees in accordance with Virginia
Standards of Quality. Goals in the Design for Excellence 2020 state the
school board's expectations for achievement outcomes for all students in
three areas: knowledge, skills, and values. Subgoals specify what students
should know and be able to do in the disciplines and reflect the skills and
attitudes required by the state as well as school board and community
expectations. The goals and subgoals are student focused and designed to
lead to the fulfillment of the mission and vision using these three categories: (1) academic achievement, (2) 21st century skills and technology,
and (3) citizenship and core values.

Following our first community forum with Gary Marx, author of
Sixteen Trends: Their Profound Impact on Our Future, we acted on key factors
and trends that are destined to reshape the world, including the astonishing shift in population demographics and its role in lifelong learning and

the role of globalization of politics and the economy that will shape our practices. We followed up on Gary's presentations with six additional community forums held during the evening in various communities throughout the county.

Each forum was led by an expert in a specific area. For example, Susan Kilrain, an engineer, former U.S. navy officer, and former NASA astronaut led a discussion about the importance of science, technology, engineering, and mathematics (STEM). John Hunter, teacher, musician, and inventor of the World Peace Game, lectured about how this generation of students can achieve world peace. The first presentation on entrepreneurship was led by one of our successful graduates, Joel Erb. He became founder, CEO, and president of INM United (a multimillion dollar company) when he was just 15 years old. Our final speaker was Dr. Michael Rao, president of Virginia Commonwealth University, who led a discussion about college readiness.

We established innovation teams comprised of community members, parents, teachers, administrators, students, and other interested citizens responsible for creating goals and subgoals to support the vision, mission, and priority goals for the district. We also established a committee responsible for data analysis to determine how best to measure the district's progress. Among our key measures of success we set advanced targets that went far beyond state and federal mandates. These targets included measurements for completion of Algebra I by eighth grade, increased enrollment in rigorous courses like advanced placement, college dual enrollment, and international baccalaureate; suspension, expulsion and graduation rates; and increased minority representation in the workforce (the minority representation measure received harsh criticism from some segments of the community).

Innovation teams met weekly to analyze the current performance of students, community expectations, legal requirements, and future needs. Next, the innovation teams drafted goals and subgoals. To ensure governance buy-in, school board and community members had an active role in the updated vision and mission development and opportunities to comment on the proposals, which were revised before final adoption. School system staff members reviewed and modified key measures of success to provide accountability expectations for the goals and subgoals.

Our school board adopted our new vision and mission statements in 2011, and these words now guide our path to 2020.

Vision: *CCPS will provide an engaging and relevant education that prepares every student to adapt and thrive in a rapidly changing world.*

Mission: *In partnership with students, families, and communities, emphasizes and supports high levels of achievement through a global education for all, with options and opportunities to meet the diverse needs and interests of individual students.*

The plan is framed around three big ideas:

1. **Blended Learning.** Merging the best of face-to-face instruction with digital-age technology allowing students anywhere/anytime learning opportunities. This is our district's big initiative to close the digital divide by offering all students access to 1:1 mobile technology.

2. **Project-Based Learning (PBL).** We partnered with the Buck Institute for Learning to bring coherence to PBL practices across grade levels and subject areas and to create relevant/real-world learning opportunities for every student.

3. **Service Learning and Citizenship.** Enhances the learning process for students by blending cognitive learning and relevant projects with community needs.

In the words of Jamie Vollmer, an award-winning champion of public education, and the author, "Schools cannot do it alone." In addition to working with organizations like the Buck Institute, we have also worked closely with a number of other organizations and professionals to support our efforts, including Partnership for 21st Century Learning, Phi Delta Kappa International, Inc., International Center of Leadership in Education, Marzano Research Laboratory, The Leadership and Learning Center, EdLeader 21, Education Trust, and Harvard University. They all helped to advise, guide, and validate our work.

DIGGING DEEPER TO UNCOVER THE REAL ISSUES

Don't expect what you don't inspect.

—W. Clement Stone, *The Success System That Never Fails*

Given the size of our school district and the complexities associated with the high-stakes accountability movement that we exist in today, it would have been impossible to determine all of the areas of needed improvements on my own. Thus, in 2007 I commissioned, with the approval of the school board, Phi Delta Kappa, Inc., to conduct a curriculum management audit of the school system. Document analysis was performed off site, as was the detailed analysis of findings from a weeklong onsite review. The audit was designed to reveal the extent to which officials and professional staff of our school district had developed and implemented a sound, valid, and operational system of curriculum management. I wanted assurances that the district was operating as effectively and efficiently as possible.

For me, the most interesting element of the process is called "years to parity" where a trend analysis of individual subgroup performance on state assessments helps predict the number of years required for each subgroup to meet parity or academic equity with their White counterparts. The lead auditor told me she was not planning to include the parity findings in their final report because after meeting with several departments and school and community groups, the audit team did not think Chesterfield County citizens were ready for such a delicate conversation. I strongly urged the lead auditor to include the parity findings, which the team eventually agreed to include. The report would have been grossly incomplete without these data. It was essential to continuing our work.

Overall, the audit team found the motivation and intent of professionals in CCPS to be student centered and forward looking. According to the report, most classrooms visited by auditors were cheerful, pleasant settings focused on learning. Auditors sensed a professional pride among both the district and school staff members in visits and interviews. However, some visual indicators of needs for teacher support in teaching to an increasingly diverse student group were noted. Some staff opinions reflected implicit socioeconomic biases and resistance to economic as well as ethnic changes in the school communities, implying that these are the excuses for some students not learning. The audit team also suggested numerous steps for improving all areas in which the status fell short of the audit criteria. Many of the 100-plus audit findings and recommendations were integrated in our original Design for Excellence.

HOW WE CLOSED THE ALGEBRA GAP

> Justice will not be served until those who are unaffected are as outraged as those who aren't.
>
> —Benjamin Franklin

At the time I arrived in CCPS, achievement gaps were rarely if ever discussed publically. In reviewing the data, there was one particular statistic that troubled me. The school system was in the early stages of implementing "Algebra for ALL" in middle schools. The goal was for all middle school students to complete algebra by the time they left eighth grade. Knowing that algebra has historically been a gatekeeper course for enrollment into rigorous high school courses and college entrance, I thought, "what a noble and ambitious goal." But when I arrived in the district, approximately 35% of middle school students were enrolled in algebra prior to high school. Yet, only about 15% of the African American and Hispanic students were taking algebra; and worse, less than 5% of the economically disadvantaged students were taking algebra in middle school. In community meetings throughout the district, I used these statistics to highlight the disparities and inequities with the school district.

One of the questions I posed to parents, community leaders, teachers, and administrators was, "Why are only 5% of economically disadvantaged students taking algebra in middle school? Is there something different in the DNA of the other 95% of these students who are not taking algebra?" Of course not! Our problem was an opportunity gap. We would never close achievement gaps if we did not close opportunity gaps. Today approximately 95% of all CCPS middle school students are taking algebra prior to entering high school, and the pass rates continue to exceed state averages. The question is, how did we do it?

We recognized and changed a long-standing tracking system that predetermined who would get an opportunity to enroll in middle school algebra often based on ethnicity or socioeconomic status. However, moving students into rigorous coursework without strong prerequisite skills necessary for success could actually do more damage than the old tracking system. Issues regarding algebra readiness were critical. Student placement had to be recalibrated.

We began the process with every elementary school offering accelerated mathematics, beginning in the fourth grade. Some teachers criticized the change, citing the lack of support from parents of low socioeconomic families, poor readiness skills of some students, and the concern for children who would be frustrated by the increased rigor. Demographic changes resulting in increased diversity in schools was also challenging for some of the veteran teachers unaccustomed to working with change. Middle school teachers also expressed concerns about the lack of readiness skills of many students who had difficulty in comprehending algebraic concepts. Some of these concerns were legitimate. Nonetheless, the district remained committed to the change and provided support to make the transition as smooth as possible. In addition to the accelerated mathematics initiative in elementary schools, all sixth- and seventh-grade middle school students received doubled the time allotted for mathematics, which resulted in the equivalence of 4 years of instruction compacted into a 2-year calendar. This work was documented in *The Algebra Solution to Mathematics Reform: Completing the Equation* by Frances R. Spilehager (2011).

FOCUS: THE KEY TO TURNAROUND

Simplicity is the ultimate sophistication.

—Leonardo da Vinci

It has been my experience that comprehensive school reform that leads to measurable academic achievement does not take a long time. It takes a leader and a team with the ability to see beyond problem analysis and understand problem identification. It requires tactical diagnosis and a proven prescription. Leaders must also recognize and comprehend the cause and effect of a problem or situation.

When I began my first year as principal of Chillum Elementary School, a low-performing Title I school in Hyattesville, Maryland, I thought I had all of the answers. I assumed that if I led by example, replicated *best practices*, and scaled up the pace, we would see immediate improvement on standardized test scores. So one might imagine how devastated I was when I received the school's test results during the summer following my first year where overall scores improved by only 2 percentage points. I thought, "How could this be?" Everyone was telling me they had never seen a principal work harder or with more passion. As I reflect back on that first year, I realize much of my time and energy was spent on adult discipline issues. The right people were not on the bus, and I allocated countless hours documenting their poor performance, which eventually led to a relatively large changeover in staff . . . this was a good thing.

In my second year, I continued to refine my focus on developing the skill sets of the teachers and microanalysis of the data. Test scores continued to make modest improvement, but overall performance was still among the lowest in the school district of 130,000 students. By the spring of my second year, things began to crystallize for me. My problem was that I was trying to fix everything. To quote my grandfather, I became "a jack of all trades and a master of none." If we were going to experience comprehensive school improvement, we really needed to simplify things and focus on being great at one thing. Reading! Our students could not read well—this would be our primary focus.

So that spring I went to the districtwide supervisor for reading and language arts and said, "Sophie, give me the names of the two best reading teachers in the school system, and I am going to hire them." At her next districtwide reading teachers' meeting she announced that this young new principal was serious about reading and was looking for excellent teachers. To my amazement, teachers from across the district expressed interest in coming to our poor little school. I actually interviewed 27 of these reading specialists. Even though we only had one vacancy, I hired four of them. To fund the positions, I eliminated all of our instructional aide positions and shifted funds from materials and professional development.

In just one year, the increases in student achievement were astonishing. At the beginning of that school year, a September districtwide pretest revealed that only 55% of our students were reading on grade level. After only 8 months of effectively implementing our reading plan, more than 89% of our students were reading on or above grade level when they tested again in May. That's right; we experienced a 34% increase in schoolwide reading scores in one school year. But something even more impressive happened. On the Maryland State Assessments, our students produced some of the highest gains in the state, with double-digit increases in all assessed areas, including mathematics, science, and social studies. Furthermore, Chillum Elementary School was recognized by the Maryland Department of Education for Outstanding Achievement that year. I was promoted to a central office administrative position following that school year, but I am proud that the momentum we built was sustained under the new principal. Several of the teachers on that staff have gone on to experience amazing successes.

Okay, so we turned one school around . . . it was really not that difficult once we learned to focus and stay disciplined in implementing our plan. The challenge for me would be to scale it up to an entire urban district like Newport News with 33,000 students or a suburban district like Chesterfield County. Along With the HOPE Foundation and a now documented process (Hargreaves & Fink, 2005; Blankstein, 2011), we did it in a short period of time, narrowing achievement gaps along the way. In Newport News we were able to double the number of schools earning NCLB Adequate Yearly Progress in one year, and by my third year as superintendent, all high schools were ranked by Newsweek magazine as among the *Best High Schools in America* for the first time.

The challenge was a little different in Chesterfield County. How could we improve the achievement of all students, including Whites, while concurrently narrowing the gap? We implemented our Design for Excellence with fidelity. We also placed a laser focus on literacy. During my first year as superintendent, we hired 60 additional reading teachers who worked directly with students. They also led professional development training in their schools.

The results are noteworthy. We have made substantial progress toward achieving our goal of raising the bar for all students while narrowing achievement gaps. Tables 13.1 and 13.2 show that in my first few years in CCPS we produced impressive gains with all student populations in reading and dramatic increases in mathematics on the Virginia Standards of Learning (SOL) assessments.

Creating a culture of excellence is difficult, and like most things in life, starting can be the toughest part of the process. Once we uncover the

Table 13.1 Virginia SOL Reading Assessment Pass Rates for All CCPS Grades

Category	2006 Results	2009 Results	Change
All Students	87	92	+5
White	92	94	+2
Black	79	86	+7
Hispanic	78	88	+10
Students w/Disabilities	67	73	+6
Economically Disadvantaged	76	83	+7
Limited English Proficient	67	85	+8

Source: Adapted from Virginia Department of Education, 2009.

Table 13.2 Virginia SOL Mathematics Assessment Pass Rates for All CCPS Grades

Category	2006 Results	2010 Results	Change
All Students	77	90	+13
White	83	93	+10
Black	64	86	+22
Hispanic	66	88	+22
Students w/Disabilities	54	73	+19
Economically Disadvantaged	61	86	+25
Limited English Proficient	66	84	+18

Source: Adapted from Virginia Department of Education, 2009.

secret ingredient, it becomes easier. I think bestselling author Jim Collins (2001) puts it well when he explains the concept of the *flywheel*. In his book, *Good to Great*, he asks his readers to picture a huge, heavy flywheel, a large metal disk that weighs about 25 tons. In our case, the flywheel is a metaphor for a school or school system. Our job is to build staff momentum to get that flywheel to move as fast as possible to meet the high-stakes accountability standards established by the Department of Education. It takes tremendous effort to move a school district. In my first year as a principal, we pushed really hard to only produce a disappointing 2-point gain. But after 2 years of sustained focus and effort, we got the flywheel to complete one entire turn. By the beginning of the third year, we had gained momentum to make complete rotations, with each rotation moving faster than the one before. We were not pushing any harder, but the flywheel was accelerating. Even when another leader followed me, the momentum of the flywheel continued its acceleration.

When I came to CCPS I had more experience. I understood the appropriate balance between force, mass, and velocity. So why doesn't every school leader simply replicate best practices? It is because every school and school system is uniquely different. Leaders must determine the right balance of force, mass, and velocity to advance the distinctive culture of the organization. Each school and school system has its own unique DNA.

In 2010, CCPS became the largest school district to have 100% of its schools fully accredited by the Virginia Department of Education for 3 consecutive years. In the years following, student performance on state assessments has leveled off. There are two primary reasons for this leveling. First, when the Virginia Department of Education changed its SOL tests beginning in 2011 to become more rigorous and elevated the passing cut score requirement, the state superintendent, Dr. Patricia Wright, predicted that pass rates would drop by approximately 25 percentage points. Second, the economic recession resulted in draconian budget cuts to our school system over the past several years. At one point, our district lost approximately $100 million in funding for operations and another $150 million in cuts to our capital improvement projects. In essence, our schools experienced significantly larger percentage cuts than almost any school system in the state. These budget cuts resulted in larger class sizes and the elimination of reading teachers, psychologists, social workers, diagnosticians, instructional assistants, academic coaches, and other professionals who support our most fragile students. Parents, business leaders, and elected officials are now starting to realize the impact of these changes and have started to advocate for increased funding for our schools. We are in the process of rebuilding support to improve equity in all schools.

I must offer one important caveat here. Student success is more than just test scores. Most educators entered the profession because they were positively influenced by a great teacher who taught them wonderful lessons that could not be measured by a standardized test. Our goal is not just to prepare students for tests; it should be to prepare them for success in life. Some of our most successful students will not likely be great test takers. I have simply offered examples of our student achievement on tests as a representation of the other accomplishments that validate student success and their preparation for good citizenship, entrepreneurship, and becoming contributing members of society.

INTENTIONAL INITIATIVES

Cultural Competency as a Vehicle for Change

> It is time for parents to teach young people early on that in diversity there is beauty and there is strength.
>
> —Maya Angelou

Chesterfield has evolved over the past several years, and cultural competency training has become an important factor in our journey toward equity and excellence. According to the most recent completed Census Report (U.S. Census Bureau, 2010), Virginia's population is on the rise. All of our minority groups are growing, as reflected in a 91.7% increase in our Hispanic population, and in our Asian population with a 68.5% upward trend. The African American population has increased during this 10-year period as well, growing nearly 12%. This was also the first time in U.S. history that people were permitted to check a box denoted "two or more races." This report shows that in 2010, 2.9% of Virginians were two or more races (U.S. Census Bureau, 2010).

As for the demographic changes in Chesterfield County, we launched our cultural competency initiative in 2009 as part of our Design for Excellence to make our staff aware of this diversity amid our shifting population.

It takes champions to lead this work, and we had three: Harold Saunders, director of professional development; Joshua Cole, principal at Ecoff Elementary School; and Laura Falcon, assistant principal at James River High School. They lead the training, including the train-the-trainer model where leaders from each school attended a series of workshops, to be taken back to their buildings for professional development. This has been effective; however, we needed more at the district and school level.

"Cultural Conversations," a two-part series for staff members, were initiated in 2013 by the department of professional development. They are designed for participants to learn about themselves, to make connections with people from different backgrounds, to recognize injustice and how to respond, and then to take these lessons immediately back to their workplace. The "Cultural Conversations" course has been presented several times throughout the year and has reached numerous CCPS employees.

Technology: The Great Equalizer

> We need technology in every classroom and in every student and teacher's hand, because it is the pen and paper of our time, and it is the lens through which we experience much of our world.
>
> —David Warlick

Many of our students have parents who read to or with them every day, who take them to museums and on European vacations, and expose them to environmentally enriching experiences beyond the school day. Mobile technology in the hands of every student, used in a safe and responsible manner and integrated with effective face-to-face instruction, has the potential to level the field and serve as the great learning equalizer.

In CCPS, implementing our innovation plan has resulted in an enormous shift in the way we educate our students. It requires a change in the way we trained our teachers and leaders. If we want our students to be 21st century learners, we need our leaders to be 21st century educators as well. Technology education is also a form of cultural competency. Given the increasing affordability of technology tools on the market today, educators have the potential to provide every child with a personalized education.

In CCPS, we are in the process of deploying 32,000 Chromebooks to our students within the limitations of our existing budget. It is hard to imagine a business thriving in a global economy without robust technology support. It seems like every businessperson, politician, parent, and educator has a mobile device or phone. Yet, moving our district to a personalized technology environment was one of the most difficult challenges of my career. As one official even said, "It will happen over my dead body." Note: this person has come around to become one of our strongest supporters.

We eventually convinced the decision makers that we would do this smarter and more cost effectively than anyone else. Staff members observed the work of districts with successful implementations, and literature reviews of the latest research on educational technology were conducted. We implemented a yearlong pilot study of six different mobile devices in our classrooms and engaged our teachers and administrators in 2 years of professional development. We also engaged our students, parents, educators, business community, and elected officials in the conversation.

The turning point was when we came up with a plan that did not require any new funding to our school district to support the plan. For 3 years, we saved money by limiting our investment in new computers, transferred funds from other capital construction projects, and cut operation costs. Then we negotiated a purchasing process that led us to one of the lowest cost laptop computers on the market with a lease purchase agreement. Throughout the process, we maintained our focus on educating our students and providing them with opportunity equity.

As a result of the anytime/anywhere learning opportunities for our students, engagement and academic achievement will continue to increase for ALL students.

CONCLUSION

Change is coming, so we had better accept it. Demographic trends in the United States indicate that the majority of citizens in our nation will be people of color within the next 25 to 30 years. Baby Boomers will be replaced by Generations X, Y, and Z. Moving forward, educators must embrace the beauty and opportunities that exist through diversity rather than lament the problems. We cannot afford anything less. Educators must plan strategically and innovatively, and effectively implement their plans. To achieve excellence through equity, we need to maintain our focus on teaching and learning; engage in the courageous conversations about culture; be transparent with our community and empower our stakeholders; and use technology to bridge the great digital divide.

REFERENCES

Blankstein, A. (2011). *The answer is in the room.* Thousand Oaks, CA: Corwin.

Collins, J. (2001). *Good to great.* New York, NY: HarperCollins.

Fullan, M. G. (2003). *The moral imperative of school leadership.* Thousand Oaks, CA: Corwin.

Hargreaves, A., & Fink, D. (2005). *Sustainable leadership.* San Francisco, CA: Jossey-Bass.

Marx, G. (2014, April). Twenty-one trends for the 21st century: Out of the trenches and into the future. *Education Week.*

Spilehager, F. R. (2011). *The Algebra solution to mathematics reform: Completing the equation.* New York, NY: Teachers College Press.

United States Census Bureau. (2010). *State and county quickfacts.* Retrieved from http://quickfacts.census.gov/qfd/states/51000.html

Vollmer, J. (2010). *Schools cannot do it alone: Building public support for America's public schools.* Fairfield, IA: Enlightenment Press.

Equity Through Expanded Learning Time

14

Lucy N. Friedman and Saskia Traill

Conversations about educational equity often focus on the hours between 9 a.m. and 3 p.m. This is a mistake. The myriad learning opportunities throughout a child's whole day—and how those opportunities connect to one another to offer deeply meaningful learning experiences—are what create excellence in education and pave a path to equity. This chapter will describe the work of The After-School Corporation (TASC), which started out just over 15 years ago to build a system of after-school supports for children of low income in New York City and evolved to establish a network of schools working in partnership with community organizations to offer a redesigned school experience. While equity has always been at the heart of TASC's mission and vision, our understanding of, and strategies to achieve, excellence through equity have changed through the years.

TASC'S FIRST 10 YEARS

When TASC was formed in 1998, we set out with the ambitious goal to make high-quality after-school programs, grounded in youth development, part of the fabric of public services in New York City. With generous seed funding from The Open Society Foundations, we funded after-school programs throughout the city and offered services and oversight to ensure quality program offerings. Other organizations shared a similar goal, motivated by the belief that poor children should have access to the same experiences children from affluent families enjoyed between 3 p.m. and 6 p.m. At the time, after-school programs for children in families with low income were primarily seen by the public and policy makers as opportunities for academic remediation or as babysitting while parents worked. Proponents of large-scale public funding for after-school programs in Boston, Providence, Chicago, and other urban areas joined forward-thinking foundations to develop quality programs for low-income young people.

Since TASC had the long-term plan to achieve broad-scale impact throughout the city primarily using public funds, we made a few key decisions about our grant-making parameters with that plan in mind. We recognized that nonprofit, youth-serving facilities were not distributed equally and were not necessarily where the greatest need was in the city. These centers had been built for newly arrived, poor immigrants one or more generations ago, in areas like Manhattan's Lower East Side and Brooklyn, areas now commanding $1 million condominiums and $20 burgers. We required that programs operate in schools, to make the most efficient use of resources that exist in every community and to ensure geographic spread.

We did not offer grants directly to schools but rather to youth-serving nonprofit organizations; we saw that community organizations were well positioned to offer high-quality programs with a youth development lens. We believed the funds would have more impact than if they became part of the school budget. We thought that school-based programs could reach children who would otherwise not participate because caregivers were unable or unwilling to get them from school to after-school programs located elsewhere. And we hoped that by locating in schools, we might gain attention from principals and also influence how they approached the hours between 9 a.m. and 3 p.m.

Spurred in part by research showing a decline in American students' abilities compared with other industrialized countries, particularly among poor students, the era of the passage of No Child Left Behind in 2001 changed the school day, most dramatically for poor kids. The federal legislation increased testing and accountability, and states, local districts, and individual schools responded by narrowing the curriculum to focus more heavily on areas to which they were held accountable, namely math and English. As the school day shifted, so did expectations about the time after school.

First, school leaders increasingly viewed the time after school as a route to offer learning opportunities that had been squeezed out of the regular school day. Time for subjects that were considered extracurricular, such as arts and sports and well as those considered core, such as science and social studies, was reduced or eliminated. For example, 40% of elementary school teachers in California reported in a WestEd survey that their students receive no more than 60 minutes of science instruction per week (Dorph, Shields, Tiffany-Morales, Hartry, & McCaffrey, 2011). In addition, the percentage of schools in New York State that meet state-mandated minimums for art education within the school day is woefully low. (In 2014, New York City Mayor de Blasio committed additional funds to boost the number of art teachers in public schools.) Parents wanted to see these subjects brought back into the day, but as time in school increased, they also wanted to ensure there was time to finish homework.

Second, recognizing the benefits of small-group instruction commonplace in most after-school programs (and required by public youth-development funds), school leaders sought to use after-school hours for tutoring. Finally, school leaders and nonprofit organizations used additional time to implement programs designed to respond to national concerns such as teen pregnancy, obesity, and other social issues.

RESEARCH ON AFTER-SCHOOL PROGRAMS

Proponents of after-school programs invested in research to understand and boost quality and to demonstrate proof of concept and provide a rationale for offering programs on a broad scale, both within schools and across school districts. In general, studies tested whether after-school participants improved socially and academically compared with their non-participating peers. (It is interesting to note that these were, in a way, studies of whether the after-school program successfully created *inequity* between participants and nonparticipants.)

Evaluations of TASC-supported after-school programs and many others showed improvements in student achievement, standardized test scores, and school attendance rates (Durlak & Weissberg, 2007; Lauer et al., 2006; Miller, 2005; Vandell et al., 2006; Russell, Mielke, Miller, & Johnson, 2007; Reisner, White, Russell, & Birmingham, 2004). The researchers found that length of time students were enrolled in TASC programs and number of days attended were correlates of educational outcomes. Students who participated in TASC-model programming for at least 2 years and attended at least 60 days of programming experienced the greatest gains on mathematics standardized test scores. In addition, Black and Latino participants and students eligible for free lunch showed the greatest academic gains, providing evidence that TASC programs helped to close the achievement gap (Durlak & Weissberg, 2007; Lauer et al., 2006; Miller, 2005; Vandell et al., 2006).

Although researchers across these studies matched participants and nonparticipants for previous academic measures, race, ethnicity, and family income, critics questioned whether participants differed from nonparticipants in ways that were not measured. We shared that concern. Families experiencing greater levels of chaos, such as housing instability, financial concerns, or medical problems, were probably less likely to enroll in programs with expectations of regular participation. Thus, while peers were experiencing gains in academic, social, and emotional development by participating in structured learning opportunities after 3 p.m., children with perhaps the fewest supports at home were continuing to fall behind because they were not enrolled.

Looking at the data and our experience, it was clear that quality mattered in reaching student outcomes. We saw that the strongest programs were those where the principal was actively involved and where students were participating regularly. Nagging at us was a concern that, especially in programs for middle school students, the hardest-to-reach children and families were not voluntarily signing up for first-come, first-served programs. TASC began developing a new approach in which every child regularly participates in expanded learning opportunities beyond the traditional school day.

MOTIVATIONS FOR EXPANDED LEARNING

In our first decade, we observed the maturation of school-community partnerships and noticed that programs with the greatest impact were in schools where the principal was highly engaged and connected to the program. These principals often viewed additional time as a platform for innovation, for both students and teachers. They saw that teachers could practice new instructional techniques or curricula. And principals realized that unallocated time could be invested in student-centered, project-based learning in which students might spend 6 to 8 weeks as agents of their own learning on projects shaped by their interests. Students could develop their talents; use technology in new and different ways to expand the school walls; and test ideas in a lower-stakes environment that enables reflection and learning from mistakes.

We were also motivated by what principals, policy makers, and others increasingly described as an opportunity gap: not in the difference between academic skills and knowledge but in exposure to new parts of a city, careers, learning environments, and ways of being. These experiences are critical for building a robust vocabulary and a nuanced understanding of context and also offer a vision for the different kinds of futures available to a young person. One of the principals with whom TASC now works closely, Ramón González of M.S. 223 in the Bronx, reported that when he surveyed his students about what other learning opportunities they'd like in the afternoon, they asked for test prep and basketball, because they hadn't been exposed to other possibilities. TASC has calculated that by sixth grade, middle- and high-income children have spent 6,000 more hours learning than children from low-income families (i.e., a 6,000 hour learning gap.).

We were also guided by research suggesting that one of the core features of successful charter school models is an increase in instructional time (Gleason, Clark, Clark Tuttle, & Dwoyer, 2010). A study including nearly all of New York City's charter school students found that the city's high-performing charter schools gave students more time to learn, especially in English language arts (Hoxby, Murarka, & Kang, 2009).

We weren't driven only by the potential benefits of rethinking the time after school; there were perceived threats on the horizon that we believed could limit students' experiences and the capacity of nonprofit youth-serving organizations to offer learning opportunities. We saw growth in extended school day programs targeted to academic remediation across the country. Miami-Dade County Public Schools, for example, extended both the school day and year in 39 schools as part of a school-reform strategy known as the School Improvement Zone (Urdegar, 2009). Students who attended "Zone" schools did not significantly outperform peers from comparison schools on reading and writing assessments (Urdegar, 2009). We felt that these types of programs exacerbated inequity twice over, in the abundance of disengaging work sheets given to children and in the increased barriers to experiential learning and enrichment that can occur with more hours in a learning day.

These motivations led to the development and implementation of a new approach to education, ExpandED Schools, in 2008.

EXPANDED SCHOOLS

In ExpandED Schools, elementary and middle schools partner with youth-serving community organizations, such as settlement houses or community-development corporations. Together, these partnerships add $2\frac{1}{2}$ to 3 hours to the conventional $6\frac{1}{2}$-hour school day through planning that includes teachers, parents, and students. The teaching artists, sports coaches, and other supports that are a given in many middle- and upper-income children's lives become part of an expanded day of learning for disadvantaged kids. These learning opportunities broaden the curriculum and offer young people a clearer picture of the exciting life ahead of them. Teachers are freed up to plan, collaborate, and deepen instruction to ensure that classroom time maximizes moments of insight and inspiration. In the 2013 to 2014 academic year, TASC supported a network of nearly 40 ExpandED Schools in New York City, Baltimore, and New Orleans.

The schools and community partners pool their resources to give students more opportunities to develop their talents, more support to overcome the challenges of poverty, and more time to achieve at the high levels essential for success in the modern workplace. ExpandED Schools incorporate the following four core elements into their redesign:

- More time for a balanced curriculum
- School-and-community partnerships
- Engaging and personalized instruction
- A sustainable cost model

Some programs use extra time to offer an explicit focus on empowerment and equity, such as leadership workshops, public speaking and debate, or problem-based learning focused on the local community. Sixth-grade students at most of these schools participate in a reading group where students choose books and read with peers, supported by a reading coach to boost their reading comprehension and engagement.

Many of the schools and community partners focus on building agency in young people. While more affluent peers may assume they are assured a role in the adult world, less affluent children—and particularly those in income-isolated communities—may not. ExpandED Schools offer learning activities that challenge and transform students' beliefs about their futures.

EARLY LESSONS

Culture shift toward collaboration takes time. From the outset, we envisioned that ExpandED Schools and their partnering community organizations would together redesign the entire school day and transform school culture. But these changes can only occur at "the speed of trust," which is slower than we anticipated. Distrust and misunderstanding can exist on both sides. For example, school leaders and teachers may doubt a community partner's ability to contribute to the school's academic goals. Community partners' distrust of school policies can restrict their willingness to offer up their resources for sharing. Despite TASC helping to find good matches between schools and community partners to ensure alignment from the outset, negative experiences in the past can leave school or community organization staff wary and critical.

Also slowing down the speed of new collaboration are accountability and high-stakes evaluations. We found these dampen school leaders' and teachers' willingness to engage in innovation and risk and limit the time they feel they can spend on areas outside of math and English. The pressure to raise test scores can push principals to forgo time and funding for a longer, more balanced school day in order to support additional test preparation. We found principals making these hard choices even when they were clearly committed to offering their students engaging experiences, real-life problem solving, and other learning opportunities that they believed would have longer-lasting effects on academic and social-emotional development. The focus on the one-time test slows the pace of change and, in some cases, creates conditions that make untenable the hope of achieving equity through expanded learning.

We tackled these issues by working to build mutual respect for each other's assets and potential contributions to school goals. Through planning sessions and on-site coaching, we helped to ensure appropriate expectations and use of resources. Community partners may stress their flexibility and nimbleness in hiring and seeking private funding. Schools can offer their considerable resources and their legal standing to add credibility to the collaboration. As partnerships mature, they may work toward shared goals and share accountability for results. To do so, they must plan collaboratively, test ideas, recalibrate, and reinvest. Implementing changes in curriculum, enrichment activities, scheduling, and staffing requires multiple forms of communication. To be effective, the process must acknowledge resistance to change, allowing stakeholders a voice in questioning their partners' decisions as well as a phase-in strategy that focuses on one or two specific change areas at a time.

Partners must break down walls they may not even have realized existed. In a school in Bensonhurst, Brooklyn, the principal and the head of the community organization describe an "invisible line" between them that neither thought was their place to cross. At the beginning of each year, they shared cell phone numbers in case of emergencies but rarely spoke to one another. Only after engaging in planning and continued conversation did they realize they could learn about and question each other's work. They now call each other almost daily. TASC continues to encourage planning conversations that take place earlier and more often to align efforts and draw on the strengths each member brings to the partnership.

Schools and districts must rethink operations. In addition to rethinking teaching and learning and shifting culture, schools must rethink operations. For example, in most schools, custodians clean unused classrooms at the same time that after-school courses are in session. When the entire school body stays until 5 p.m. or 6 p.m., custodians find it difficult to get into unused rooms. Schools had to develop detailed plans for using and cleaning classrooms and other spaces. Second, after-school programs serve snacks or supper only to their participants, but in ExpandED Schools, a third meal is served to every student. Cafeterias are often used at capacity to serve lunch throughout the school day, and getting a third meal in before 5:30 p.m. or 6 p.m. can be a challenge.

District support is critical in streamlining the complex regulations and policies that stand in the way of school redesign and flexibility. For example, ExpandED Schools have been working to shift pupil-transportation systems to later hours, rather than relying on parent pickup as most optional after-school programs do. And they sought technology supports from the district to add two additional periods to the day.

Funding requirements are often coupled with administrative burdens. Youth-development funds brought in to pay for extra time bring additional requirements, including licensing, program monitoring visits, evaluation, and grant reporting. Some of these conflicted with district requirements. For example, one ExpandED School used 21st Century Community Learning Center funds and local after-school funds from the New York City Department of Youth and Community Development to offer learning activities in the afternoon. Each grant required program staff to enter participant information into a separate data system in addition to the school's system.

Schools, districts, and community organizations need clarity to use public funds in innovative ways. Lack of clarity about the appropriate use of public funds inhibits school-community partnerships from using funds in innovative ways. We found that district personnel needed clarification of the regulations concerning education funds, such as Title I and III, which may be used in innovative ways to support a longer school day. After-school funds, for the most part, may not be used during the school day. As the lines between community-partner-led enrichments and the traditional school day increasingly blur, so do specifications about when and how funds may be used.

One source of after-school funding that may now be used for expanded learning time is 21st Century Community Learning Centers, administered by the state from federal Title I allocations. In New York and some other states, regulations now allow 21st Century funding to be used for activities during the school day, provided they supplement rather than supplant existing school funds. Defining the difference between supplementation and supplantation is often a subtle and subjective process, one that may deter some school leaders and their community partners from trying to use funds in new ways. Similarly, policy makers have a tendency to distribute public funds broadly, which may leave out the neediest children in a given school or community. Garnering multiple grants for one school may have the perception of double-dipping and requires strong, coordinated budgeting to ensure that those perceptions are dispelled.

STRATEGIC AREAS TO DRIVE EXCELLENCE THROUGH EQUITY

We believe expanded learning provides a powerful opportunity to redefine educational excellence, by recognizing what affluent families regularly organize for their children—learning opportunities that act as recharging stations to make education exciting and fun, boosting desire for challenge and helping kids bounce back from failure. Building a collective demand for equity in joyful learning would do more to build a nation of creative problem solvers, engaged citizens, and global leaders than small increases on standardized test scores. Employers recognize the value of these skills in the workplace and have repeatedly called on K–12 and higher education to build them.

While not letting up on the importance of skills and knowledge in math and English language arts, there are two areas particularly conducive to interventions in expanded learning: (1) social and emotional development and (2) science, technology, engineering, and math (STEM).

First, we have found principals, teachers, funders, and policy makers are all eager to understand how to infuse social and emotional learning into the school day. The federal government has made social and emotional learning a priority in competitive grants and in public discussion. TASC has worked to help schools measure how students are progressing in their social and emotional development. We collaborate with school teams to develop processes of analysis and reflection that drive personalization of the learning day. Personalization ensures that students' individual areas for growth are addressed. Research on motivation and on the importance of believing in intellectual growth through hard work has fueled interest in social and emotional development to help close academic achievement gaps (Dweck, 2006). A report from the Chicago Research Consortium about so-called "noncognitive" factors (Farrington et al., 2012) has also helped to provide a framework for discussion. There is an ongoing tension between two desires: (1) to have social and emotional metrics viewed on par with academics and (2) to avoid policies that would encourage high-stakes accountability of social and emotional learning.

Second, the National Research Council's *Framework for K–12 Science Education* (2012) and the ensuing Next Generation Science Standards

(2014) make clear the beneficial impact that scientific practice and engineering design have on education. These practices, in which students experiment, tinker, and fail, can be difficult to include within the confines of a regular school period. Thanks to the Noyce Foundation, Mott Foundation, and others, STEM has emerged among after-school providers as a critical area, and many after-school educators are now adept at using after-school science curricula that engages, inspires, and complements school-day instruction. TASC has implemented a STEM Educators Academy, similar to other STEM initiatives around the country, spearheaded by intermediaries such as Boston After-School and Beyond and the Providence After School Alliance. In the STEM Educators Academy, teachers and community educators train together over the summer guided by a cultural institution grounded in science content and skills and hands-on techniques to make STEM come alive. Educators then work together throughout the year aligning their practice and teaching collaboratively to maximize their collective effect.

The NRC *Framework* articulated the importance of the affective domain in learning science, and research from Eric Jolly, Robert Tai, and others has shown clearly the important effect that science engagement and interest in exploration can have on entrance into science-related careers. These lessons take root in science and related disciplines but can extend to all content areas. The youth-development perspective in after-school programs can help meet the affective challenge, not only through explicit instruction in social and emotional skills but also through learning activities that provide opportunities to build those skills, such as group projects and presentations in which students present theories developed from evidence they have collected.

CAUSE FOR OPTIMISM

We believe expanded learning time has the power to facilitate the transformative, and perhaps revolutionary, thinking and design processes of what school will look like in another 15 years. Students and educators will feel less constrained by time and space and less pressure from high-stakes testing. They will be better able to offer a learning day that allows students to pose and answer challenging questions; argue and debate; fail and reflect; and test and apply their knowledge and skills. Technology supports for learning can help us reduce inequities by encouraging learning anytime, anywhere. Without effectively harnessing the power of technology, we stand to exacerbate divides between children from affluent families and their less affluent peers.

Principals are the lead change agents in this process. Michael Fullan (2014) describes the principal as a lead learner, both pushing and pulling other stakeholders toward success and ownership of success. Principals engaging in expanded learning must master the skills required of a change agent, in collaboration with a supportive leadership team. Through peer learning opportunities, we hope this first cohort of ExpandED Schools principals can help those who aspire to expand the school day to do so without reenacting mistakes and with a reduced ramp-up time.

We look to schools of education to ensure future teachers and school leaders expect to lead collaboration and culture change in their jobs and to demand it of the districts in which they work. Schools of education and districts can also think of these longer school days as opportunities for innovation and testing by student teachers, who should spend time working in small groups with young people and try out curriculum and instructional techniques in settings that aren't restricted by pressures of carefully scripted scope and sequence.

TASC is working to ensure that expanded learning is accepted as a strategy available to all schools, and to all children, to achieve equity and meet academic, social, and emotional goals for young people. We hope that expanded learning is viewed as a core strategy in ensuring that young men and women of color have access to vibrant, engaging education. As initiatives such as the president's initiative, *My Brother's Keeper*, draw national attention to what is necessary for boys of color to succeed, we hope they will more explicitly articulate the role that expanded learning can play in helping young people reach their full potential.

We hope school leaders, parents, teachers, students, and community educators will be able to decide together whether and how to transform their school. In particular, we hope funding will move toward consolidated, multiyear awards; simplified reporting requirements; and flexibility in options for transportation, special needs, nursing, and food service. These flexibilities will help drive innovation and excellence through equity.

REFERENCES

Dorph, R., Shields, P., Tiffany-Morales, J., Hartry, A., & McCaffrey, T. (2011). *High hopes—few opportunities: The status of elementary science education in California*. Sacramento, CA: The Center for the Future of Teaching and Learning at WestEd. Retrieved from http://www.wested.org/resources/high-hopes-mdash-few-opportunities-full-report-the-status-of-elementary-science-education-in-california/

Durlak, J. A., & Weissberg, R. P. (2007). *The impact of after-school programs that promote personal and social skills*. Chicago, IL: Collaborative for Academic, Social, and Emotional Learning.

Dweck, C. (2006). *Mindset: The new psychology of success.* New York, NY: Random House.

Farrington, C., Roderick, M., Allensworth, E., Nagaoka, J., Seneca Keyes, T., Johnson, D. W., & Beechum, N. O. (2012). *Teaching adolescents to become learners: The role of noncognitive factors in shaping school performance: A critical literature review.* The University of Chicago Consortium on Chicago School Research. Retrieved from https://ccsr.uchicago.edu/sites/default/files/publications/Noncognitive%20Report.pdf

Fullan, M. (2014). *The principal: Three principles to maximizing impact.* San Francisco, CA: Jossey-Bass.

Gleason, P., Clark, M., Clark Tuttle, C., & Dwoyer, E. (2010). *The Evaluation of charter school impacts, June 2010.* Washington, DC: US Department of Education, Institute of Education Sciences, National Center for Education Evaluation and Regional Assistance. Retrieved from http://ies.ed.gov/ncee/pubs/20104029/pdf/20104029.pdf

Hoxby, C. M., Murarka, S., & Kang, J. (2009). *How New York City's charter schools affect achievement: Second report in series.* Cambridge, MA: New York City Charter Schools Evaluation Project. Retrieved from http://www.nber.org/~schools/charterschoolseval/how_NYC_charter_schools_affect_achievement_sept2009.pdf

Lauer, P. A., Akiba, M., Wilkerson, S. B., Apthorp, H. S., Snow, D., & Martin-Glenn, M. L. (2006). Out-of-school-time programs: A meta-analysis of effects for at-risk students. *Review of Educational Research, 76*(2), 275–313.

Miller, B. M. (2005). Pathways to success for youth: What counts in after-school. *Massachusetts After-School Research Study (MARS).* Retrieved from http://supportunitedway.org/files/MARS-Report.pdf

National Research Council. (2012). *A framework for K–12 science education standards.* Washington, DC: National Academy Press.

Next Generation Science Standards. (2014). http://www.nextgenscience.org/

Reisner, E. R., White, R. N., Russell, C. A., & Birmingham, J. (2004). *Building quality, scale, and effectiveness in after-school programs.* Washington, DC: Policy Studies Associates.

Russell, C. A., Mielke, M. B., Miller, T. D., & Johnson, J. C. (2007). *After-school programs and high school success: Analysis of post-program educational patterns of former middle-grades TASC participants.* Washington, DC: Policy Studies Associates.

Urdegar, S. M. (2009). *Miami-Dade County Public Schools: School improvement zone final evaluation report.* Miami, FL: Miami-Dade County Public Schools, Office of Program Evaluation. Retrieved from http://media.miamiherald.com/smedia/2009/05/14/18/Zone.source.prod_affiliate.56.pdf

Vandell, D. L., Reisner, E. R., Pierce, K. M., Brown, B. B., Lee, D., Bolt, D., & Pechman, E. M. (2006). *The study of promising after-school programs: Examination of longer term outcomes after two years of program experiences.* Report to the Charles Mott Foundation. Retrieved from http://www.gse.uci.edu/childcare/pdf/afterschool/PP%20Examination%20in%20Year%203.pdf

PART VII

Coda

The previous sections have exemplified the principles of Courageous Leadership in action. The book concludes the way it began—with a call to action for courageous leaders to take the first steps for their journey to ensure the economic, educational, and overall quality of life for all of our citizenry by promoting excellence through equity. Pulling from his vast knowledge and the experiences of three European countries, Andy Hargreaves presents eight recommendations for policy makers. He advocates for an abandonment of failed policies and the pursuit of policies that uplift our children.

The Iniquity of Inequity

15

And Some International
Clues About Ways to Address It

Andy Hargreaves

THE URGENCY OF EQUITY

In early 2014, the global book market was topped by an unexpected bestseller: a 685-page hardback tome written by a hitherto obscure and, outside academic circles, utterly unknown French economist. Thomas Piketty's *Capital in the Twenty-First Century* took the publishing world by storm and brewed up a storm of controversy in the process (Piketty, 2014).

Poring over vast global databases of previously unconnected statistics of income and wealth over several centuries, Piketty came to a stunningly simple conclusion that a worldwide audience of disillusioned middle-class readers had more than suspected for years: the distribution of wealth has become concentrated in fewer and fewer hands, especially in the United States. Although the 3 decades after World War II saw social policies, government investment, and demographic growth create greater equity in economic and educational terms, from the 1980s, Piketty claims, the United States witnessed a "resurgence of inequality" (p. 20) on a scale that typified the early 20th century.

This inequality has been defined not merely by income but increasingly by how it has been differentiating those who own property, land, and wealth from those who do not. In this new world, Piketty's work shows, the passing on of accumulating assets from generation to generation has slowed social mobility, reduced the impact of public education, and tied

273

social and family advantage to inheritance more than achievement. In many respects, over the past 3 decades and more, the United States and nations like it have been turning into de facto aristocracies of the wealthy. There is not yet class warfare, but the existence of the extremely affluent 1% in America and elsewhere is not an illusion or an exaggeration.

However, not everyone agrees that inequity, even extreme inequity, is a bad thing. Some say inequity is a generational question. When the young get promoted, earn more, and save, then eventually they become wealthy, too. But, as Piketty points out, most economic inequalities occur within generations, not between them.

Others argue that when privilege is earned, it is a fair reflection of the relationship between effort and reward that defines the best parts of capitalism. Surely, it is believed, the indolent and the incompetent should not reap the same returns as the rest of us. What we should therefore seek is not equality but meritocracy—a society in which everyone has a fair chance to succeed but where those who demonstrate talent, merit, and effort receive extra income compared with the rest. Singapore, for example, has unashamedly built its economic development on this basic principle—that if everyone is provided with the basic security of subsidized shelter and adequate health care along with equal educational opportunities in an almost entirely state-run system, those who work hard and perform well should be rewarded handsomely for their labors (Kwang et al., 2001; Yew, 1998).

But even meritocracy has three fundamental flaws. First, as Michael Young brilliantly argued in his satirical depiction of *The Rise of the Meritocracy*—in a society where everyone truly is rewarded according to their abilities, those with lesser abilities (and, we might add, active disabilities) will become despondent and resentful when the lottery of genetic inheritance or early upbringing places a ceiling on their advancement and opportunity (Young, 1958). Second, when wealth concentrates into smaller and smaller groups, the rules of political and economic influence and interconnection increasingly tilt the playing field in favor of the already advantaged, in terms of everything from the manipulation of electoral boundaries (termed gerrymandering after Governor Gerry of Massachusetts in 1812), to the alteration of tax regulations so that they benefit the wealthy, and to reduced levels of public investment that would otherwise assist the disadvantaged and the poor—including investment levels in public education. Eventually, meritocracy turns into plutocracy (Piketty, 2014). The upper middle class becomes the ruling class.

Then there is a third objection. Even if the freedom to be unequal is a defining belief of a society and the rights of citizens within it, when the degree of inequality exceeds a certain level, extremely serious and damaging consequences ensue for the quality of life in society as a whole.

Among all the international comparisons that have been published on the differences between nations in economic and social terms, two British academics—epidemiologist Richard Wilkinson and anthropologist Kate Pickett—have presented some of the most compelling data.

In *The Spirit Level: Why More Equal Societies Almost Always Do Better*, Wilkinson and Pickett (2009) examine variations in social and health outcomes between nations and between U.S. states. These outcomes include rates of depression, anxiety, alcoholism, teenage pregnancy, drug dependency, obesity among children and adults, educational achievement, rates of incarceration and severity of sentences for particular crimes, violence, suicide, gun ownership, levels of distrust, infant mortality, and social mobility. The authors explore and consider a range of variables that might explain these variations. The major predictor of differences in social and health outcomes, they conclude, is economic. More importantly, above a minimal level that defines extreme poverty, the factor that most explains differences in health and social outcomes is not variations among countries and states in their overall levels of wealth but rather the degrees of income inequality that exist within those countries and states.

Consider just one example. Wilkinson and Pickett (2009) constructed a composite index of all the health and social problems and then looked at the relationship of this index to levels of income inequality in different countries and states. By country, the nations with the fewest problems turn out to be the ones with the lowest levels of income inequality: Norway, Sweden, the Netherlands, Finland, and Japan. Among U.S. states, the low problem/low inequality states are New Hampshire, North Dakota, Vermont, Minnesota, and Iowa. At the opposite end of the scale, the nations with severe social and health problems are also the ones with the greatest inequalities—the United Kingdom, Portugal, Greece, New Zealand, and, almost off the chart altogether, the United States. Among states, the unhealthy and unequal states of Louisiana, Mississippi, and Alabama are far worse than all the rest.

Similar patterns are evident in the United Nations Educational, Scientific, and Cultural Organization's (UNESCO's) 5-yearly international surveys of child well-being and lack of well-being in families, schools, and communities at age 15 in the more developed countries. Topping the table are the Northern European nations with strong social states: the Netherlands, Norway, Iceland, Finland, Sweden, and Germany. The United States finds itself in 26th place—just above Lithuania, Latvia, and Romania and immediately below Slovakia and Greece (UNICEF, 2013).

So how do we put an end to extreme inequity and the social and health iniquities that it visits upon poor families and their children? Piketty concludes there are no automatic mechanisms of self-correction that bring society back toward the middle when inequities have gone too far. Clearly, we cannot just wait for things to turn around by themselves. Instead, the response of those who resent excessive and exclusive privilege may be revolution, as it was for the French in 1789. Great wars can also provoke a corrective response when those of different rank who have fought side by side for their country seek and demand a fair and just society on their return from the front line. The period following World War II is a prime example of this.

But if we cannot depend on self-correction and should not wish upon ourselves another Great War, what other options exist instead? In times of social reform driven by principles of fairness and distributive justice, says Piketty, progressive taxation can help to redistribute some of the wealth from the highest echelons to the lowest reaches of society. Some of this can be directed toward public education and the public good to improve the conditions of and opportunities for the disadvantaged and the poor.

Some of America's leading educational academics, such as David Berliner (2006, 2009) and Diane Ravitch (2011), repeatedly remind us that most of the variance in student achievement is explained by factors outside the school and beyond the ambit of educational policy and strategy. Poverty, poor infant care, lack of statutory maternity or paternity support, environmental toxins, neighborhood violence, financial insecurity and resulting instability among the working poor—these are the kinds of factors that are the greatest predictors of student underachievement in the United States. Conversely, outside Asia, the highest performing countries on the international Performance in Student Assessment (PISA) tests of educational achievement have strong social states that protect the poorest families and especially their children from hardship and insecurity through strategies of progressive taxation and strong public investment. In these societies, schools and their teachers are not left to fight poverty single-handedly (Organisation for Economic Co-operation and Development [OECD], 2011).

EQUITY AND EDUCATIONAL EXCELLENCE

In light of all these social and economic inequities in the United States, you might expect there to be poor quality in overall educational achievement. Many high-profile critics complain that the United States' performance on international assessments such as PISA is mediocre at best, and that America should start to model its educational reforms on the systems already in place among its high-performing Asian competitors like Singapore and China (Tucker, 2011). But America's middle-ranking performance in education is in many ways a significant accomplishment and a tribute to the nation's teachers given the immense social privations and deprivations that many American children have to overcome such as poverty, homelessness, racism, and poor infant medical care (Sahlberg, 2014). And some states, such as Massachusetts, are a match for the very highest performing countries and systems in the world, as even business critics acknowledge (MBAE, 2014). So it's hard to blame America's teachers for the nation's educational inequities. But it is possible to look to those same teachers and their schools as resources for reducing inequity and improving quality still further.

As the OECD has pointed out, despite all the important influences on educational achievement that originate from outside the school, the relationship between educational equity and excellence can still be affected both positively and negatively, by deliberate educational policy and strategy (OECD, 2011). The strategies that nations adopt inside the educational system as well as outside it do matter, especially in combination, as we can see from three international examples.

Finland: High Quality, High Equity

In January 2007, I went to Finland as part of an OECD thematic review of the relationship between policies and practices of educational leadership and systemwide educational performance (Hargreaves, Halasz, & Pont, 2008; Hargreaves & Shirley, 2009). Finland had been a top performer on PISA since the origin of the tests and was being inundated with visitors, yet the reasons for the nation's high performance were something of a mystery, including among Finns themselves.

We were able to provide one of the first coherent and globally known narratives of the reasons for Finland's success. These included a strong vision of and value for public education in which most Finnish children participate as the creators of Finland's future society; resulting in a high status for the country's teaching profession whose members are stringently selected through rigorous university-based teacher education programs that confer master's degrees on all of them; a widespread culture of collaboration in curriculum development among teachers in each school district; an equally robust culture of collaboration among all partners in strong local municipalities where most curriculum and other policy decisions are made; and a system of widespread cooperation and trust instead of U.S.-style test-based accountability.

In addition to all these strategies that improve educational quality by raising teacher quality and supporting strong collaborative leadership in local municipalities, Finnish author Pasi Sahlberg adds a further factor:

the focus on equity (Sahlberg, 2011). Since the mid-1980s, but especially after a major economic collapse in 1992 that had seen unemployment rise to nearly 20%, the concentration in Finnish educational policy was not on what we would now call raising the bar of overall achievement but on narrowing the achievement and opportunity gap between children from economically more and less prosperous families. This was evident in the creation of a strong social welfare state so that child poverty now stands at only 4% compared with 20% in the United States, for example. Voluntary participation in free preschool by 98% of children, generous paid family leave for parents to care for their own children through the first 3 years of life, and the direction of intense attention to diagnosing and intervening in response to children's early learning difficulties all help provide a more equal start in formal education.

Abolition of streaming or tracking in the 1980s removed differences between subjects studied or levels of difficulty in each subject that had led to pronounced gaps in educational outcomes. An unusually inclusive special education strategy where any child requiring support with an aspect of their learning is provided with special assistance—so that around 50% of students have received special support at some point before the end of high school—also contributes to an unending assault on inequity. The consequence, Sahlberg (2011) has observed often, is that from the 1990s, Finland first improved its performance on equity, and then, as the gaps closed, found that this also led to significant improvements in overall standards or quality.

In Finland, it appears, deliberate and sustained attention to equity as the priority has been eliminating gaps and difficulties and made it easier to deliver eventual higher quality. This seems to suggest that instead of raising the bar and then narrowing the gap, it might be better to narrow the gap first in order to raise the bar (but not instead of raising the bar, as we shall see next).

Wales: Strong Equity, Weaker Quality

A country with some similarities to Finland is Wales. Wales is a small nation with a population of just over 3 million—about half the size of Finland. Geographically, a lot of the country is rural in nature but with a concentration of urban communities near the sea, in the south. Wales and Finland are both flanked by larger neighbors with whom they have had a long history of close yet fraught relationships. National identity and autonomy are therefore issues of continuous concern.

There are also some similarities in educational performance between the two countries. Both have fully comprehensive public educational systems. And like Finland, Wales is a strong performer in educational equity on the PISA tests: "student performance is less dependent on a student's school and socioeconomic background than the OECD average" (OECD, 2014, p. 7).

But the similarities end there. Despite its exemplary record in educational equity, Wales is in the bottom third of all the countries who participate in PISA, it is the lowest ranking of all the four U.K. countries, and it is the only one of these to differ by a statistically significant degree (OECD, 2014). Wales is high on equity, but its results are disappointing in overall excellence or quality. Why is this?

In October 2013, the Welsh Government invited the OECD to undertake a visit to review its improvement strategy, and I was one of two experts who served on the five-person team that did this work. Our report was published in May 2014 (OECD, 2014). Three of our four recommendations are relevant to this chapter.

One recommendation was to "define and implement policy with a long-term perspective." Unlike Finland, which set out, through education, to develop a society and economy of creative knowledge workers, Wales seemed to have no obvious vision that was driving educational provision or change other than trying to improve its rankings on international assessments. As the BBC news headlined our review: "Welsh government lacks education 'long-term vision'" of the kind of learners it wants its students to be (BBC, 2014). Overall, our review team said, the Welsh government should "develop a shared vision of the Welsh learner, reflecting the government's commitment to quality and equity, and translate it into a small number of clear measurable long-term objectives" (OECD, 2014).

A second recommendation was that Wales should create a coherent assessment and evaluation framework. After devolution from England, Wales disposed of its standardized tests. England was not an international high performer, and no high-performing systems had testing processes on a scale of those that were being used in England/Wales and the United States. So ending the tests seemed to make sense educationally as well as making a statement culturally and politically, perhaps. Moreover, the strong performers of Finland had no standardized testing except to test confidential samples for monitoring purposes.

But getting rid of a bad thing is not the same as instituting a good thing. Teachers in Wales had little training in classroom assessments, processes to moderate those assessments across teachers were not strong, and grade inflation began to occur year upon year as teachers felt they should be improving all the time.

The Welsh government then reacted and perhaps overreacted by reintroducing standardized testing for Grades 2 to 9, so we advised reviewing and refining this strategy by working to minimize unintended effects such as teaching to the test and suggested that in time the tests may be reduced to no more than a couple of grades, as in high-performing countries such as Singapore and Canada, using the money saved to provide higher quality training in classroom assessments.

Third, as Wales was undertaking its improvement planning process, its approach to developing quality in teaching had been different than in Finland. Finland had long been able to attract high-quality teachers into teaching by the power of its national educational vision, the status that teachers were accorded in the society as a whole, and the fact that all Finnish teachers were selected from the top 10% of applicants and had master's degrees. Wales, by contrast, had struggled to attract teachers from above the lower reaches of the university graduation range, and it had only recently embarked on a government-funded master's program for early career teachers (which we suggested it should continue and extend).

Wales was finding it harder than Finland to develop the professional capital of its teachers. In our review of Finland, we found that teachers believed they were able to know their students well (a basic condition of being able to evaluate their progress effectively) because they did not have to respond constantly to external initiatives. In Wales, though, professional capital in teaching was being depleted by feelings of overload among teachers who felt they had to implement too much too fast. We therefore advised that they should learn from the mistakes of other jurisdictions such as England and sequence their literacy and numeracy strategy into literacy, then numeracy, or vice versa, so they would not have to make changes in almost everything they taught, all the time.

Finally, Wales and Finland differed in the social capital of teachers—in how well teachers worked together. As we have seen, in Finland, collaboration among teachers is integrated into their work through joint curriculum planning for which teachers, not bureaucracies, have prime responsibility, more time to meet with their colleagues in the school day than in any other developed country, and the possession of a genuine sense of collective responsibility for students' success beyond any teacher's own class or grade level. By contrast, Wales had tried to develop teacher collaboration by training school teams in how to build professional learning communities (PLCs). Despite extensive investment in this initial process, the PLCs had no clear or consistent focus (in Finland it was curriculum development; in Wales it might have been classroom assessment or literacy implementation), and there was no continued funding to make them sustainable after the initial training process by increasing teachers' time in the school day to meet and work with colleagues. The social capital of teacher collaboration within schools to meet all students' needs was therefore less effective than in high-performing Finland.

One key area for developing strong social capital among teachers is to be found in how schools learn from and support each other. In Finland, the OECD team had seen in the city of Tampere how secondary schools shared resources and ideas to support the success of all students in the city together. Collaboration, not competition, is a key part of the Finnish professional ethic in education. In Wales, the Welsh government had started to make initiatives in school-to-school collaboration, but as our own review and one before it found, these arrangements were in their very early stages (Hill, 2013), they were crisis driven as a way to turn around failing schools rather than being embedded in a whole collaborative system culture, the models of school-to-school collaboration were overly dependent on and derivative of London exemplars rather than drawing on several international examples as a basis for a unique "made-in-Wales" solution, and some schools were confused and overwhelmed by being expected to participate in different school-to-school initiatives, especially when they were categorized as high performers in some groups and lower performers in others.

So whereas Finland was able to combine equity with excellence, it seems that Wales struggled to combine equity with excellence because it lacked an inspiring national vision of what it wanted its next generation of learners to be, because it was unable to inspire teachers of sufficiently high quality to come into the profession, and because it had not yet provided the conditions and culture where teachers and their schools could collaborate to support all students' high-quality learning on a systemic and sustainable basis. New, deliberate policies will be needed to move Wales closer to Finland in its strategies and results including developing and articulating a national vision, strengthening the professional capital of teaching by extending the existing master's degree qualification, reducing the quantity and frequency of external initiatives, providing more in-school time for collaboration to become a routine part of teachers' professional culture, and developing a made-in-Wales approach to collaboration across schools so that improved quality and equity become embedded in the system's professional culture.

Sweden: Declining Equity and Quality

Next to Finland is its former colonizer: Sweden. Once a poster child for social democratic excellence and equity, in the past decade, following its aggressive introduction of decentralization and market-driven educational reforms in the 1990s, Sweden has experienced the greatest deterioration in

PISA scores out of all OECD countries who were performing above average in 2003. Sweden also shows the greatest deterioration in educational equity between these dates. Sweden's educational reforms, especially its profit-based "free" schools (many of them owned by hedge fund companies), are similar in some respects to the Anglo-American reforms of England and the United States. So it is interesting and important to note that Sweden's educational performance is falling further and further behind the other high-performing Scandinavian countries and moving more toward the low performers of England and the United States, whose strategies are more similar to Sweden's own.

Writing for *Slate* magazine, Columbia business professor Ray Fisman (2014) argues that Sweden's "race to the bottom" is at least in part attributable to grade inflation in the private free schools as educators try to attract more and better students and increase their schools' market share. "It's the darker side of competition that Milton Friedman and his free-market disciples tend to downplay: If parents value high test scores, you can compete for voucher dollars by hiring better teachers and providing a better education—or by going easy in grading national tests" (Fisman, 2014). Noting that Sweden has a higher proportion of "free" or charter schools than U.S. cities like New York, Fisman says that the Swedish reforms should serve as a warning to U.S. reformers because when charter schools increase in volume, they become harder to regulate, and corruption in the system becomes more likely.

Critics of the Slate article from the Friedman Foundation for Educational Choice and London's Center for Market Reform in Education argue that private schools are currently insufficient in number to explain a decline in the whole system, that the private system fares no worse and arguably marginally better than the public system, and that the corruptions of the system are a result of poor implementation rather than being inherent to the model (Sahlgren, 2014; Sanandaji, 2014). Moreover, they claim, the problem may be that the market reforms have not been pursued vigorously enough and that they remain tainted with lingering centralized controls in areas like school discipline where students retain the right to carry smart phones and wear hats! Teacher quality, they point out, is low in Sweden because of poor salaries. And the decline in performance coincides with the introduction of "progressive" pedagogies in the 1990s.

This back-and-forth response is reminiscent of an analysis for the Brookings Institute of some people's tendencies to overinterpret the dramatic improvements in the educational performance of being a result of the abolition of tracking or streaming.

Poland's 1999 education reforms were not limited to tracking. Instead, they involved a complete overhaul of the Polish school system, including decentralization of authority and greater autonomy for schools, an increase in teacher salaries, a new system of national assessment, adoption of a core curriculum and national standards, reform of teacher education at the university level, and a new system of teacher promotion. Any one of these policies—or several in combination—may have produced Poland's gains on PISA. Some may have even produced negative effects, dragging down achievement, while others offset the losses with larger gains. The point is this: no single reform can be plucked from several reforms adopted simultaneously and declared to have had the greatest positive impact. The data do not allow it (Loveless, 2012, pp. 28–29).

Loveless (2012) is correct in saying that no single reform should be selected arbitrarily or ideologically as being responsible for exceptional improvement or, as in Sweden's case, decline. But a nihilistic multivariate answer arguing that it could be any, many, or none of them is not satisfactory either and in many ways an abrogation of social scientific duty to understand how variables can and do interact together.

In the case of Sweden's market reforms, the exceptions cited by the reforms' defenders may actually be the rule that undercuts those reforms. If poorly paid teachers with weak professional capital are disillusioned by disruptive reforms that appeal to individual market interests rather than a more Finnish-like vision of human development and wider public good, they are unlikely to deliver high quality in either pedagogy (especially ones that are more complex and student-centered) or classroom assessment (as in Wales). And in a competitive market system of all against all, rather than Finland's all for one mentality, the social capital of school-to-school collaboration and assistance will be weakened, losses will not be confined to any one sector, and the corrupting effects of what is widely known as Campbell's Law will inexorably and eventually prevail where "the more any quantitative social indicator is used for social decision-making, the more subject it will be to corruption pressures and the more apt it will be to distort and corrupt the social processes it is intended to monitor (Campbell, 1976).

With an election looming in September 2014, major political parties responded to growing public unrest with Sweden's educational decline in a number of ways. Elevating the status and quality of teachers was one of them. Proposals included raising teachers' salaries, reducing the administrative burdens on teachers, and raising the bar for teacher qualifications so teachers would not come from the lowest ends of the graduation range. Introducing more regulations for privately owned schools was another response in terms of proposals such as insisting on longer-term ownership of schools, removing the rights of profit making from public schools or insisting that profits should be reinvested in the schools, and repealing school choice altogether.

Given strong similarities between Swedish and U.S. market-based reforms in a world where no market-driven reform program other than the Netherlands' (which is paradoxically within the context of a strong welfare state) has yet produced strong performance on the international tests of student achievement, U.S. school reformers should keep a very close eye on Sweden's precipitous decline and the policy-induced contributions to it.

THE IMPLICATIONS FOR EQUITY AND EXCELLENCE IN AMERICA

So we have looked at three countries (all of them democracies) that vary in the relationships they demonstrate between educational excellence and equity. Finland remains one of the top two performing nations in the world outside Asia and has the best record of all of them on equity. All this appears to be the result not of small size or geographical latitude but of a quarter century of deliberate educational and social policy. Wales has a strong record on equity in a fully comprehensive educational system but is a much weaker performer in educational quality. Sweden was once a high performer in both quality and equity, but in a period paralleled and in some ways prompted by the onset of aggressively market-driven reforms in education, it has experienced the most rapid decline of all developed nations in both quality and equity. What can America learn from these three international examples when we consider them together? Eight desirable directions are outlined below.

1. **Invest in local public schools.** All high-performing countries make strong investments in their public systems. Their private systems are small or negligible, except in the Netherlands where there is a proliferation of faith-based alternatives that are historically enshrined in legislation. Charter schools are not a serious option in high-performing nations. In general, in the United States, as in Sweden, despite all the policy and resource incentives and after all the disruptive effects on the regular public system, charter schools do not outperform other public schools to any significant degree, they often rob local schools of teacher and student capacity, and most charter schools turn out to be more traditional than the public schools they replaced (Goldring & Cravens, 2006). If all U.S. schools were good, as they are in Finland, the vast majority of parents would choose their local district school.

2. **Revive local commitment and control.** All high-performing educational systems, including Finland, have high local control of their schools either as city-states, like Hong Kong or Singapore, or through their local districts. But as Sweden and Wales illustrate, not all systems that exhibit strong local control are high performers. Yet there is no evidence up to this point that improved performance in developed economies can be achieved with market-based solutions that destroy or diminish local districts. School districts are not only the cornerstones of high-performing systems; they are also a foundation of American public democracy. If districts are too tiny, too corrupt, or divided from each other by race and by residence, the answer is to reform them, not to remove them from the system.

3. **Introduce fairer funding.** High-performing systems do not make the quality of their schools primarily dependent on the residential inequities of property taxes. Although, ever since Lyndon Johnson's Elementary and Secondary Education Act, federal funding has been designed to offset these inequities, it increasingly comes with strings attached, meaning that schools already dealing with deep social disadvantages have to implement multiple and shifting initiatives and also endure the distractions of constant grant writing so that the resources they need can come to them. The United States should therefore move core funding of public schools away from property taxes, and the inequities they create between districts, toward other forms of taxation.

4. **Invest in and circulate professional capital.** To increase the human capital of our students, we must invest in the professional capital of our teachers (Hargreaves & Fullan, 2012). Top-performing countries like Finland draw their teachers from the top third or better of the graduation range, they train them in rigorous university preparation programs where they undertake deep research into their practice, and they have to undergo extensive practice-based experience in schools. America must communicate strong and positive messages about the value of teachers and teaching and also back them up by articulating a compelling vision for America's students and their schools, by improving the working conditions for teachers—especially teachers' opportunities to collaborate with each other—and by according more flexibility to teachers to design curriculum and develop pedagogical expertise together. Paradoxically, giving teachers more time to collaborate with each other can yield better achievement results than providing extended learning time for students who have been falling behind (Bailey, 2014). Teachers will also have time to know their students well and attend to their mental health and well-being if they are not overwhelmed with top-down reforms and initiatives. They will be able

to conduct classroom assessments effectively rather than degenerate into grade inflation if they have the support to develop assessment expertise together and if they do not fear for the survival of their schools and their jobs in high-threat systems of win-lose competition. Last, if they are rigorously trained and able to continuously upgrade their own skills with their colleagues, they will be able to differentiate their instruction for diverse students rigorously rather than implementing student-centered pedagogies in an ineffective way.

5. **Strengthen cross-school collaboration.** The United States can do better at turning around low-performing schools. High-performing systems improve their schools not by having intervention teams descend in from a great height but by building collective responsibility where strong schools assist weaker neighbors, where resources are disbursed from the district or the state department to schools to make this assistance possible, and where these collaborative efforts run across district boundaries (Fullan & Boyle, 2014).

6. **Put responsibility before accountability.** High-performing countries understand there is no substitute for strong, high-quality teachers who work together to develop good teaching and who exercise shared responsibility for all students in their schools. U.S. testing must become more prudent if we are to see improvements in the quality of teaching that avoid teaching to the test, rotating teachers and principals in and out of already unstable schools, and falling prey to other perverse incentives predicted by Campbell's Law that have included outright cheating among Atlanta educators that became part of the ever-present panic to lift the scores (Aviv, 2014). If professionals are expected and supported to exercise collective responsibility for all students' success, a great deal of otherwise time-consuming accountability will take care of itself.

7. **Develop uplifting leadership.** The drive for equity needs disciplined and dedicated leadership. Martin Luther King said "all labor that uplifts humanity has dignity and importance and should be undertaken with painstaking excellence." Equity is about uplift as an end; it is about the struggle for justice and opportunity that has, for example, defined African American history for 150 years (Gaines, 1996). Equity also requires uplifting leadership as a process—to inspire multitudes, not just a few individuals, to have the courage, commitment, and tenacity to lift up those around them (Hargreaves, Boyle, & Harris, 2014). In Finland, uplifting leadership is evident in how all teachers lead in taking collective responsibility for student achievement and how their principals, often elected from among those teachers, see their task as being one of

facilitating this process rather than driving it. In Ontario, in Canada, expert leadership is evident throughout a high-performing system where leaders in the province's administration take responsibility for literacy reform, where 72 district directors or superintendents have been behind the inspirational transformation of the province's approach to special education inclusion, and where teacher unions have worked with government to support teacher-designed innovations among thousands of teachers in the province (Hargreaves & Braun, 2012). By contrast, in Wales, in Sweden, and in America too, leadership has been giving way to performance management. In the United States, what is misguidedly labeled instructional leadership has actually turned out to be capacity to fill out observational checklists of classroom competence in order to provide the objective evidence that will justify termination of a few incompetent teachers (Fullan, 2014). It is time for U.S. education to bring school and system leadership back in as a driver of change, not as an afterthought—for leadership to be about a new vision of what American learners should be, not about how to manage a system as it races competitively toward a numerically defined top.

8. **Redefine urgency as opportunity.** Many educational reformers in the United States and elsewhere have been inspired and emboldened by Harvard business professor John Kotter's influential idea of a "sense of urgency." But urgency has too often been interpreted as crisis or panic. In *Accelerate: Building Strategic Agility for a Faster-Moving World*, Kotter (2014) argues that if urgency is depicted in doom-mongering terms, people become anxious and afraid for their jobs and their futures and are unable to make the huge-step changes that their organizations might require. At the University of San Diego, Alan Daly (2009) has shown this is exactly what happens in high-threat reform environments in the United States that makes principals rigid and risk-averse and unable to engage in long-term thinking as they concentrate on their personal and institutional survival.

But if urgency is interpreted as a big, if extremely challenging, opportunity, then whole communities can be inspired to raise their energy, volunteer their time, and transform their practice in order to achieve a higher purpose and common cause together. This is what U.S. educational reformers now need to do.

What do these elements of equity-driven educational reform add up to? They don't mean that the United States should become Finland, or Singapore, or even Canada. They don't mean that American reformers should contemplate taking directions they have never taken before. Instead,

Americans could do no better than revisit and recast the educational policy achievements of Lyndon B. Johnson, 36th president of the United States. After the life-shaping influence of being a public school teacher at the start of his career, Johnson built and left an immense educational legacy in the early childhood education reforms of Operation Head Start and in the Elementary and Secondary Education Act that assigned federal resources to offset local inequities. Standing at a crossroads of educational and social change, Johnson was clear about the path that America should take. "Education is not a problem," he declared. "Education is an opportunity."

The opportunity for all Americans is to articulate and believe in an inspiring vision of educational change that is about what the next generation of America and Americans should become, not about a target or ranking that the nation should attain. The opportunity for Americans everywhere is to clamor to get their children into their local public schools because these are the best schools that are available to them. The opportunity is for Americans to attract and develop vast numbers of high-quality teachers for all the nation's children, rather than perseverating on eradicating an incompetent few. Most of all, the opportunity is for America to find its direction and lead once more in creating an inspiring, equitable, and inclusive future that it will entrust to a new generation of outstanding teachers who will come to be known and admired internationally as the very best in the world.

REFERENCES

Aviv, R. (2014). Wrong answer: In an era of high-stakes testing, a struggling school made a shocking choice. *The New Yorker, XC.* Retrieved July 28, 2014, from http://www.newyorker.com/magazine/2014/07/21/wrong-answer

Bailey, M. (2014). Lessons from a school that scrapped a longer student day and made time for teachers. *Hechinger Report.* Retrieved July 28, 2014, from http://hechingerreport.org/content/lessons-school-scrapped-longer-student-day-made-time-teachers_16663/

Berliner, D. (2006). Our impoverished view of educational research. *Teachers College Record, 108*(6), 949–995.

Berliner, D. C. (2009). *Poverty and potential: Out-of-school factors and school success.* Tempe, AZ: Education Policy Research Unit.

Campbell, D. (1976). *Assessing the impact of planned social change.* Kalamazoo: Evaluation Center, College of Education, Western Michigan University.

Daly, A. (2009, April). Rigid response in an age of accountability: The potential of leadership and trust. *Educational Administration Quarterly, 45*(2), 168–216.

Fisman, R. (2014, July 15). Sweden's school choice disaster. *Slate.* Retrieved July 28, 2014, from http://www.slate.com/articles/news_and_politics/

the_dismal_science/2014/07/sweden_school_choice_the_country_s_
disastrous_experiment_with_milton_friedman.html

Fullan, M. (2014). *The principal: Three keys to maximizing impact.* San Francisco, CA: Jossey-Bass.

Fullan, M., & Boyle, A. (2014). *Big city reforms.* New York, NY: Teachers College Press.

Gaines, K. K. (1996). *Uplifting the race: Black leadership, politics, and culture in the twentieth century.* Chapel Hill: University of North Carolina Press.

Goldring, E., & Cravens, X. (2006). *Teacher's academic focus for learning in charter and non-charter schools.* Nashville, TN: Vanderbilt University.

Hargreaves, A., Boyle, A., & Harris, A. (2014). *Uplifting leadership: How organizations, teams, and communities raise performance.* Hoboken, NJ: Wiley.

Hargreaves, A., & Braun, H. (2012). *Leading for all: A research report of the development, design, implementation and impact of Ontario's "Essential for some, good for all" initiative.* Ontario, Canada: Council of Ontario Directors of Education.

Hargreaves, A., & Fullan, M. (2012). *Professional capital: Transforming teaching in every school.* New York, NY: Teachers College Press.

Hargreaves, A., Halasz, G., & Pont, B. (2008). The Finnish approach to system leadership. In B. Pont, D. Nusche, & D. Hopkins (Eds.), *Improving school leadership: Vol. 2. Case studies on system leadership* (pp. 69–109). Paris, France: OECD.

Hargreaves, A., & Shirley, D. (2009). *The fourth way.* Thousand Oaks, CA: Corwin.

Hill, R. (2013). *The future delivery of education services in Wales.* Cardiff, UK: Robert Hill Consulting.

Kotter, J. P. (2014). *Accelerate: Building strategic agility for a faster-moving world.* Boston, MA: Harvard Business Review Press.

Kwang, H. F., Ibrahim, Z., Hoong, C. M., Lim, L., Lin, R., & Chan, R. (2001). *Lee Kuan Yew: Hard truths to keep Singapore going.* Singapore: Straits Times Press.

Loveless, T. (2012). *How well are American students learning?* Washington, DC: Brookings Institute.

MBAE. (2014). *The new opportunity to lead: A vision for education in Massachusetts in the next 20 years.* MA: MBAE.

Measuring devolution: Carwyn Jones on record and future. (2014). BBC News. Retrieved July 28, 2014, from http://www.bbc.com/news/uk-wales-27811294

Organisation for Economic Co-operation and Development (OECD). (2011). *Strong performers and successful reformers in education: Lessons from PISA for the United States.* Paris: OECD.

Organisation for Economic Co-operation and Development (OECD). (2014). *Improving schools in Wales: An OECD perspective.* Paris: OECD.

Piketty, T. (2014). *Capital in the twenty-first century.* Boston, MA: Harvard University Press.

Ravitch, D. (2011). *The death and life of the great American school system: How testing and choice are undermining education.* New York, NY: Basic Books.

Sahlberg, P. (2011). *Finnish lessons: What can the world learn from educational change in Finland?* New York, NY: Teachers College Press.

Sahlberg, P. (2014). *Five U.S. innovations that helped Finland's schools improve but that American reformers now ignore. Answer Sheet.* Retrieved July 28, 2014, from http://www.washingtonpost.com/blogs/answer-sheet/wp/2014/07/25/five-u-s-innovations-that-helped-finlands-schools-improve-but-that-american-reformers-now-ignore/

Sahlgren, G. (2014). *Is Swedish school choice disastrous—or is the reading of the evidence?* The Friedman Foundation for Educational Choice RSS. Retrieved July 28, 2014, from http://www.edchoice.org/Blog/July-2014/Is-Swedish-School-Choice-Disastrous-or-Is-the-Read

Sanandaji, T. (2014). Sweden has an education crisis, but it wasn't caused by school choice. *Slate.* Retrieved July 28, 2014, from http://www.national review.com/agenda/383304/sweden-has-education-crisis-it-wasnt-caused-school-choice-tino-sanandaji

Tucker, M. S. (2011). *Standing on the shoulders of giants: An American agenda for education reform.* Washington, DC: National Center on Education and the Economy (NCEE).

UNICEF. (2013). *Child well-being in rich countries: A comparative overview.* Innocenti Report Card 11. Florence: UNICEF Office of Research.

Wilkinson, R., & Pickett, K. (2009). *The spirit level: Why more equal societies almost always do better.* London, UK: Allen Lane.

Yew, L. K. (1998). *The Singapore story: Memoirs of Lee Kuan Yew.* Singapore: Simon & Schuster.

Young, M. (1958). *The rise of the meritocracy.* Harmondsworth, UK: Penguin Books.

Index

Related ASCD Resources: *Excellence Through Equity*

Below are some of the ASCD resources on related topics that were available at the time of publication (ASCD stock numbers appear in parentheses). For up-to-date information about ASCD resources, go to www.ascd.org. Search the complete archives of *Educational Leadership* at http://www.ascd.org/el.

Print Products

- *Aim High, Achieve More: How to Transform Urban Schools Through Fearless Leadership* by Yvette Jackson and Veronica McDermott (#112015)
- *The Big Picture: Education Is Everyone's Business* by Dennis Littky with Samantha Grabelle (#104438)
- *Breaking Free from Myths About Teaching and Learning: Innovation as an Engine for Student Success* by Allison Zmuda (#109041)
- *Creating the Opportunity to Learn: Moving from Research to Practice to Close the Achievement Gap* by A. Wade Boykin and Pedro Noguera (#107016)
- *Detracking for Excellence and Equity* by Carol Corbett Burris and Delia T. Garrity (#108013)
- *The Differentiated Classroom: Responding to the Needs of All Learners, 2nd ed.* by Carol Ann Tomlinson (#108029)
- *Educating Everybody's Children: Diverse Teaching Strategies for Diverse Learners, Revised and Expanded 2nd Edition* edited by Robert W. Cole (#107003)
- *Meeting Students Where They Live: Motivation in Urban Schools* by Richard L. Curwin (#109110)
- *Personalizing the High School Experience for Each Student* by Joseph DiMartino and John H. Clarke (#107054)
- *Raising Black Students' Achievement Through Culturally Responsive Teaching* by Johnnie McKinley (#110004)
- *School Climate Change: How do I build a positive environment for learning? (ASCD Arias)* by Peter DeWitt and Sean Slade (#SF114084)
- *Teaching English Language Learners Across the Content Areas* by Judie Haynes and Debbie Zacarian (#109032)
- *Teaching with Poverty in Mind: What Being Poor Does to Kids' Brains and What Schools Can Do About It* by Eric Jensen (#109074)
- *Unlocking Student Potential: How do I identify and activate student strengths? (ASCD Arias)* by Yvette Jackson and Veronica McDermott (#SF115057)
- *A World-Class Education: Learning from International Models of Excellence and Innovation* (2012) by Vivien Stewart (#111016)

PD Online® Courses

- Achievement Gaps: The Path to Equity (#PD09OC64)
- An Introduction to the Whole Child (#PD13OC009M)

Videos

- *Breaking Through Barriers To Achievement* (#605133)
- *Educating English Language Learners: Connecting Language, Literacy, and Culture* (#610012)
- *Educating Everybody's Children* (#600228)
- *How to Involve All Parents in Your Diverse Community* (#607056)
- *How to Use Students' Diverse Cultural Backgrounds to Enhance Academic Achievement* (#608031DL)
- *Teaching with Poverty in Mind: Elementary and Secondary* (#610135)

For more information: send e-mail to member@ascd.org; call 1-800-933-2723 or 703-578-9600, press 2; send a fax to 703-575-5400; or write to Information Services, ASCD, 1703 N. Beauregard St., Alexandria, VA 22311-1714 USA.

WHOLE CHILD
TENETS

1 **HEALTHY**
Each student enters school healthy and learns about and practices a healthy lifestyle.

2 **SAFE**
Each student learns in an environment that is physically and emotionally safe for students and adults.

3 **ENGAGED**
Each student is actively engaged in learning and is connected to the school and broader community.

4 **SUPPORTED**
Each student has access to personalized learning and is supported by qualified, caring adults.

5 **CHALLENGED**
Each student is challenged academically and prepared for success in college or further study and for employment and participation in a global environment.

THE WHOLE CHILD

The ASCD Whole Child approach is an effort to transition from a focus on narrowly defined academic achievement to one that promotes the long-term development and success of all children. Through this approach, ASCD supports educators, families, community members, and policymakers as they move from a vision about educating the whole child to sustainable, collaborative actions.

Excellence Through Equity relates to **all five** tenets.

For more about the ASCD Whole Child approach, visit **www.ascd.org/wholechild.**